THE MOOHUMMUDAN LAW OF INHERITANCE

THE

MOOHUMMUDAN LAW

OF

INHERITANCE,

ACCORDING TO

ABOO HUNEEFA AND HIS FOLLOWERS.

BY

NEIL B. E. BAILLIE

GYAN

Published by

Gyan Publishing House
5, Ansari Road
Daryaganj, New Delhi-110002
Phone: 011-47034999, 9811692060
E-mail: books@gyanbooks.com

Distribution Network
gyanbooks.com
India, USA, Canada, UK, Australia, France

ISBN: 978-81-212-7947-5 (PB)
First Published, 1832

2nd Impression 2023

Printed at: Gyan Press, Delhi.

THE MOOHUMMUDAN LAW
Author: NEIL B. E. BAILLIE

THE MOOHUMMUDAN LAW OF INHERITANCE,

ACCORDING TO

ABOO HUNEEFA AND HIS FOLLOWERS.

WITH

AN APPENDIX,

CONTAINING AUTHORITIES FROM THE ORIGINAL ARABIC.

BY

NEIL B. E. BAILLIE,

Member of the Asiatic Society; a Pleader in the Presidency Court of Sudder Dewanny Adawlut, and an Attorney of His Majesty's Supreme Court.

Calcutta:

PRINTED AT THE BAPTIST MISSION PRESS, CIRCULAR ROAD: SOLD BY MESSRS. THACKER AND CO., CALCUTTA; AND MESSRS. SMITH, ELDER AND CO., CORNHILL, LONDON.

1832.

TO

LIEUT.-COLONEL JOHN BAILLIE,

A MEMBER

OF

THE HONORABLE THE COURT OF DIRECTORS, FOR THE AFFAIRS
OF THE HONORABLE EAST INDIA COMPANY;

AND FORMERLY

PROFESSOR OF THE ARABIC AND PERSIAN LANGUAGES,
AND OF MOOHUMMUDAN LAW, IN THE COLLEGE
OF FORT WILLIAM,

THE FOLLOWING PAGES

ARE MOST RESPECTFULLY DEDICATED.

ADVERTISEMENT.

The following Treatise has been compiled in a great measure from two Arabic works of high celebrity among the Moohummudans of India—the *Sirajiyyah*, and its commentary the *Shureefeea;* and is little more than a condensation of their contents, reduced to an English form. The *Sirajiyyah* is very brief and abstruse; and, without the aid of a commentary, or a living teacher, to unfold and illustrate its meaning, can with difficulty be understood even by Arabic scholars. It is not therefore matter of surprise, that its Translation by Sir William Jones should be almost unknown to English lawyers, and be perhaps never referred to in His Majesty's Supreme Courts of Judicature in India. With the assistance of the *Shureefeea*, it is brought within the reach of the most ordinary capacity; and if the abstract Translation of that commentary, for which we are also indebted to Sir William Jones, had been more copious, nothing further would have been requisite to give the English reader a complete view of this excellent system of Inheritance.

The Moohummudan law is founded on the *Kooran*, and traditionary decisions of the Prophet and his companions. With respect to the authenticity or meaning of some of these decisions, there may be a doubt in the minds of true Moohummudans. But in matters of Inheritance, I believe, there is less difference of opinion between the four great sects that divide the orthodox Moohummudan world, than on any other branch of the law. The doctrines which are here adduced are those of *Aboo Huneefa* and his disciples *Aboo Yoosuf* and *Moohummud*, which are received by the orthodox Moohummudans of India, and alone formed the law of this country, while under the sway of the Moghul Emperors. The *Imameea* Code is now administered by the Honorable Company's Courts to *Shias*, when both parties are of that persuasion. But the general law of the country is still that of *Aboo Huneefa*, and I am not aware that any other has ever been administered to Moohummudans by His Majesty's Supreme Court.

Besides the *Sirajiyyah* and *Shureefeea*, other works are occasionally referred to throughout this essay; but they are chiefly on matters which do not strictly form a part of the Law of Inheritance. The important subjects of parentage, treated of in the third chapter, and of the powers of executors, comprehended in the first, have been drawn entirely from other sources.

The *Sirajiyyah* and *Shureefeea* are printed together, and form one book, the text being distinguished from the Commentary by a line drawn over the former. The references are to the edition published at Calcutta in the year 1236 of the Hijree, the pages of which do not always correspond with the recent reprint. The extracts from the *Koodooree* are in general from a manuscript in my own possession; but with the exception of that in the fifth chapter, they may be usually found in the *Hidaya*, which is little more than a commentary upon that work. The quotations from the *Hidaya* have been made from the Arabic edition printed at Calcutta. Of Mr. Hamilton's Translation from the Persian, which is also referred to by the volume and the page, for the greater satisfaction of the English reader, there is, I believe, only the quarto edition, published at London, in 1791. The *Jowhurrut-oon Nuyyerah*, another commentary on the *Koodooree*, is still to be found only in manuscript, though it well deserves in my opinion to be printed. It is of later date than the

Hidaya, and is perhaps more valuable in other respects. The extracts are from a copy which belonged to the late *Kazee-ool-Koozzat*, and I have been able to indicate them only by citing the book or chapter in which they may be found, in case the reader should have an opportunity, and think it worth his while, to bring them to the test of actual collation. The references to the *Inayah*, a commentary on the *Hidaya*, (itself only a comment as already observed,) and the valuable collection of decisions called the *Futawa Alumgeeree*, are made to editions now in the course of publication from the Education Press. The only other work referred to is the *Futawa Sirajiyyah*; and the extracts have been taken from the edition published in 1827 at Calcutta.

On appearing before the public as the author of even so humble a work as the present, it becomes me to apologize for the errors which, notwithstanding my utmost care, it may be found to contain. No pains have been spared to render it as correct as possible. I have anxiously compared the text several times with the works which are quoted in support of it, and have rigidly discarded every thing for which there did not appear to be sufficient authority. Of my own opinions, the reader will find that I have been sparing; having hazarded an argument but seldom, and then chiefly on the meaning of my authorities, which it has been my sole object to place before him in the plainest language. It is not without much diffidence, and a painful sense of the responsibility which will attach to me as a member of the legal profession, if I should unhappily become the means of perverting the judgments of my brethren on points which deeply affect the interests of their Moohummudan fellow subjects, that I now venture to give my performance to the world. From the Attornies of the Supreme Court, for whose use it was originally undertaken, I am sure of meeting with every possible indulgence. I do not expect less from the candour of the Gentlemen of the Bar. And if my performance should meet with their united approbation, I shall not be apprehensive for the ultimate judgment of the public at large.

CONTENTS.

THE

MOOHUMMUDAN LAW

OF

INHERITANCE.

CHAPTER I.

Of the General Application of a Moohummudan's Estate.

THE property of a deceased Moohummudan is applicable in the first place to the payment of his funeral expenses; secondly, to the discharge of his debts; thirdly, to the payment of legacies as far as one-third of the residue; and the remaining two-thirds, with so much of the other third as is not absorbed by legacies, are the patrimony of his heirs*.

Funeral expenses payable before debts.

The funeral of a Moohummudan comprehends the duties of washing, shrouding, and interring his body; all of which are to be performed in a manner suitable to his condition†, and even in preference to the payment of his debts, where his property is inadequate to both purposes‡; with the exception however of such debts as have been charged by pledge

* Sirajiyyah, Appendix, No. 1.

† Shureefeea, Appendix, No. 2.

‡ Ibid, No. 3.

or otherwise on particular property, for the payment of which such property is primarily liable*.

Debts preferred to legacies.

Debts of every description take precedence of legacies and the claims of heirs, but debts acknowledged on death-bed are postponed to all others, unless they appear to have been incurred for known and sufficient reasons†. With this exception all debts are on an equal footing; no creditor being preferred to another, but all receiving the full amount of their respective claims, or a ratable share of the property where it is inadequate to the complete discharge of all the debts‡. By a provision perhaps peculiar to the Moohummudan law, debts not actually due at the time of the debtor's death, become payable immediately on the occurrence of that event. This is founded on the consideration that the privilege of postponement is a personal right of the debtor, which dies with him; and, accordingly, the death of a creditor is not attended with the same effect, because the person to whom the right of delay belongs is still alive§.

Effect of debtor's death on debts not immediately payable.

Legatees how far preferred to heirs.

A dispute for priority can seldom arise between the heirs and legatees whose interests attach to different portions of the estate. But if such a case should occur, the author of the *Shureefeea* observes, that the legatee would be entitled to the preference so far as

---

* Sirajiyyah, Appendix, No. 4.

† Jowhurrut-oon-Nuyyerah, Appendix, No. 5, and Shureefeea, ibid, No. 6.

‡ Shureefeea, Appendix, No. 7.

§ Jowhurrut-oon-Nuyyerah, Appendix, No. 8.

a third of the property[*]. Thus, if the legacy were a third of the testator's *dirhems*, or his goats, and two-thirds of them should happen to perish, leaving the remaining third still within a third of his whole estate, the legatee would be entitled to it[†]. It is only, however, when the articles out of which the legacy is to be paid are homogeneous, as money, goats, and generally such commodities as are estimable by weight or measurement of capacity, that the precedence of the legatee to the heirs can be of any avail to him; for if the articles be of different kinds, as for instance a bequest of a third of the testator's apparel, the apparel being of various descriptions, the legatee would be entitled to no more than a third part of the remainder, in the case of loss, even though the whole of the remainder should still fall within a third of the general estate[‡].

Gifts on death-bed how far lawful.

The law is so careful of the interests of the heirs, that it protects them against the gratuitous acts of their ancestor upon death-bed, as well as against his bequests, beyond a third of the clear residue of his estate, after the payment of funeral expenses and debts. Accordingly, gifts made in these circumstances must not, together with legacies, exceed the third, unless confirmed by the heirs after the donor's death[§]; and it is material to observe, that assent

* Shureefeea, Appendix, No. 9.

† Hidaya, Appendix, No. 10, and see Mr. Hamilton's translation, vol. iv. pp. 488 and 489.

‡ Hidaya, Appendix, No. 11. Translation, vol. iv. p. 490.

§ Hidaya, Appendix, No. 12. Translation, vol. iii. p. 162.

before death is not sufficient*. And neither gifts in a last sickness nor legacies are valid to any extent unless so confirmed, where the person in whose favor they are made is also an heir. In like manner, the law is so jealous of the partiality of the deceased for any particular heir, that acknowledgments of debt made on death-bed in favor of an heir are utterly void, unless afterwards assented to by the other heirs†. As the law has placed no controul over a husband's power of divorce, he might, by exercising it in his last moments, deprive a wife who had incurred his displeasure of her right of inheritance; but that is obviated by a provision, that a divorced wife shall retain her right of inheritance, unless her husband survives the completion of her *iddut*, or the period during which it is unlawful for her to enter into another marriage‡. There is one way, however, in which a husband can even upon death-bed materially reduce the share of the inheritance to which his wife would be entitled, that is, by marrying or acknowledging a marriage with another woman, by which means the widow's share would be divided

Death-bed divorce.

Its effect on widow's right of inheritance.

---

* Because their right has not yet accrued, and the assent may be annulled upon the death of the testator. Hamilton's Hidaya, vol. iv. p. 470.

† Jowhurrut-oon-Nuyyerah, Appendix, No. 13. Hidaya, Appendix, No. 14. Translation, vol. iii. p. 164.

‡ Hidaya, Appendix, No. 15. Translation, vol. i. p. 279. The *iddut* of a divorced woman is in general about three months, when she is not pregnant. Of a pregnant woman, the *iddut* is not accomplished until her delivery. Ibid, p. 359 and 360.

among both equally. The wife newly married or acknowledged would also be entitled to a reasonable dower; but that as a debt would fall on the general estate*.

Women are not entrusted with the power of divorce, but, in the acquisition and disposal of property, even those who are married do not labor under any disabilities, but such as are common to both the sexes. The rules for the succession to a woman's estate are the same as those for the succession to a man's, with this exception, that the share of a husband in his wife's inheritance is double that of a widow in her husband's, as will be seen more fully hereafter.

Executors.

Though a Moohummudan is disabled from disposing of more than a third of his property by will, or by death-bed donation, he is nevertheless at liberty to appoint an executor for the administration of the whole, and an important question arises as to the nature and extent of the executor's power over the property. The executor of a father is the guardian of his minor children†, and is in that capacity invested with powers over their property, which are not possessed by ordinary executors. That he may lawfully sell so much of it as is movable, there is no doubt, nor any confliction of authorities upon the point. But his power of disposing of the immovable property of his wards, except under circum-

Executor of a father; his power over the property of minor children.

* Hidaya, Ap. No. 12. Translation, vol. iii. p. 162.

† Hamilton's Hidaya, vol. iii. p. 520.

stances of necessity or extraordinary advantage, is perhaps open to question. Some difference exists between the older and later writers on this subject, though I have not been able to ascertain the precise sentiments of the former, the only authorities with which I am acquainted being contradictory. In the extract from the *Inayah* cited below*, it is stated that the sale by an executor of the immovable property of a minor heir was lawful according to the ancients, while, in a passage quoted by Mr. Macnaghten† from the *Ashbaho Nuzair*, it is represented as their opinion, that such a sale is unlawful. With respect again to the sentiments of the moderns, we are informed by the author of the *Inayah*, in the extract last referred to, that "they have said an executor may lawfully sell the immovable estate of a minor heir, when the deceased has left debts which cannot be otherwise discharged, or the price is required for the supply of the minor's necessities, or a purchaser is willing to give double the value for the property." The language of this extract is less strong than that of the *Ashbaho Nuzair*, where the sale of a minor's immovable property is said to be positively forbidden by the moderns, except in the three cases above-mentioned, and in four others of similar expedience or necessity. It is still possible, however, that the circumstances

---

* Appendix, No. 16.

† Principles and Precedents of Moohummudan Law, Appendix, Chap. viii. Sec. 14.

mentioned by both the authors may be intended only as marks or guides for the father's executor in the exercise of a general discretion which the law has conferred on him, and are not to be considered as indispensable to the creation of such an interest in the immovable estate of his ward as would entitle him to dispose of it. This view of the case is strengthened by two other passages of the *Inayah**, in which the author speaks of the executor's power to sell the immovable property of a minor without any reserve or qualification, assumes and reasons upon it as a thing generally known and admitted, contrasts it with his more limited controul over the estates of major heirs, and deduces from it his farther power of making a partition of the deceased's immovable property so far as relates to the portions of minors. The case of partition merits particular attention, because it involves the interests of third parties. The author supposes the deceased to have bequeathed a third of his estate to a stranger, and to have left heirs of the remainder, some of whom are of age and absent, and the others are minor. In these circumstances, if the executor should make a partition of the estate, giving to the legatee his third, and reserving two-thirds for the heirs, the partition is lawful and binding on all the heirs with respect to the movable property, but on the minors only, as to the immovable. "This difference between the

* Appendix, Nos. 17 and 18.

movable and immovable property, arises (as the author informs us) from the fact, that when the heirs are minor, the executor has the power of selling their portions, both of the movable and immovable estate; but when they are of age, he has not the power to sell the immovable estate so far as they are concerned, his authority extending no farther than to the sale of the chattels: and such being the case in sale, so also is it in partition, which is but a species of sale." The executor being invested with a general power of making a partition of immovable property on behalf of a minor, it may be inferred, that he is placed under no other restraint with respect to the sale of such property, than the obligation of shewing its necessity or expediency, and that an advantage to the minor much more moderate than double the value of the property, would justify him in disposing of it.

The power of a father's executor over the property of adults.

With respect to heirs, who have arrived at majority, a father's executor has no power over their property when they are present; but in their absence he is invested with the general power of preservation, under which he may sell their movable estate, the price being more easily preserved than the actual articles themselves*. It is only, however, with respect to such movables, as have been left to the absent adult by his father, that the executor is invested with this power†.

---

* Hidaya, Appendix, No. 19. Translation, vol. IV. p. 553.

† Futawa Sirajiyyah, Appendix, No. 20.

The executor of a mother, brother, or paternal uncle, is invested with the same general power over the portions of minors and absent adults, as the executor of the father possesses over the property of the latter; i. e. the power of preservation, under which he may sell so much of it as is movable*. But his authority is strictly confined to the property left to the heirs by his testator†.

The executor of a mother, &c.

When the deceased has left debts or legacies which the heirs decline to discharge, the executor may lawfully sell so much of his testator's estate as is requisite for their liquidation, whether the heirs be minor or adult, and however they may have been related to the deceased. Upon these points there is a general agreement of authorities‡. But whether an executor may lawfully sell the whole of his testator's estate when it is not entirely absorbed by the claims upon it, is a question upon which there is some difference of opinion. That he may lawfully sell the whole of the movables, all concur. But with respect to immovable property, according to *Aboo Yoosuf* and *Moohummud*, no more of it can be sold by an executor than is necessary for the payment of debts and legacies. *Aboo Huneefa*, on the other hand, considered, that a power to sell a part implies a power over the whole, and that

Executor's power for payment of debts and legacies.

* Futawa Sirajiyyah, Appendix, No. 21. Hidaya, Appendix, No. 22. Translation, vol. iv. p. 554.

† Inayah, Appendix, No. 23.

‡ Inayah, Appendix, No. 24. Futawa Alumgeeree, Ap. No. 25.

the remainder may also be lawfully sold by an executor*. In this, as in the case of a guardian, it is proper to distinguish between the strict legal right, and its discreet and judicious exercise ; and it would seem that though an executor be actually possessed of funds of the deceased, adequate to the discharge of his debts, yet that if he do proceed to sell his immovable estate, the sale is notwithstanding lawful†.

Power of a single executor when several are appointed.

When two executors have been appointed, one of them cannot lawfully act without the concurrence of the other, according to *Aboo Huneefa* and *Moohummud,* except in the following instances ; viz. the purchase of requisites for the funeral, and of food and clothes for young children, the restoration of articles which had been deposited with the testator, or usurped by him, or acquired under defective contracts of sale, the general preservation of his property, the payment of debts, the discharge of specific legacies, the manumission of a specific slave, the litigation of the deceased's rights, the acceptance of gifts, the sale of articles to which any loss or damage may be

---

* Inayah, Appendix, No. 26. Futawa Alumgeeree, Appendix, No. 27.

† Futawa Alumgeeree, Appendix, No. 28. This point is of so much importance, that I subjoin a literal translation of the authority. "An executor sold land to pay a debt of the deceased with its price, having property in his hands sufficient to the discharge of the debts: this sale was lawful. So in the *Khuzanut-ool-Mooftieen.*"

apprehended, and generally of all perishable commodities*.

Aboo Yoosuf was of opinion, that executors may act singly in all cases, though appointed together; and there is no doubt that they may do so when they have been appointed separately†. So also, where it is clearly indicated from other circumstances, that such was the intention of the testator. When they are appointed separately.

Upon the death of one of two executors, the rights enjoyed by both do not accrue to the survivor, whose powers are suspended until the appointment by the *kazee* of a successor to the deceased executor, unless the deceased executor had himself nominated the survivor or some other person to be his executor. And even, when so nominated, *Aboo Huneefa* was of opinion, that the survivor cannot lawfully act until the *kazee* has appointed another executor, because if the testator had been content with the discretion of one person in the management of his affairs, he would not have committed it to two persons‡. Power of the survivor.

When a sole executor dies, having appointed an executor of his own will, the person so appointed becomes also the executor of the original testator, according to the general consent of the followers of *Aboo Huneefa*§. The executor of an executor.

---

* Hidaya, Appendix, No. 29. Translation, vol. iv. p. 544 and 555.

† Hidaya, Appendix, No. 30. Translation, vol. iv. p. 546.

‡ Jowhurrut-oon-Nuyyerah, Appendix, No. 31.

§ Ibid, Appendix, No. 32.

The heirs. The clear residue of the estate, after the payment of funeral expences, debts, and legacies, descends to the heirs; and among these the first are persons for whom the law has provided certain specific shares or portions, and who are thence denominated Sharers. *Sharers**. In most cases there must be a residue after the sharers have been satisfied; and this passes to another class of persons who from that circumstance may Residuaries. be termed *Residuarics*†. The name, however, is not always appropriate, for it may happen that the deceased has not left any relative of the class of sharers, and then the whole will pass to one or more individuals of the second class. When there are sharers but no residuaries, the surplus, which would have passed to the latter, reverts to the former with two exceptions, being divisible among them, according to the respective amounts of their shares; and this right of reverter constitutes what is technically call- The return. ed the return‡. It can but seldom happen that the deceased should leave no individual connected with him who would fall under one or other of the classes already mentioned. But to guard against this possible contingency, the law has provided another class of persons, who, though many of them are nearly related to the deceased, have yet been deno-

* Sirajiyyah and Shureefeea, Appendix, No. 33.

† Sirajiyyah, Appendix, No. 34.

‡ Sirajiyyah and Shureefeea, Appendix, No. 35.

minated *distant kindred*, by reason of their remote position with respect to the inheritance*. Distant kindred.

Of the three classes of heirs before-mentioned, the two first are by far the most important, as none of the distant kindred can ever be admitted to a participation in the inheritance so long as there is a single sharer or residuary to claim it. The heirs of a Moohummudan, might therefore, for all practical purposes, be divided into two classes, sharers and residuaries; and these are so distinct from each other, and the rules for their succession also so entirely dissimilar, that we may be apt to infer that the law respecting them was drawn from different sources. This conclusion seems to be justified by the manner in which the two classes are treated of in the Kooran. The sharers and their portions are specifically laid down in that book, while of the residuaries there is only incidental mention as *usubat* or heirs†; the name by which they are still distinguished by Moohummudan lawyers. They are, however, alluded to in such a manner, that it is obvious their rights were sufficiently understood and acknowledged by the persons to whom the Kooran was addressed. Heirs divisible into two classes, sharers and residuaries.

---

* Sirajiyyah, Appendix, No. 36. Arabic *Zuwee-l-urham*, which may be more literally translated, *uterine relatives*.

† "The *Arabic* verb *âs'sába* primarily signifies *to collect and bind together the branches of a tree*: hence the secondary sense, *to constitute the heir and head of a family*." Note to Translation of the *Bigyato'l b'ahith*, by Sir William Jones. Quarto edition of works, vol. iii. p. 496.

And the law respecting them is in fact referred to traditionary decisions of the prophet and his companions. In the *Bigyato'l b'ahith,* which professes to contain the doctrine of inheritance as delivered by *Zeid* the son of *Thabit,* the residuaries and the order of their succession are as distinctly stated as in the *Sirajiyyah.* And *Zeid* was not only one of the prophet's companions, but was expressly recommended by him to his followers as their instructor in the law. How then shall we account for the omission of so important a class of heirs in the Kooran, comprehending, as it does, those who by the common consent of mankind are the best entitled to the succession of a deceased person, namely his sons? To me it seems probable, that the law respecting the residuaries is a relic of the old system of inheritance of the Pagan Arabs, and that the doctrine of shares was superinduced by Moohummud, or if it existed previously to his time, was at least so materially altered by him, as to require, in his opinion, the divine sanction to secure its reception by his countrymen*.

---

* Upon this supposition, there would appear to have been a strong resemblance between the law of inheritance of the old Arabs, and the system of the Romans, before it was remodelled by Justinian. It is impossible to trace the analogy without anticipating the subjects of the fourth and fifth chapters ; but the point is curious and interesting, and the reader will pardon me for dwelling on it for a few minutes. The foundation of inheritance under the law of the Twelve Tables was the preservation of families, and, as daughters became by marriage members of other families, their

Should there be neither sharer nor residuary, nor any of the distant kindred alive and capable of in- Successor by contract.

descendants were constantly excluded. Thus the heirs were, first children, next the children of sons, then the children of sons' sons, and so on *ad infinitum*. It was a saying of the *Khuleef Allee*, that the children of his sons were his own children, but those of his daughters, the children of other men. And the reader will find hereafter that the residuaries of the Moohummudan law are, first sons, then their sons, then the sons of their sons, and so on without limit. As the law now exists, females are residuaries with males of the same degree, that is, daughters with sons, and sons' daughters with sons' sons, &c.; but this may have been an addition made by Moohummud, as the residuary rights of females are founded on a text of the Kooran; though it is also possible that he only revived a provision of the old law. It is not improbable that both by the old Romans and the Arabs, as well as other partially civilized nations, the rights of females were originally little regarded, and that daughters were in practice left dependant on sons under both systems, though perhaps not positively excluded by either. By one of the strongest peculiarities of the old Roman law, the *patria potestas*, children were incapable of acquiring property during the life of the ancestor in whose power they happened to be; and the succession passed as a matter of necessity from descendants to collaterals, among whom it was regulated by the same constant principle of the exclusion of the descendants of females. Thus, the first of the collateral heirs were brothers and sisters, then the children of brothers, and so on, in the same manner, through the remoter branches. There is no trace of the *patria potestas*, in the Arabian system, and, after exhausting the line of descendants, the inheritance ascends; but here the succession is still marked by the same uniform selection of males and persons connected with the deceased through males. Thus among ascendants, the first residuary is the father, the next his father, and so on *ad infinitum*. The rights of the mother and grand-mothers are blended with those of the father and grand-fathers, in the same manner as the

heriting, "the estate goes (unless there be a widow or widower who is first entitled to a share) to him

---

rights of female descendants are mixed with those of males of the same degree. But this also may be said to have been superadded by Moohummud to the old system, for it is a consequence of a rule which is found in the Kooran. In the collateral line the residuaries are first brothers, with whom sisters are united in the same way as daughters with sons; next the sons of brothers, and so on without limit through their descendants, and then in like manner through the remoter lines. But for the exclusion of ascendants under the civil law, and the principle of representation which seems to have existed in it from the earliest times, the residuary system of the Moohummedans, and the law of inheritance of the Twelve Tables, would have been not so much similar as identical. The leading characteristic of both laws, the constant exclusion of the descendants of females, was gradually relaxed among the Romans by the edicts of prætors and the constitutions of some of the emperors; but not finally abolished until the time of Justinian, who placed relatives connected with the deceased through females, or cognates, on the same footing with those connected through males, or agnates, and opened the succession to ascendants, after the line of the descendants is exhausted. The alterations of Moohummud were less sweeping, but perhaps not less just and wise. He not only modified the severity of the old law, by admitting females to a participation in the inheritance with males of the same degree, but, by his doctrine of shares, which allows of the simultaneous succession of relatives of different lines, that is, of ascendants with descendants, he provided for *all* who, by their age, sex, and propinquity may be supposed to have been dependant upon the deceased, while in other respects he left the law as he found it. Justinian, on the other hand, may be said to have entirely reconstructed the Roman Law of Inheritance, yet his system requires the entire exhaustion of one line before any individual of another can be called to the slightest participation in the

who may be called the *successor by contract**." The form of this contract is as follows: if a person of unknown descent say to another, "Thou art my *Mowla*, (master,) and shalt inherit to me when I die, paying my fine when I commit an offence," and the other answer, "I have accepted," the contract is valid; and if the person addressed be also of unknown descent, and make the same proposal, which is in like manner accepted, they become mutually liable for the fines of each other, and the survivor is the heir of his fellow. The maker of a contract of this kind may, however, at any time retract, until his *mowla* has actually paid a fine on his behalf†.

Acknowledgment of kindred.

Next to the successor by contract is a person in whose favor the deceased has made an acknowledgment of kindred, but of such a nature as not to establish his consanguinity, and has persisted in such acknowledgment to his decease‡. To render an acknowledgment of this kind valid, three conditions must be observed. First, it must be in such terms as

Conditions of its validity.

---

succession, and the parents of the deceased are thus left entirely unprovided for, so long as there is a single descendant, however remote. *For the references to the Civil Law in this note, see Justinian's Institutes, Lib.* iii. *Tit.* i. *and* ii.—*and Heineccius' Elementa Juris Civilis, Lib.* iii. *Tit.* i. *et seq.*

* Commentary on the Sirajiyyah by Sir W. Jones. Works, quarto edition, vol. iii. p. 558.

† Sirajiyyah and Shureefeea, Appendix, No. 37.

‡ Sirajiyyah, Appendix, No. 38.

at least to imply the descent of the person acknowledged from some other person than the acknowledger himself. Thus, if one acknowledges as his brother a person of unknown descent, the term implies that the person acknowledged is the child of the acknowledger's father*. But if the acknowledgment were in terms so vague as our English expression cousin, for instance, without any thing to qualify it by which the descent might appear, it would seem to be defective under this condition. Secondly, the acknowledgment must be such as not to establish the descent of the person acknowledged; for if it were sufficient to the latter purpose, (as for instance an acknowledgment of one as a brother *assented to by the acknowledger's father*, which under some exceptions would establish the paternity,) its effect would be to give him an interest in the inheritance on a distinct ground from the acknowledgment, namely as brother to the deceased†. And the third condition is, that the acknowledger should die without retracting the acknowledgment, the reason of which is obvious‡.

When the remoteness of the contingency is considered, it may be thought that too much has been said on this subject. But in a country so extensive as Hindoostan, still composed of different states, whose

---

* Shureefeea, Appendix, No. 39.

† Shureefeea, Appendix, No. 40.

‡ Shureefeea, Appendix, No. 41.

inhabitants are frequently moving from one extremity of it to another, and subject to the influx of strangers from all parts of the world, it must occasionally happen that a person dies without leaving any known relatives, and in such a case it is by no means unusual to exercise the power in question*.

Though the law does not allow a Moohummudan the power of disposing by will of more than a third of his property, still if he has appointed a legatee of the whole, and has left no known heir, nor successor by contract, nor person acknowledged as last mentioned, such legatee is permitted to take the property; for the prohibition against bequeathing more than a third exists solely for the benefit of the heirs†. Universal legatee.

Last of all, when there is none of the persons before mentioned to claim the property, it falls to the *Beit-ool-mal*‡, which is usually, and with sufficient propriety, translated the "public treasury," and for which the British Government has, I believe, The Beit-ool-mal, *ultimus hæres*.

---

* In one of the most important cases that has occurred in this country, since it fell under our dominion, as well for the amount of the property in dispute, as on account of its connection with the judicial administration of Bengal, the heir was a person who claimed as having been acknowledged in this manner by the deceased. I mean the great Patna cause, decided in the time of Mr. Hastings, if it can be said to be yet fully decided, for a claim to part of the property is still under appeal to the Lords of the Privy Council.

† Sirajiyyah and Shureefeea, Appendix, No. 42.

‡ Sirajiyyah, Appendix, No. 43.

substituted itself in this country as *ultimus hæres* to its subjects. The *Beit-ool-mal* is not the property of the ruling power, but that of all Moohummudans, for whose benefit it must be administered; and it may perhaps be questioned, how far our Government, in taking possession of the property of one of its Moohummudan subjects as an escheat, would be justified, under the Moohummudan law, in applying it to the general purposes of the state, or in any other way, than for the exclusive benefit of Moohummudans.

CHAPTER II.

Of Impediments to Inheritance.

Four impediments to inheritance.

THERE are four impediments to inheritance under the Moohummudan law: slavery, homicide, difference of religion, and difference of country*.

1. Slavery.

1. Slavery is either perfect or imperfect; and of imperfect slaves there are three descriptions; the *Mookatub*, whom his master has agreed to emancipate for a specified ransom; the *Moodubbur*, to whom he has promised gratuitous emancipation after his death; and the *Oom-i-wulud*, who has borne a child to her master, and is thence entitled to her liberty at his death. But bondage, whether absolute or qualified, is equally a bar to inheritance; because a slave is incapacitated from acquiring property by any means; and because, if he were capable of inheriting from his own relatives, their succession would fall to his master, to whom everything in his hands belongs, and who might thus in effect succeed to the property of a person to whom he was an absolute stranger†.

Whether absolute or qualified.

---

* Sirajiyyah, Appendix, No. 44.

† Shureefeea, Appendix, No. 45.

Slave partially emancipated. It occasionally happens that a slave, who is the property of several persons, is emancipated by some, and retained in servitude by others. In this situation he is entitled to complete emancipation, on performing emancipatory labor for a due proportion of his value*. Yet even under circumstances comparatively so favorable, the incapacity to inherit is not removed according to *Aboo Huneefa*. Both *Aboo Yoosuf* and *Moohummud*, however, consider that a slave who is partly emancipated is in effect free, and enjoys the right of inheritance with the other privileges of freedom†.

2 Homicide. 2. Homicide is so far an impediment to inheritance, that the slayer is precluded from succeeding to the property of the person whom he has slain; but this consequence attaches to such homicides only as are punishable by retaliation, or require to be expiated in one of the modes prescribed by law‡. Of homicides of this description there are

Intentional. three kinds. First, *intentional* homicide, which subjects the perpetrator to retaliation, and is committed when a human being is wilfully and illegally struck with some deadly instrument, and death is the consequence. According to *Aboo Huneefa*, the instrument must be either a weapon, or something which may be employed instead of a weapon for separating the parts of the body, as a sharpened

---

* Hidaya, Appendix, No. 46; Translation, vol. i. p. 440.

† Shureefeea, Appendix, No. 47.

‡ Sirajiyyah, Appendix, No. 48.

piece of wood or stone; but the disciples reject this distinction, and account the homicide intentional, if the instrument be of such a nature that death would generally ensue from its blow, as a large stone*. Second, homicide which from its similarity to the first is called *quasi intentional*, and differs from it only in the instrument of violence being of such a nature, that its blow would not generally produce death†. Of this offence the penalty is expiation, by emancipating a Moohummudan slave, or fasting for two months in succession; besides a heavy fine of a hundred female camels, of different ages, which is leviable from the *Akila*, or neighbourhood of the slayer‡. The third species of homicide which operates as an impediment to inheritance is, where a person is killed by mischance, as if one shooting at game should hit a human being instead, or a person were to roll over another in his sleep and kill him, or fall down upon him from a terrace, or let a stone drop from his hand upon him, and death should ensue§. In all these cases, it will be observed, that however innocent of any intent to kill or inflict injury, the slayer is the immediate cause of the sufferer's death; and he is consequently liable to a penalty by way of expiation; his neighbourhood being at the same time subject to a fine, which differs only in a trifling

Quasi Intentional.

Accidental.

---

* Shureefeea, Appendix, No. 49.

† Shureefeea, Appendix, No. 50.

‡ Hamilton's Hidaya, vol. iv. pp. 329 and 330.

§ Shureefeea, Appendix, No. 51.

degree from that already mentioned*. But when a person is merely the occasion of another's death, as by digging a well in ground not his own into which one falls, or placing a stone upon it against which one stumbles, and death is the consequence in either case, he is neither liable to expiation nor subject to the incapacity of inheritance; though the neighbourhood is still liable to a fine†, which, as in the former cases, sinks into the estate of the deceased, and forms a part of his succession.

Case of a son killed by his father.

There is one instance of intentional homicide, where the crime induces the incapacity of inheritance, though the offender is not subject to retaliation. This is the case of a son murdered by his father. But it is properly an exception to the law of retaliation, the crime having been originally subject to this highest penalty, though it was remitted by the prophet‡.

3. Difference of religion.

3. Difference of religion is such an impediment to inheritance, that an infidel cannot, in any case, be heir to a believer, nor a believer to an infidel‖. All infidels, however, who, in questions of inheritance are considered of one religion, are capable of inheriting to each other, however different their actual

---

* The expiation for homicide by misadventure is the same, as for *quasi* intentional. Hamilton's Hidaya, vol. iv. p. 329.

† Shureefeea, Appendix, No. 52.

‡ Shureefeea, Appendix, No. 53. On the different kinds of homicide, see Hamilton's Hidaya, vol. iv. pp. 271, 274, and 276.

‖ Shureefeea, Appendix, No. 54.

creeds may happen to be*. *Ibn-Abee Luela* received the latter doctrine with some degree of qualification. He was of opinion, that Jews and Christians might succeed to each other, because they agree in the two important points of the unity of God, and the divine legation of Moses ; but that neither of them could inherit from a *Mujoosee*, nor he from them, because he denies the unity, recognising two Gods, *Yuzdan* and *Ahrimun*†, and neither acknowledges the mission of the prophets, nor possesses any of the Sacred Scriptures‡. Others carry the distinction so far as to deny, that Jews and Christians can inherit to each other, because they differ as much with respect to Christ, as Moslems do from both respecting Moohummud§. Free-thinkers are not disabled from inheriting to Moohummudans, because they concur in the belief of the Prophets and the Scriptures, and differ only in their interpretation of the latter, and of the traditions‖. But apostates are declared to be incapable of inheriting to any one, even to apostates like themselves¶; partly as a punishment for their guilt in abandoning the faith, and also because they are not considered to be of any religion; the law refusing

Apostasy.

---

* Shureefeea, Appendix, No. 55.

† The principles of good and evil.

‡ Shureefeea, Appendix, No. 56.

§ Shureefeea, Appendix, No. 57.

‖ Shureefeea, Appendix, No. 58.

¶ Sirajiyah, Appendix, No. 59.

to acknowledge them as belonging even to that to which they have apostatized*.

Succession to apostates.

The Moslem heirs of an apostate are not deprived of their right of inheritance, with the exception of a husband or wife, who are excluded, because the marriage, which is the basis of their right, is dissolved by the apostasy of either party†. Apostasy being a voluntary act, a husband is not excluded from the succession to his wife, if she has apostatized *in extremis*‡, nor a wife from the succession to her husband, if, before the expiration of her *iddut*, he is put to death for his apostasy, or dies naturally, or is judicially pornounced to have taken refuge in a hostile country§.

Punishment of apostasy in males.

A male apostate is liable to be put to death, if he continues obstinate in his error‖; for which *Aboo Huneefa* has assigned this among other reasons, that he is to be viewed in the light of an enemy who has entered the Moohummudan territories without protection. An enemy in such circumstances is deprived of the use of his property, his power over which is suspended until it is determined whether he shall be put to death or reduced to slavery; and, according to *Aboo Huneefa*, a male apostate is in like manner disabled from selling or otherwise disposing of his

Power of a male apostate over his property.

* Shureefeea, Appendix, No. 60.

† Shureefeea, Appendix, No. 61.

‡ Hidaya, Appendix, No. 62. Translation, vol. ii. p. 232.

§ Hidaya, Appendix, No. 63. Translation, vol. ii. p. 232. For an explanation of the term *iddut*, see Note, p. 4.

‖ Futawa Alumgeeree, Appendix, No. 64.

property. But *Aboo Yoosuf* and *Moohummud* differed from their master upon this point; considering a male apostate to be as competent to the exercise of every right, as if he were still in the faith*. There was also a difference of opinion between the master and his disciples, with respect to the distribution of a male apostate's property at his death, or escape to a hostil country and judicial declaration of that fact. *Aboo Huneefa* distinguished between acquisitions made before and subsequent to the apostasy, declaring the former to be the property of the heirs, and the latter to belong to the *Beit-ool-mal*; while *Aboo Yoosuf* and *Moohummud*, rejecting this distinction, maintained the right of the heirs to the whole property†.

Acquisitions before and after apostasy.

Apostasy in females.

A female apostate is not subject to capital punishment, though she may be kept in confinement until she recants‡; and with respect to her property, the whole of it, without distinction, and by the general consent of the learned, descends to her Moohummudan heirs§, with the exception of her husband, as already mentioned. There seems to be a like uniformity of opinion regarding the validity of a female apostate's disposal of her property, the argument of *Aboo Huneefa* in the case of males being inapplicable to women, who can never be considered enemies‖.

* Hidaya, Appendix, No. 65. Translation, vol. ii. p. 235.

† Sirajiyyah, Appendix, No. 66.

‡ Hidaya, Appendix, No. 67. Translation, vol. ii. p. 227.

§ Sirajiyyah, Appendix, No. 68.

‖ Hidaya, Appendix, No. 69. Translation, vol. ii. p. 238.

When the apostate has taken refuge in a hostile country, he becomes an alien enemy, and his Moohummudan heirs are precluded from succeeding to any property which he may have acquired subsequently to that period, by the next impediment to inheritance, which is difference of country. In this respect, male and female apostates are on the same footing by the general concurrence of the learned*.

Rule as to the religion of infants.

The general rule respecting infant children is that they are to be considered of the same religion with their parents. But where one of the parents is a Moohummudan, and the other of a different persuasion, as a Christian or Jew, the infant shall be accounted a Moohummudan, on the principle, that where the reasons are equally balanced, the preference is to be given to that religion as the more worthy in the eye of law†.

Difference of country.

IV. The last impediment to inheritance is difference of country; which is either actual, as between an enemy and a *Zimmee*‡; or constructive, as between a *Zimmee* and a *Moostamin*§, or between two

---

* Desertion to a foreign country and judicial declaration of the fact amount to *civil death;* hence the right of the deserter's heirs to take immediate possession of his property, as in the case of natural demise. Apostasy has not that effect; and the distinction is of some consequence in this country, where the capital penalty cannot be enforced.

† Hidaya, Appendix, No. 70. Translation, vol. i. p. 177. Shureefeea, Appendix, No. 71.

‡ Tributary infidel.

§ Literally "one who has sought protection," but applied to all foreigners living by permission in the Mohummudan territories.

Moostamins from different countries*. When an enemy dies in a hostile country, leaving within the Moohummudan territories, a father or son who is a *Zimmee,* or a *Zimmee* dies in the Moohummudan territories, leaving a father or son who is an enemy and residing in an hostile country, neither can succeed to the other, though they should be of the same religion, because their countries are *actually* different, the *Zimmee* being to all intents and purposes a subject of the Moohummudan state†. The case is so far different with respect to a *Zimmee* and a *Moostamin,* that for the time they are both inhabitants of the same country; but their condition is not the same, the *Zimmee* being, as already observed, the subject of the Moohummudan state, to which he pays tribute and owes allegiance, and being no longer at liberty to return to the place of his birth. The *Moostamin,* on the other hand, is only on sufferance in the Moohummudan territory, where he is not permitted to remain longer than a year, and during that time he neither pays tribute, nor is debarred from returning to the country from whence he came, and to which he is held to belong. It is not to be wondered at, therefore, that the *Zimmee* and *Moostamin* should be accounted in law as of different countries, and consequently incapable of inheriting the one to the other‡.

Actual.

Constructive.

* Sirajiyya, Appendix, No. 72.

† Shureefeea, Appendix, No. 73.

‡ Shureefeea, Appendix, No. 74. For the law respecting Moostamins, see the Translation of the Hidaya, vol. ii. Book of Institutes, chap. vi.

In what the difference of country consists.

Countries differ from each other by having different sovereigns and armies* ; but Moohummudans, though no longer subject to the sway of one prince, are still accounted of the same country, being connected together by the tie of their common religion. Difference of country is consequently no impediment to inheritance, so far as they are concerned†. It is also liable to some modification with respect to unbelievers. In the early ages of the Moohummudan religion, all who were not for it were considered to be against it, and every infidel was an enemy, on whom it was the sacred duty of the true believer to wage war until he embraced the faith or consented to pay tribute. In later times some practical relaxation of this doctrine became necessary ; and we accordingly find the Turks and some other Moohummudan nations entering into treaties of peace, and even offensive and defensive alliances, with people of a different faith. Difference of country is no impediment to inheritance, between the subjects of kingdoms between which there subsist engagements for mutual assistance against enemies‡ ; and a simple treaty of peace would probably have the same effect, though the authorities are not so express upon this point. The reason assigned by the author of the *Sirajiyyah*, for the difference of country being a bar to inheritance, is the want of mu-

---

* Sirajiyyah, Appendix, No. 75.

† Shureefeea, Appendix, No. 76.

‡ Shureefeea, Appendix, No. 77.

tual protection to the subjects of different states *; and it is applicable only to a state of actual warfare, which was probably the condition of the whole world, so far as the author was acquainted with it, at the time that he wrote. The comment on the text also implies a state of hostilities; for it supposes by way of illustration, that if a soldier of one of the states fall in the way of the troops of the other, they may lawfully put him to death†. It seems therefore probable that in the present age of the world, the subjects of different countries may lawfully inherit to each other, if there be no other legal impediment, unless their governments be positively opposed in actual warfare.

Of all the disqualifications above enumerated, the effect upon the person subject to them is absolute exclusion from the right of inheritance, and upon all others the same, as if the disqualified person were actually dead‡. This certainly appears to be the natural consequence, according to our ideas, and would probably be taken for granted by the reader at this stage of his progress. But he will see hereafter, that while the existence of a particular heir has the effect of entirely excluding from the inheritance some persons who would otherwise be entitled to participate in it, it merely reduces the shares of others from a higher to a lower degree, which is called in law par- Effect of disqualification.

* Sirajiyyah, Appendix, No. 75.

† Shureefeea, Appendix, No. 78.

‡ Sirajiyyah and Shureefeea, Appendix, No. 79.

Peculiar opinion of *Ibn Musood.*

tial exclusion. *Ibn Musood* contends, that a disqualified person, though he is himself incapable of deriving any benefit from his relationship to the deceased, is nevertheless the means of partially excluding others*. Thus, to take a case which actually occurred in the time of the *Khuleef Alee*, the fourth successor to *Moohummud*, a Moohummudan woman died, leaving a husband and two half-brothers by the same mother, all of whom were of the faith, and a son who was an unbeliever. Here the son was of course disabled from inheriting by reason of his unbelief; but according to *Ibn Musood*, his mere existence ought to have partially excluded the husband by reducing his share from a half to a fourth. The *Khuleef*, however, and *Zeid Ibn Thabit*, decided that the son was to be considered in the same light as if he were dead, and they awarded one-half of the inheritance to the husband, one-third to the brethren, and the remainder to the residuary heirs†. This decision was approved by *Aboo Huneefa* and his followers, and they have accordingly adopted the principle on which it was founded.

---

* Sirajiyyah, Appendix, No. 80.

† Shureefeea, Appendix, No. 81.

CHAPTER III.

Of Parentage.

Relation between persons the foundation of inheritance.

THE right of inheritance depends in every case on the existence of some relation, either natural or artificial, between the deceased and the person who claims to be his heir. The few artificial relations which confer the right of inheritance have been sufficiently noticed in the first chapter, with the exception of marriage, into the consideration of which I could not enter without too great a departure from the proper subject of this essay. It is besides fully treated of in the *Hidaya;* and to the translation of that work by Mr. Hamilton, I beg leave generally to refer the reader, though some incidental notice of the evidence necessary to the establishment of marriage will be found towards the close of this chapter. All natural relations may be ultimately reduced to that which subsists between parent and child; and a good deal respecting it may also be found in the *Hidaya*, but it is dispersed through different parts of the work; and I have never met with a connected view of the subject in any treatise on Moohummudan Law. I therefore propose to collect in this place, some of the most important passages from the principal authorities on this branch of the law, placing them to the best of my power before the English reader in the order that appears to me to be the most natural.

The relation between parent and child how established.

The relation between a mother and her child is held to be sufficiently established by evidence of its birth, whether it be the fruit of lawful intercourse, or not*. The descent of a child, on the other hand, from a particular man can never be established, where his intercourse with its mother was not lawful†. There is an obvious difference between the two facts considered with respect to their susceptibility of proof, which appears to be the ground of this marked distinction in the law‡.

What intercourse of the sexes is lawful.

All intercourse between the sexes is unlawful, where there is neither marriage nor the semblance of it between the parties, and the man has neither a right of property, nor the semblance of such right in the woman§. A man may lawfully have at one time so many as four wives, provided that they are of his own faith, or Christians, or Jews; and the law has prescribed no limit to the number of slaves with whom he may legally cohabit. But intercourse between the sexes, where the woman is neither the wife nor slave of the man, is *zina* or fornication‖, and is severely punishable; being visited, in its more ag-

Fornication.

---

* Futawa Sirajiyyah, Appendix, No. 82.

† Jowhurrut-oon-Nuyyerah, Appendix, No. 83.

‡ Inayah, Appendix, No. 84.

§ Jowhurrut-oon-Nuyyerah, Appendix, No. 85.

‖ Hidaya, Appendix, No. 86. Translation, vol. ii. p. 18.

gravated form of adultery, on the married party, with the heaviest penalty of the law, or stoning to death. To constitute moral guilt, there must be a guilty knowledge on the part of the agent, and whenever that knowledge is absent, the specific punishment of fornication is not inflicted: but the waiving of the punishment does not legalise the act; and it is only in cases where a doubt attaches to the illegality of the intercourse, or as before expressed, where there is a semblance of marriage, or of a right of property in the woman, that even an express acknowledgment or claim by the man, of the children who are the fruit of the intercourse, can establish their descent from him*. The cases in which such a doubt of the illegality exists, as to render the establishment of the children's descent possible, are the following, as stated in the authorities cited below†. 1. Where the woman is the slave of the man's son, or of his son's son. 2. Where she is in her *iddut* after a complete divorce by implication. 3. Where the woman is a slave sold by the man, but not delivered to the purchaser. So also where she is the slave of his *Mookatub*‡, or of his licensed slave§. 4. Where she is a slave

Its punishment.

When waived.

Cases of doubtful legality, where the paternity of a child may be established.

---

* Hidaya, Appendix, No. 86. Futawa Alumgeeree, Appendix, No. 87.

† Hidaya, Appendix, No. 88. Translation, vol. ii. p. 21. Futawa Alumgeeree, Appendix, No. 89.

‡ See page 21.

§ That is, a slave licensed by his master to trade.

assigned to a wife as her dower, but is still undelivered. 5. Where she is a slave held by the man in common with other persons as partners. 6. Where she is a slave impledged, and is carnally enjoyed by the pledge. In the above cases the descent of the child, which is the fruit of the intercourse, is established from the man, if he claim or acknowledge it; but otherwise not. To these may perhaps be added the case of a marriage contracted without witnesses, and one where the woman is still in her *iddut* after separation from another man*. Marriage in these circumstances is not strictly legal, but there is such a semblance of legality as appears to withdraw the intercourse from the opprobrium of fornication, and to render the offspring the husband's if claimed by him. It must be observed, however, with respect to the former, that the presence of witnesses is essential to the actual constitution of marriage†, which seems to be inconsistent with even such a shade of legality as would render the establishment of the descent possible.

By the acknowledgment of its putative father.

Legality of intercourse has reference to the period of the child's conception.

To establish the descent of a child from a man, it is necessary that the relation between its parents, which legalises their intercourse, should have subsisted at the supposed period of its conception. Accordingly, if a married woman should produce a child within six months from the date of her marriage, which is the shortest period of gestation in the

* Jowhurrut-oon-Nuyyerah, Appendix, No. 35.

† See post. page 48.

human species, according to the Moohummudan lawyers, its descent is not established from her husband unless he claims it* ; and even in the event of his claiming it, if he should admit that it was the fruit of fornication, its descent is not established†. In like manner, the child born to a slave girl, within six months from the day on which she was purchased, does not belong to the buyer, but to the seller. The slave herself also reverts to the seller, to whom she has now become an *oom-i-wulud* by bearing him a child, which renders the sale unlawful; and it is accordingly cancelled and the purchase-money restored‡.

According to the followers of *Aboo Huneefa*, there are three steps or degrees in the establishment of descent; meaning the descent of a child from a man, for with respect to its mother, proof of its birth, as already observed, is all that the case requires or admits of. The first step is a valid marriage, or a marriage of which (though defective in some respects), the defect is not such as to reach any thing essential to the contract. The second is the peculiar relation which subsists between a master and his slave, when she has already borne him a child, and becomes his *oom-i-wulud*. The third is the simple relation of master and slave. Marriage, which is the first degree, differs from the others in so much that the descent

Three steps or degrees in the establishment of paternity.

1. Marriage.

2. Where the child's mother is an *oom-i-wulud*.

3. Where simply a slave.

* Futawa Alumgeeree, Appendix, No. 90.

† Futawa Alumgeeree, Appendix, No. 91.

‡ Hidaya, Appendix, No. 92. Translation, vol. iii. p. 124.

Difference between marriage and other degrees.

of a child is established from the husband of its mother, without any claim or acknowledgment upon his part; (that is, where the birth has taken place at a due time after the solemnization of the marriage ;) and cannot be repudiated by a simple denial, nor any thing short of the solemn form of *lian* or imprecation*; whereby the husband formally charges his wife with adultery, repudiates her offspring, and imprecates curses on his own head if he has accused her falsely. It is only where both the parties are free, adult, of sound mind, and Moosulmans, that the case is susceptible of *lian* †, and it is only in cases to which the *lian* is applicable, that a child, born at a due time after marriage, can possibly be repudiated by the husband of its mother ‡. To guard against the abuse of so extraordinary a power, the husband is allowed but a short time for its exercise. According to *Aboo Huneefa*, the child's descent is established, unless denied by the husband previous to its birth; and though his disciples *Aboo Yoosuf* and *Moohummud* have allowed of a slight enlargement of the period for coming to a determination on so important a point as the rejection of offspring, they both agree that it should not be long §.

Child begotten in marriage can be repudiated only by *lian*.

Paternity of a child born to an *oom-i-wulud* established without express claim.

When a slave has already borne a child to her master, her condition is materially improved. She

---

* Futawa Alumgeeree, Appendix, No. 93.

† Hamilton's Hidaya, vol. i. p. 344.

‡ Appendix, No. 93.

§ Hamilton's Hidaya, vol. i. p. 352.

can no longer be sold, and is entitled to her freedom at his death. She thus acquires the character of a fixed member of his family, and any child whom she may subsequently bring forth, is so far presumed to have been begotten by him, that its descent is established without any claim or acknowledgment upon his part. Its condition, however, differs in one respect from that of a child begotten in marriage, that it is liable to repudiation by a simple denial*. But there is a limit to the exercise of this power; for if the paternity has once been judicially declared, or a long time has been allowed to elapse after the birth of the child, it can no longer be repudiated†. When it is said that the child of an *oom-i-wulud* is presumed to be her master's, this must be understood with some qualification; for if, at the supposed period of the child's conception, the intercourse of the master had, by reason of any supervening circumstance, ceased to be lawful, as for instance, by his entering into an agreement with her of *kitabut*, or emancipation for a specific ransom, or having sexual intercourse with her mother or daughter, the child must be claimed in order to establish its descent from the master of the *oom-i-wulud*‡.

May be repudiated by simple denial.

The last degree in the establishment of the paternity of a child is when it is born to a slave girl, who has never before borne a child to her master; and in that case, it is not accounted his without an express claim or acknowledgment of it as his offspring§.

Express claim requisite to establish the paternity of a child born to a mere slave.

* Appendix, No. 93. † Ibid. ‡ Appendix, No. 93. § Ibid.

Who are legal slaves.

The only legal slaves are captives in religious warfare, or wars undertaken for the propagation of the Moohummudan faith, and the descendants of such captives. Of these, there are probably very few in the British dominions in India ; and to constitute the legal descent of a child from a man in this country, it must therefore, in general, be necessary, that it should have been begotten in marriage. It does not follow, however, that in all cases of disputed paternity, the marriage of the child's parents must be proved. The constitution of the relation and its proof are obviously distinct. The latter, as a branch of the general subject of evidence, does not fall within the limits of this essay : but a few words on the effect of acknowledgment, considered as a means of establishing the relation of persons to each other, may not be superfluous in this place. And to these I shall add some observations respecting the indirect means of inferring marriage, and consequently the descent of children, afforded by the continued cohabitation of parties.

Acknowledgment a means of establishing parentage. Its conditions.

Acknowledgment is in some instances sufficient evidence of parentage ; but there are three conditions necessary to its validity. 1. The ages of the acknowledger and the person acknowledged must be such, as to admit at least of the possibility of their standing to each other in the relation of parent and child. 2. The person acknowledged must be of unknown descent. And 3. he must believe or assent to the fact of his being the acknowledger's child*.

* Inayah, Appendix, No. 94.

To bring an acknowledgment within the limits of the first condition, the acknowledger, if a female, must be nine years and a half, and if a male, twelve years and a half, older than the person acknowledged*. The second condition guards the doctrine of acknowledgment from being made a means of adoption, to the prejudice of the proper heirs; as a descent which is established from one person cannot be transferred to another†. The third condition is to be understood with some qualification; for the assent of an infant, too young to be able to give any account of himself, is not requisite to the validity of an acknowledgment‡.

First condition.

Second condition.

Third condition.

When the preceding conditions concur in an acknowledgment of parentage, the person acknowledged becomes an heir of the acknowledger, and is entitled to a full participation in his inheritance with the other heirs of the same description; even though he were sick at the time when the acknowledgment was made §.

The person acknowledged is entitled to a full share of the inheritance.

The doctrine of acknowledgment is applicable to the establishment of other degrees of kindred, besides that of parentage. The acknowledgment of a man is valid with respect to his father, mother, child, wife, and emancipator; whether made in health or in sickness: but the assent of all the persons ac-

Other relations established by a man's acknowledgment.

---

* Jowhurrut-oon-Nuyyerah, Appendix, No. 95.

† Ibid. Appendix, No. 96.

‡ Ibid. Appendix, No. 97, and see Hamilton's Hidaya, vol. iii. p. 170.

§ Jowhurrut-oon-Nuyyerah, Appendix, No. 98.

knowledged is necessary to the establishment of the relation between the parties, subject to the limitation already noticed with respect to the assent of children*. The acknowledgment of a woman is also valid with respect to her father, husband, and emancipator†; but not so with respect to her child, because its effect, if allowed, would be to impute the child to her husband‡. This exception is to be understood only of a woman who is married, or in her *iddut;* and even with respect to a *femme coverte,* her acknowledgment is valid, if credited by her husband, or confirmed by the testimony of the midwife; for all that is necessary is evidence of the actual birth, to which the testimony of one woman is sufficient§, the ascription of the child to the husband being an inference of law from the fact of marriage, as already observed, which can be rebutted only by the *lian* or imprecation. Where a woman has no known husband, there ceases to be any reason against the validity of her acknowledgment of a child, and it is accordingly held to be sufficient to establish its descent from herself‖. In most of the authorities, a woman's acknowledgment is stated to be valid with respect to both her parents;

By a woman's.

Her acknowledgment not valid with respect to a child.

Exception.

* Jowhurrut-oon-Nuyyerah, Appendix, No. 99. Inayah, Appendix, No. 100.

† Jowhurrut-oon-Nuyyerah, Appendix, No. 101. Inayah, Appendix, No. 102.

‡ Inayah, Appendix, No. 103. Jowhurrut-oon-Nuyyerah, Appendix, No. 104.

§ Appendix, No. 103 and 104.

‖ Jowhurrut-oon-Nuyyerah, Appendix, No. 104.

but the author of the *Jowhurrah* justly observes, that it ought to be restricted to her father; for if it were valid with respect to her mother, the mother's assent being all that is farther necessary to complete the evidence, a woman's acknowledgment would thus in all cases be good for establishing the descent of a female child from herself; which it is not, when she is *vestita viro*, or in her *iddut*, according to the concurrence of all authorities*.

In what cases the assent requisite to acknowledgment may be given after the acknowledger's death.

The assent of the person acknowledged, which is necessary to the proof of kindred by acknowledgment, may in a case of descent be interposed after the death of the acknowledger, because descent is not rendered void by death. So also where the acknowledgment is made with respect to a wife, because one at least of the rights or consequences of the marriage remains after her husband's death, that is the *iddut*†. Where the person acknowledged is the husband, his assent cannot be received after his wife's death, according to *Aboo Huneefa*, the marriage and all its rights or consequences being at an end. But *Aboo Yoosuf* and *Moohummud* maintained the validity of the acknowledgment in this case also, on the ground that inheritance, which is one of its rights, remains‡.

Implied acknowledgment.

We have hitherto been speaking of express acknowledgment, but there is one case of what may

---

* Jowhurrut-oon-Nuyyerah, Appendix, No. 104.

† Inayah, Appendix, No. 105.

‡ Jowhurrut-oon-Nuyyerah, Appendix, No. 106.

be called implied acknowledgment, which deserves some consideration from the frequency of its occurrence. I mean the case of a man and woman living together and having children, where there is no evidence of actual acknowledgment on the part of the man, though his whole conduct may indicate nevertheless that he always looked upon the children as his own. If it can be shewn, that the woman is one with whom a Moohummudan cannot lawfully have intercourse, (as an idolatress, for instance,) the most express acknowledgment by the man would not be sufficient to establish their descent from him, as already noticed. So also, if it could be proved, that the woman was the wife of another during the time of the intercourse of which the children were the fruit, the intercourse would in like manner be *zina*, and express acknowledgment insufficient. But the proof of the latter issue is less easy than might at first strike the English reader, for the woman, though once married, might have been divorced, and it may frequently be difficult to *prove* that there was an actually subsisting marriage with another person at the time of the children's conception. Much less can it be proved, that the intercourse was unlawful, where the woman may legally be the wife of the person from whom it is desired to establish the descent of her children; that is, one of the same religion, and who is neither related to him within the forbidden degrees, nor the wife of another; the man himself, too, having no more than his legal complement of wives. Let us suppose that in such circumstances, where there is a mere absence of any evidence of marriage, and on the other hand, no proof of the illegality of the intercourse, that the man expressly acknowledges the children to be his. The legal effect of the acknowledgment is not limited to the establishment of their descent, or to the obligation of continuing to maintain them as his children; (both which consequences may probably be in his contemplation, as the acknowledgment implies a conviction in his own mind that the children are actually, if not legally, his own;) but it also exposes him to the severe penalty attached to fornication, amounting in some cases to capital punishment, if it should subsequently transpire, that the woman was not in fact related to him in such a manner as legalized his intercourse with her. No such consequence could attach to the tacit acknowledgment implied in his conduct. Nothing short of the evidence of four male witnesses, or the positive confession of the accused, can establish the fact of fornication*; and whatever suspicion may be excited, by a person bringing up as his own the children of a woman who is not his wife nor his slave, that he is conscious of having had criminal intercourse with their mother, yet there is nothing in that, even coupled with the fact of his notoriously living with her, that the law can properly lay hold of as a proof of his guilt. An express acknowledgment is thus

General consequence of express acknowledgment.

* Hidaya, Appendix, No. 107. Translation, vol. ii. p. 203.

Difference between express and implied acknowledgment considered as evidence of paternity.

viewed only in the light of evidence, entitled to a weight which cannot be allowed to one that is only implied. And I am not aware of any authority that supports the proposition, that the want of an express acknowledgment of descent can be supplied by inferences drawn from the conduct of the party. Indeed it is quite undisputed, that where the woman is the slave of the man, and not his *oom-i-wulud*, nothing short of a direct claim or acknowledgment of the children can establish their descent from him. And it is only when the slave has previously borne him a child, that even his acquiescence for a *long time* in the ascription of her subsequent children to him, can preclude him from afterwards disclaiming them. It would seem to follow *a fortiori*, that a positive claim or acknowledgment is necessary where the woman cannot be shown to have been related to him in any way that would render their intercourse lawful.

Case of constructive marriage.

It seems fair that the most liberal construction should be put on the admission of a fact, so as to avoid if possible the imputation of a collateral crime, which it is not the intention of the party to confess. Thus, where a man acknowledges a child produced by his wife within six months after his marriage, though there is strong reason to suspect that it must have been begotten in fornication, yet the descent is established, unless the acknowledger expressly admit it to be the fruit of unlawful intercourse*. It is, however, carrying the indulgence

---

See *ante*, page 37.

too far to reject the distinct testimony of a third party, because its tendency, if true, would be to impute a crime. Least of all, can there be any necessity for doing so, when the crime is of such a description that the law has required the evidence of several persons to establish it, and the testimony of one, however positive, can infer only a suspicion of its having been committed. Yet this appears to have been done by one of the Law Officers of the *Sudder Dewany Adawlut*, in the important case cited by Mr. Macnaghten at page 299 of his Principles and Precedents of Moohummudan Law; where the descent of children was held to be sufficiently established from a man, though there was no evidence of acknowledgment upon his part, and some of the witnesses positively declared that he was not married to their mothers. The latter fact being rejected by the *Kazee-ool-Koozzat* for the reason mentioned, the way was cleared for a constructive marriage between the mothers and the putative father of the children, and the latter were accordingly declared to be his heirs. But the Court is said to have gone further than the particular case, and to have decided, among other things, the general point, " that a marriage may be proved by something short of ocular proof, such as continual cohabitation, notoriety, hear-say, or circumstantial evidence*." It would be

---

* Principles and Precedents of Moohummudan law.—Note to page 302.

too great a digression to enter into a full examination of all the particulars which are here mentioned, and I shall confine myself to a few observations on the value of continual cohabitation, considered as an evidence of marriage, which is of too much importance to be entirely omitted.

Proof of marriage.

It may be observed in general, with respect to the proof of marriage, that the Moohummudan law has made ample provision for the preservation of direct evidence respecting it. Where the parties are Moosulmans, it is necessary that the ceremony be performed in the presence of two male, or one male and two female witnesses, who are free, sane, adult and Moosulmans*. And the presence of these is required, as a condition essential to the constitution of the contract†. It would seem, however, that the object was publicity or something more than evidence, for the character of the witnesses, which is so carefully investigated in other cases, is here of no account; the presence of a person who has undergone the specific punishment for slander, and whose evidence is not generally admissible, being expressly declared to be sufficient‡.

---

* Hidaya, Appendix, No. 108, Translation, vol. i. p. 74.

† Budaye and Buhr-oor-Raik, as cited in the Futawa Alumgeeree, Appendix, No. 109.

‡ Buhr-oor-Raik, as above, Appendix, No. 110.

Now there is nothing in the fact of cohabitation, from which it can be inferred, that a contract of this special description has been entered into. If we imply that the intercourse of persons cohabiting together is legal, it is surely all that can be required in the most liberal indulgence for their situation. But it is not necessary for this purpose that we should suppose them to be married. If the woman be the slave of the man, their intercourse will be just as lawful as if she were his wife; and it is at least fully as probable that they should have been living together in a relation, which may be constituted by sale or gift, or any other of the numerous ways that property is acquired, as that they should have entered into a contract requiring formalities which almost ensure its publicity; and yet that not a trace of that contract should remain in the recollection of any person who can be produced as a witness*. It is true, that in this country, where there are so few legal slaves, the probabilities are less that the parties are in the predicament of master and slave. But it must be remembered, that we are considering the effect of cohabitation under the Moohummudan law, which was not made for this country, but for a state of society where legal slavery was common. It is farther to be observed, that the value of cohabitation, as an inference of

General value of cohabitation as a fact from which the contract of marriage may be inferred.

* The reader will keep in view, that if the woman were the slave of the man, the marriage would be *illegal*, and *express* acknowledgment by him of her child unquestionably necessary to the establishment of the paternity.

marriage, depends on the moral feelings of the community, and there is no reason to doubt, that though the number of legal slaves in the British dominions in India must be very small in the strict sense of the Moohummudan law, yet that there are persons who in the common parlance of the country are called slaves, and that the intercourse of these with their masters is just as lawful in the estimation of all good Moohummudans, with the exception perhaps of such as are versed in their law, as if they were slaves in the most rigid sense. In the case under discussion, the mothers of the children, whose descent was held to be established, were declared by the witnesses to be slaves of this description to their putative father.

Grounds of the *Kazee-ool-Koozaat's* opinion investigated.

The above reasoning, it must be admitted, is at variance with the opinion expressed by the *Kazee-ool-Koozzat*, and the decision of the court, which was in accordance with it; and it becomes necessary to examine the authorities adduced by the learned *Kazee* in support of his opinion. The first of these, from the *Khoolasut-ool-Mooftieen*, is to the following effect: "Generally speaking, hearsay evidence is not admissible, except in four cases. Regarding death, or descent, or marriage, or with respect to a *Kazee*. To instance this in a case of descent: when a person hears from others, that such a one is the son of such a one, it is competent to him to give his evidence to that effect, although he may not have witnessed the birth in that person's family; in the same manner as we at this day testify, that *Aboo Bucr* (on whom be the mercy of God) was the son of *Quhafa*, although we never saw *Quhafa*. To instance marriage: when a man sees another living in a state of cohabitation with a woman, and it is rumoured that she is his wife, it is competent to him to give evidence, that the woman is the wife of that person, although he may not have been present when the marriage was contracted. And when persons give evidence under such circumstances, declaring, that they are not eye-witnesses to the fact, but that it is notorious, their testimony will we received as valid*." Upon this quotation, so far as relates to marriage, I have to observe, that the fact of cohabitation is coupled with a *rumour* (in itself no slight degree of evidence), that the parties are married, and that it is merely stated to be *competent* to the person who has this double ground of conviction, to bear testimony to the fact. While it is only when the rumour has risen to *notoriety* (in some cases a very high species of evidence), that testimony will be received to the fact of marriage, when the persons giving it admit that they were not eye-witnesses. So that it would appear, that whenever the defective grounds of belief are exposed to the judge, and the testimony is found to rest on no better foundation than the cohabitation of the parties, and a rumour of their marriage, it will be rejected as insufficient to establish the fact. That this is the true meaning

* Principles and Precedents of Moohummudan Law, p. 301.

of the passage is obvious from the parallel passage of the Jowhurrut-oon-Nuyyerah cited below*, where it is distinctly stated, that, in the four cases in which it is lawful for a person to bear testimony to a fact which he has not seen, he must have received the information from two male, or one male and two female, credible witnesses; the information must have been communicated to him in the formal words of testimony; he must believe it in his heart to be true; and finally, that he must not explain the grounds on which his testimony rests; for if he does explain it, as for instance if he say, "I bear witness from hearsay," it is incumbent on the *Kazee* to reject his testimony. This is confirmed by the only other authority quoted by the *Kazee-ool-Koozzat* from the *Hidaya*, though he has not given the passage at length. Thus, "it is not allowable for witnesses to depose to any thing which they have not seen, except in cases of descent, marriage, death, jurisdiction of a *Kazee*, and sexual intercourse. It is competent to a person to depose to a fact which may have been communicated to him by another in whom he has confidence. This proceeds upon a favorable construction." The *Kazee's* quotation then proceeds: "Thus, for instance, a person sees a man and woman living in the same house, and cohabiting with each other after the manner of husband and wife. In such case he may depose to the marriage†." But the quotations are widely apart in the

* Appendix, No. 111.

† Principles and Precedents of Moohummudan Law, p. 301.

original, being separated by what in the translation is a whole quarto page, and partly by a passage which contains the very distinction that I have alluded to. This passage, including the reference to cohabitation, is as follows: "When a person, in any of the above cases, gives evidence from creditable hearsay, it is requisite that he give it in an *absolute* manner, by saying, for instance, 'I bear testimony that A is the son of B,' and not, 'I bear testimony so and so, *because I have heard it*,' for in that case the *Kazee* cannot accept it; in the same manner as if a person, having seen a thing in the hands of *A*, were to say, 'This thing is the property of A,' in which case his testimony is valid: but if he should state that 'he gives evidence *because he has seen the thing in the possession of A*,' the *Kazee* could not accept his testimony. So also, if a person see another sitting in the court of justice, deciding in a suit between plaintiff and defendant, it is lawful for him to give evidence that 'that person was a Kazee;' or if a person see a man and woman dwelling in the same house, and conducting themselves towards one another in the manner of husband and wife, he may lawfully give evidence of their being husband and wife; in the same manner as it is lawful for a person who sees a melon in the hand of another, to give evidence that it is the property of that person*." The distinction between the statement of a witness and the grounds of his belief

* Hidaya, Appendix, No. 112. Translation, vol. ii. p. 678.

does not exist in our law, where the latter are always the subject of careful investigation. But whether it be that the Moohummudan lawyers, as they are more careful about the character of the persons admitted to give testimony, so they place greater reliance on human testimony when given, and are less in the habit of cross examining witnesses, there is no question that the distinction exists in the Moohummudan law. That the practice of cross-examination is not entirely unknown, appears from the comment of the *Inayah* on the passage just quoted from the *Hidaya*. The author puts the case, that the *Kazee* should interrogate the witness who speaks to the marriage of persons whom he sees cohabiting together as man and wife, if he was present at the marriage. If he should answer in the negative, he may still have heard it in such a manner as to justify him *in foro conscientiæ* in positively asserting the fact, and his evidence is not rejected, because the assertion, until it is actually discovered to rest on the defective ground of hearsay, is entitled to be received. But if the inquiry is pushed farther, and it is found that the foundation of the belief is in reality no better than hearsay, it is at once rejected*. Here it is obvious, that the fact of cohabitation, separated from the rumour of marriage, is not taken into account at all, as forming any ground from which a rational inference can be drawn†.

* Inayah, Appendix, No. 113.

† There is something so defective in hearsay, as a channel of

If what has been above offered be considered sufficient to explain away the two passages cited by the *Kazee-ool-Koozzat*, in support of his opinion in favor of cohabitation, then there has nothing

---

communication, that its admission into the Moohummudan law is not calculated to raise that system in the estimation of the English lawyer. The term hearsay, however, conveys a very imperfect idea of the Arabic word *istimau*, of which it is nevertheless a literal translation. Testimony is of two kinds: direct, when given by the actual witnesses of a transaction; and indirect, when transmitted by persons who have heard the declarations of the actual witnesses. The last is entirely rejected by the Moohummudan law in cases that "drop in consequence of a doubt," (Hamilton's Hidaya, vol. ii. p. 709;) as where a person is accused of a crime which induces retaliation or a specific punishment. It is also rejected in all other cases, unless the original witness be dead, absent at a distance, or sick, (ibid. p. 712.) And when received at all, it is guarded with every precaution which can secure its accuracy. Thus, the original witness must have given his testimony to the secondary in the "same manner that he would have done in the assembly of the Kazee," (ibid. p. 711;) that is with the solemn words "I bear witness," which carry a peculiar sacredness, and are all that the law requires from the primary himself. 2nd. He must have expressly called on the secondary to receive his testimony, (ibid. 710.) And 3rd, there must be two secondary witnesses to the testimony of each primary, (ibid. p. 710.) In the four cases mentioned in the text this strictness is so far relaxed, that the positive call of the primary witness on the secondary to receive his testimony is not required. But then the hearsay ceases to be a legal channel of communication to the mind of the judge, and is sufficient only to the justification of a witness *in foro conscientiæ*, and his protection from the punishment due to false testimony, if he should take upon him positively to assert the fact which has been communicated to him.

been adduced to impair the general effect of the reasoning by which I have attempted to shew that it is not a fact from which a Moohummudan marriage can be fairly inferred. The passage quoted from the *Hidaya* is indeed a direct authority the other way, going the full length of declaring cohabitation to be insufficient; for the author says expressly, with respect to the possession of a thing, that seeing it in the hand of a person is no evidence of right of property, though perhaps enough to justify a witness in making the assertion; and of cohabitation he says, that it is lawful for the person who has seen it to bear testimony to the marriage of the parties, only, "in the same manner as it is lawful for a person who sees a melon in the hand of another, to give evidence that it is the property of that person."

Under the English and Scotch laws it is necessary, that the person who claims to be an heir should prove the legitimacy of his birth. When this is required in the Moohummudan law, it is only for the purpose of establishing descent. And in all cases whenever a claimant has established his descent, he becomes entitled to such portion of the inheritance as the law has appropriated for his degree of kindred to the deceased.

CHAPTER IV.

Of Shares and Sharers.

Number of shares and the persons entitled to them.

THE shares mentioned in the *Kooran* are six in number; viz. a half, a fourth, an eighth, two-thirds, one-third, and a sixth. And there are twelve classes of persons for whom they are appointed; of which four are male, namely, the father, true grand-father*, half-brother by the same mother, and husband; and the remaining eight are female, viz. the wife, the daughter, daughter of a son how low soever, that is, of any male descendant connected with the deceased entirely through males, sister of the full blood, or by the same father only, or the same mother only, the mother and true grand-mother†.

Some of the sharers liable to partial and others to total exclusion.

The persons above enumerated do not all succeed simultaneously, nor are their shares constantly the same. On the contrary, some of them are in the most ordinary cases entirely excluded, and the shares of the others, though they are always entitled to some participation in the inheritance, are liable in certain circumstances to reduction. The latter class

---

* For an explanation of this and the term true grand-mother, see *post* pp. 63 and 65.

† Sirajiyyah, Appendix, No. 114.

includes the husband and wife, father, mother, and daughter; and the former includes the true grand-father and true grand-mother, the daughter of a son how low soever, the full sister, and the half-sister whether by father or mother, and the half-brother by the same mother. The exclusion of these persons is founded upon and regulated by two general principles, applicable alike to sharers and residuaries. The one is, that a person who is related to the deceased through another, has no interest in the succession during the life of that other; with the exception of half brothers or sisters by the mother, who are not excluded by her. And the other principle is, that the nearer relative to the deceased excludes the more remote*. Thus, a grand-father is excluded by a father upon both principles, being more remote, and also connected through him with the deceased; and a grand-son is excluded by a son upon both principles, when that son is his father, and upon the second principle, when he is his paternal uncle.

Some of the sharers may also be residuaries.

Having premised these few general observations, the reader will be able to follow without difficulty the details of the different shares as they are presented to his notice. But here it is proper to remark, that some of the persons above-mentioned are occasionally residuaries, as well as sharers, and will appear in the former character in the next chapter. I ought, perhaps, in strictness to confine myself in this place to a consideration of their claims as sharers; but it

* Sirajiyyah and Shureefeea, Appendix, No. 115.

may be convenient to the reader to have all their rights in the inheritance placed before him in one view; and I will therefore notice, as I proceed, the residuary rights of such of the sharers as may become residuaries, following in this respect the example of the author of the *Sirajiyyah*, though perhaps at the expence of some repetition. It is of little consequence in what order we consider them, and I shall take them according to their propinquity to the deceased, beginning with the husband.

Share of the husband.

The share of a husband is one half; but it is reduced to a fourth when there is a child or child of a son how low soever*, that is, any male descendant connected with the deceased entirely by males. And to one or other of these shares the husband is always entitled, being one of the persons who are never entirely excluded, as already noticed.

Share of the widow.

The share of a wife is precisely the half of a husband's in similar circumstances; being an eighth when there is a child or child of a son, how low soever, and a fourth when there is none. Though a man may have as many as four wives, the provision for two or more is the same as that for one; the fourth or eighth, as the case may be, being divisible among them equally†.

Share of the daughters.

A daughter's share, where there is only one, and no son, is a half of the property; and the share of

---

* Sirajiyyah, Appendix, No. 116.

† Sirajiyyah, Appendix, No. 117.

two or more daughters in the same predicament is two-thirds, which are of course divisible among them equally. When there is a son, they lose their character of sharers and become residuaries with him*, by reason of a principle laid down in the *Kooran*, which requires that the portion of a son shall be double that of a daughter. A compliance with this rule would be plainly impossible, if the daughters were to retain their shares, and the expedient has been adopted of merging the shares in the residue. In this case, the sons are said to render their sisters residuaries, and the proportion of the inheritance to which they are entitled must depend upon the amount of the residue, which will of course vary according to the number of the other sharers who may be in existence. Whatever the residue may be, it is to be divided in the proportion of two shares to each male, and one share to each of the females†.

They become residuaries with a son.

Share of the son's daughters.

When the deceased has left neither son nor daughter, nor son's son, the share of the inheritance appropriated to daughters passes to the daughters of the son, who then come into the place of daughters in every respect ; the share of one being a half, and of two or more two-thirds, as above-mentioned‡. When there happen to be in the same degree with the daughters of the sons, one or more males who

* Sirajiyyah, Appendix, No. 118.

† Shureefeea, Appendix, No. 119.

‡ Sirajiyyah, Appendix, No. 120.

are residuaries; as their own brother, or the son of their paternal uncle; the shares of the son's daughters are merged in the residue by reason of the principle already mentioned, and they are said to be rendered residuaries, in the same way as the daughters of the deceased are made residuaries by the existence of a son*.

Become residuaries with a son's son.

As the shares of daughters sink into the residue when there is a son, there can be nothing to pass to the series of heirs beyond them, and the sons' daughters are therefore always excluded by the existence of a son. They are likewise excluded as *sharers* when the deceased has left two or more daughters though no son†, because the whole of the two-thirds appropriated to daughters is then exhausted by themselves. But where there is only one daughter and no son, the complement of the two-thirds after deducting her moiety, being one-sixth of the estate, passes to the daughters of the son‡.

Entitled to a sixth with a single daughter.

Though sons' daughters are entirely excluded as *sharers*, when there are two or more daughters, they are nevertheless in some instances admitted to a trifling participation in the inheritance by the operation of the rule already noticed. This happens when there is a male or males in the same or a lower degree entitled to the residue§. Suppose, that the

May occasionally participate to a small extent though there are two or more daughters.

* Shureefeea, Appendix, No. 121.

† Sirajiyyah, Appendix, No. 122.

‡ Ibid. Appendix, No. 123.

§ Appendix, No. 122.

deceased has left no son, but two or more daughters, and grand-children both male and female by a son. Here two-thirds being set apart for the daughters, there is nothing to pass to the sons' daughters as *sharers*; but if there be no other legal sharers, the remaining third is divided, as residue, between the grand-children, in the ratio of two parts to a male, and one to a female. In strictness, the operation of this rule ought to be confined to the case where the residuary is in the same degree with the daughters of the son. But it has seemed hard, that they should be deprived by a more remote relative, of an advantage which they enjoy with one who is nearer, and the rule has been extended accordingly*. The extension however is limited to cases where the more enlarged construction is beneficial to them; for whenever they happen to be legal sharers, it is only by a male of the same degree, that they can be made residuaries†.

It seems unnecessary to follow the line of female descendants farther, as the reader, if I have succeeded in rendering the principles which regulate the succession of the sons' daughters intelligible to him, will have no difficulty in applying the same principles to the daughters of the grandson, and so on.

Share of the father.

Of ascendants, the first in degree, as in importance, is the father of the deceased, whose legal share is a sixth; but it will be seen hereafter, that he may be a residuary also. So that there are three states or

---

* Shureefeea, Appendix, No. 124.

† Sirajiyyah and Shureefeea, Appendix, No. 125.

conditions appropriate to a father. He is simply a sharer, being entitled to a sixth of the estate, as abovementioned, when the deceased has left a son, or son's son how low soever. When there are only daughters, or son's daughters, he is both a sharer and residuary; and simply a residuary where there is no child, nor child of a son how low soever*.

The true grand-father is defined to be a male ancestor, into whose line of relationship to the deceased a female does not enter†; and the first true grand-father is of course the father's father. He is entirely excluded by the father ‡; but if the father be dead, comes into his place; and his interest in the inheritance is the same, with this difference, that being more remote, he is liable to be differently affected by the rights of the mother and grand-mother. Thus a paternal grand-mother, who is entirely excluded by the father, is capable of inheriting with the true grand-father; and a mother who, when there is a father and a husband or wife, gets no more than a third of the remainder, after deducting the share of the husband or wife, is entitled to one-third of the whole, when there is a grand-father instead of the father §.

The true grand-father.

His share.

The share of a mother is a sixth when there is a child living, or the child of a son how low soever, or two or more of the brothers and sisters,

Share of the mother.

* Sirajiyyah, Appendix, No. 126.

† Ibid. No. 127.

‡ Ibid. No. 128.

§ Sirajiyyah and Shureefeea, Appendix, No. 129.

whether of the whole or half blood. And in all other cases, with only two exceptions, her share is a third. The exceptions are when the deceased has left a husband, or wife, and both parents*. In these circumstances, the husband being entitled to a half, and the wife to a fourth, if the mother received a third, there would remain no more than a sixth for the father in the one case, and five-twelfths in the other, while the law generally requires that the share of a male shall be double that of a female when they succeed together. To avoid this inconsistency, the share of the mother is reduced to one-third of the remainder, after deducting the portion of the husband or wife; by which means the proper ratio is preserved between the shares of the father and mother; for the former, being in this case the residuary, will take the remaining two-thirds, or exactly double the portion of the latter.

When there is a father, the benefit of the reduction of the mother's share occasioned by the existence of two brothers or sisters, devolves on him.

It has been observed, that the mother's share, when there are two or more brothers and sisters, is a sixth. It will be seen hereafter, that brothers and sisters are entirely excluded by the existence of the father; yet it may be asked, if the other sixth, which they are thus the means of cutting off from the mother, shall not belong to themselves, or if it must devolve on the father? This question has given occasion for much discussion, and a variety of opinions among the learned; but the sect of *Aboo Huneefa* have determined in favor

* Sirajiyyah, Appendix, No. 130.

of the father, assigning the following text of the *Kooran* as the ground of their decision; "but if he have no child, and his parents be his heirs, then his mother shall have the third part; and if he have brethren, his mother shall have a sixth part*." Here it is contended, that as the father is undoubtedly entitled under the first clause of the sentence to the remainder, after deducting the mother's third, so the latter part of the sentence ought to be taken as if it had stood thus: "and if he have brethren, *and his parents be his heirs*, his mother shall have a sixth part, *and his father the remainder*†.

True grand-mothers.

The true grand-mother is any lineal female ancestor in whose line of relationship to the deceased a false grand-father does not enter‡; and a false grand-father is a lineal male ancestor between whom and the deceased a female is interposed. Thus in the first degree, the mothers of both parents are necessarily true grand-mothers; and in the second degree, there are three true grand-mothers, viz. the father's grand-mothers on both sides, and the mother's maternal grand-mother, her paternal grand-father being excluded by the interposition of her father, who is obviously a false grand-father.

Their share.

The share of a true grand-mother is a sixth, which, if there be more than one of them in the same degree, is divided between them equally§.

---

* Sale's Kooran, (Edition 1801) page 94.

† Shureefeea, Appendix, No. 131.

‡ Appendix, No. 114.

§ Sirajiyyah, Appendix, No. 132.

Excluded by a mother.

True grand-mothers of any description are excluded by the existence of the mother; those on her own side for two reasons; first, because they are connected with the deceased through her, and second, because they have but one common cause of succession, namely, maternity. She excludes the paternal grand-mothers for the latter reason only. These are also excluded by the existence of the father, or the paternal grand-father; but the maternal grand-mothers are not excluded by them*.

The nearer excludes the more remote.

Amongst grand-mothers the more remote are excluded by the nearer, even though she should be incapable of taking any part of the inheritance. Thus the paternal grandmother is excluded by the father, but she is nevertheless capable of excluding the mother of the mother's mother, though the latter would not, as already noticed, be excluded by the father himself†.

Difference of opinion as to the portion of an ancestor related to the deceased through both parents.

In the higher stages of ascent, an ancestor is occasionally connected in two ways with the deceased. Thus, suppose that the deceased has left two great-grand-mothers, one the mother of his father's mother, and the other the mother of his mother's mother, and that the latter is also the mother of his father's father; thus making his paternal grand-father and maternal grand-mother brother and sister‡. The three relationships above-mentioned are each a ground of inheri-

* Sirajiyyah and Shureefeea, Appendix, No. 133.—N. B. The words كذلك بالجد have been omitted at the end of the extract.

† Sirajiyyah and Shureefeea, Appendix, No. 134.

‡ Sirajiyyah, Appendix, No. 135.

tance in itself, and two of them being united in the person of one of the great-grand-mothers, *Moohummud* considered that she was entitled to two-thirds of the sixth; the remainder being the portion of the other; but, according to *Aboo Yoosuf*, the sixth is, notwithstanding the double relationship of one, to be equally divided between both*. We are informed by the *Imam Surukhsee* that there is no authentic report of *Aboo Huneefa's* opinion upon this point; but it is mentioned in the book of inheritance of *Husn*, the son of *Abd-oor-Ruhman*, the son of *Abd-oor-Ruzzaq*, *Ash-shashee*, a follower of *Shafei*, that *Aboo Huneefa* and *Malik*, as well as his own master, were of the same opinion as *Aboo Yoosuf*†.

Share of full sisters.

There are five conditions in which full sisters may be found. Three of these occur, when there are neither children nor children of a son how low soever; one full sister being entitled to a half of the property in that predicament, and two or more of them to two-thirds; while they lose their character of sharers when there are full brothers, whose existence renders them residuaries‡, the portion of each female then becoming half the portion of a male.

Excluded by a son or son's son, father or true grand-father.

In all the preceding cases, however, the share of the sisters is liable to be intercepted by a father, or true grand-father; by whom they are absolutely excluded, as well as by a son or son's son how low soever§.

---

* Sirajiyyah, Appendix, No. 136.

† Shureefeea, Appendix, No. 137.

‡ Sirajiyyah, Appendix, No. 138.

§ Ibid, No. 139.

Become residuaries with two or more daughters.

When there are two or more daughters, or daughter's of a son how low soever, there can be nothing to pass to the deceased's sisters, though there be neither son nor son's son, father or true grand-father to exclude them. In this case, it seems hard that they should be denied all participation in the inheritance, to give place to a residuary less closely connected with the deceased than themselves. The prophet himself has anticipated and obviated this hardship, by directing that sisters in the case supposed, shall be residuaries with daughters, or the daughters of a son* ; and their portion will be either one-half or a third, as there is one or more of these in existence. It is not to be supposed, however, that the full sisters can supersede the husband or wife, mother or true grand-mother. These being legal sharers must be satisfied before any thing can pass to a residuary, and as the sisters are rendered merely residuaries in the case in question, they can have no better right than the legal residuary in the same circumstances.

Share of half-sisters by the father.

Half-sisters by the father come into the place of full sisters, when there are none ; that is, the share of one is a half and of two or more two-thirds†, while with daughters or son's daughters, they become residuaries‡. With one full sister, whenever she is entitled to a half, they take the complement of two-thirds, or one sixth ; and by two or more full sisters

---

* Sirajiyyah, Appendix, No. 140.

† Sirajiyyah, Appendix, No. 141.

‡ Ibid, Appendix, No. 142.

they are entirely excluded, unless there happens to be a half-brother by the father who makes them residuaries, when they become entitled to participate in the residue in the ratio of two parts to a male, and one to a female*.

Share of half-brothers and sisters by the mother.

Half-brothers and sisters by the same mother, are entirely excluded from the inheritance by the existence of a child, or the child of a son how low soever, or of a father or true grand-father; and in all other cases, the legal share of one is a sixth, and of two or more one-third. There is no distinction in this case in favor of the stronger sex, both males and females having the same right and succeeding equally†. The learned author of the Principles and Precedents of Moohummudan law observes, however, that "the general rule of a double share to the male applies to their issue‡." The issue of half brothers and sisters by the same mother are no where mentioned as sharers in their own right; and the learned author has himself observed, that the right of representation has no place in the Moohummudan Code §. It will be found in the following chapter, that the proper residuaries are all connected with the deceased through males; a condition which obviously excludes the children of half-brothers or sisters by the mother.

---

* Sirajiyyah, Appendix, No. 141.

† Sirajiyyah, Appendix, No. 143.

‡ Page 5, § 30.

§ Preliminary Remarks, p. viii. and Principle 9, page 2.

The only other description of heirs in which it seems possible to include them, is that of distant kindred, and in that character, they may occasionally be found entitled to a participation in the inheritance; but according to the better and more general opinion, their succession as distant kindred is regulated in the same way, as that of their parents, without any distinction on account of sex.

---

* See chapter of Distant Kindred.

CHAPTER V.

Of Residuaries.

The surplus of the estate after the shares have been satisfied passes to the residuaries.

In most of the cases mentioned in the last chapter, there is a residue after the portions of the legal sharers have been separated from the estate. This residue passes to a class of persons, who from that circumstance have been termed residuaries by Sir William Jones, in his translation of the *Sirajiyyah*, and the name has been adopted by Mr. Macnaghten in his Principles and Precedents of Moohummudan law. There is some reason to suppose, as already observed in the first chapter, that the persons who are now generally classed as mere residuaries, were originally the sole heirs of an intestate person. The term by which they are designated in the Arabic language, was first rendered "heirs," by Sir William Jones, in his translation of the *Bigyatol bahith*, though he afterwards substituted for it the word "residuaries," in the translation of the *Sirajiyyah*. A name is not perhaps of much importance; but if I had felt myself at liberty to depart from two such high authorities, I might have ventured to suggest the term "agnate" of the civil law, as approaching nearer to the definition of the Moohummudan Code*.

Three classes of residuaries.

Residuaries have been divided by the author of the *Sirajiyyah* into three different classes; residuaries in their own right; residuaries in the right of another; and residuaries with another †.

Residuaries in the right of another, and with another.

With the two last classes the reader has been made acquainted in the preceding chapter; the residuaries in right of another being daughters, son's daughters, full sisters, and half-sisters by the father; all of whom lose their character of sharers and become residuaries, when there exist one or more males in the same or a lower degree; and residuaries with another being sisters with two or more daughters or daughters of a son how low soever; in which case the former are entirely excluded from the inheritance as sharers, but admitted to participate in the character of residuaries. Upon these two classes it is unnecessary for me to say more in this place, and I shall confine myself to the consideration of those who are residuaries in their own right.

Residuaries in their own right.

The residuary in his own right is defined to be "every male in whose line of relation to the deceased no female enters‡;" and such residuaries may be divided into three classes; viz. descendants, ascendants, and collaterals. By a metaphor not peculiar to the Moohummudan law, the deceased is consider-

---

* See Note, page 14.

† Sirajiyyah, Appendix, No. 144.

‡ Ibid, Appendix, No. 145.

ed to be a tree, of which his descendants are the *branches*, and the ascendants the *roots*. Without straining the metaphor too far, we may be permitted to term the collaterals *offsets*. The branches or descendants come first in the order of succession, and they are the sons, then their sons how low soever ; next follow the roots or ascendants, who are the father, then the true grand-father how high soever ; and last succeed the *offsets*, or collaterals, who are first the sons of the father, that is, brothers ; then their sons how low soever ; and next the issue of the true grand-father, or paternal uncles, and their sons how low soever*.

Distinction between sharers and residuaries.

There is this marked difference between sharers and residuaries, that, while several distinct classes of the former are capable of succeeding together, the existence of the nearer residuary entirely excludes the more remote†. Thus, a son's son can never participate in the inheritance with a son, nor the father with either as a residuary, though he is not excluded from his proper sixth as a sharer. When there are two persons equally near of kin to the deceased, but one related to him through both parents, and the other only through one, the master of two propinquities, as he is termed, is preferred‡.

The reader who has attentively perused the chapter on sharers, will have no difficulty in determin-

* Sirajiyyah, Appendix, No. 146.

† Ibid.

‡ Ibid, No.147.

ing the amount of the residue in every case that can occur. Yet to facilitate reference, I will take a short view of the residuaries in the order of their succession, noticing, though at the risk of some repetition, the sharers who are entitled to participate in each particular case.

Sharers with the son as residuary.

When the residuary is a son, the only other persons who are entitled to participate in the inheritance are the parents (or their substitutes among the more remote ancestors), each of whom has a sixth, the husband whose share is a fourth, or the wife who is entitled to an eighth. Daughters, if the deceased has left any, are residuaries with the son or sons, the share of each male being double that of a female.

Sharers with the son's son as residuary.

In default of a son, the son's son is the residuary; and in that case, all the sharers mentioned in the last paragraph are entitled to participate, with the addition of the daughters; the son's daughters becoming residuaries with their brothers or cousins, and taking according to the usual rule of distribution among males and females. In the subsequent stages of descent there is the same difference; the females of the higher grade being sharers when the two-thirds appropriated to daughters are not exhausted, and in other cases participating in the residue according to the general rule.

Sharers when the father is residuary.

When the father is the residuary, the daughters, and their substitutes the daughters of a son how low soever, are sharers to the extent of two-thirds, the husband is entitled to a half, the wife or wives to one-fourth, and the mother or her substitutes among the grand-mothers to a sixth, though the portion of the mother is liable to some variation in this case as already noticed.

Sharers when the paternal grand-father is residuary.

In default of the father, the paternal grand-father is the residuary, and the sharers are the same as in the last case, with a slight difference in the rights of the mother, which has been adverted to under the head of her share. The same observation is applicable to the more remote ancestors, whose condition is in all respects the same as that of the first grand-father, except in so far as it may be affected by the claims of intermediate grand-mothers.

When there is neither in the descending nor the ascending line a male who is connected with the deceased through males, the residue passes to the children of the father, or brothers, among whom the master of two propinquities, or full brother, is preferred, as already noticed, to the brother by the father alone.

Sharers with a full brother as residuary.

When a full brother is the residuary, the sharers are the same as with a residuary grand-father, with the addition of half-brothers and sisters by the mother only, who are now first entitled to a share, which, as formerly noticed, is a sixth for one and a third for two or more. The full sisters are residuaries with their brother or brothers, and share according to the general rule of distribution among males and females.

Sharers with a half brother by the father as residuary.

When a half-brother by the father is the residuary, the sharers are the same as in the last case, with the addition of full sisters, who are not made residuaries by half-brothers, and retain their own character of sharers.

Sharers when the son of a full brother or of a half brother by the father is residuary.

With the sons of the full brother for residuaries, there is the further addition of half-sisters by the father only as sharers; and so with the sons of the half-brother by the father, and all subsequent descendants of the father, the females of the preceding grade being sharers when the two-thirds appropriated to daughters are not exhausted, and in other cases dividing the residue according to the general rule of distribution among males and females.

Sharers with a paternal uncle as residuary.

After we have passed the descendants of the father, all the sharers except the husband and wife disappear, and the first residuary among the descendants of the grand-father, that is the paternal uncle, is liable to be reduced by all the sharers in existence, none of whom are excluded by him. Among uncles, as among brothers, the master of two propinquities is preferred to the master of only one, and the paternal uncle, who is the full brother of the father, is accordingly called to the succession before him, who is connected with the father through one parent only*. The further descendants of the grand-father are called to the succession in the same manner as those of the father.

No limit to lineal residuaries, whether in descent or ascent.

In the right line, whether of ascent or descent, it is universally agreed, that there is no limit to the per-

* Sirajiyyah, Appendix, No. 148.

sons who may be called to the succession, provided that they are males, and connected with the deceased through males, according to the definition already given of the term residuary. I am disposed to think that, with this qualification, the succession of residuaries in the collateral line is equally unlimited. It must be admitted, however, that the learned author of the Principles and Precedents of Moohummudan Law seems to entertain a different opinion, and that his opinion appears to be supported by the translator of the *Sirajiyyah.* Whatever respect may be due to the sentiments of these two distinguished persons, it is hardly necessary to apprize the reader that they cannot be received as authority upon a point of this kind, except in so far as they are founded upon what has been delivered by the original writers, and to these I will presently beg to direct his attention.

Difference of opinion as to limit in the collateral line.

The passage of the Principles and Precedents, in which the opinion that I have adverted to seems to be contained, is as follows: "When there is no son nor daughter, nor son's son, nor son's daughter however low in descent, nor father, nor grand-father, nor other lineal male ancestor, nor mother, nor mother's mother, nor father's mother, nor other lineal female ancestor, nor widow, nor husband, nor brother of the half or whole blood, nor sons how low soever of the brethren of the whole blood, or of those by the same father only, nor sister of the half or whole blood, nor paternal uncle, nor paternal uncle's son how low soever, (all of whom are termed either sharers or residuaries,) the daughter's children and the children of the son's

Stated.

daughters succeed; and they are termed the first class of distant kindred*." The text of the *Sirajiyyah* quoted by the author at the end of his book, and bearing the same number as the above passage, can have been intended only as an authority for the succession of the distant kindred; but it is here given entire, as translated by Sir William Jones, for the further satisfaction of the reader. "A distant kinsman is every relation, who is neither a sharer nor a residuary. The generality of the prophet's companions repeat a tradition concerning the inheritance of distant kinsmen, and according to this our masters and their followers (may God be merciful to them) have decided. The first class is descended from the deceased, and they are the daughter's children, and the children of the son's daughters†."

Authority examined.

The only passage in the translation of the *Sirajiyyah*, bearing directly on the point, that I am aware of, is the following, which does certainly seem to countenance the doctrine of the limitation of residuaries in the collateral line to the descendants of the grand-father, though it is at the same time obviously

---

* Page 7, § 43.—There is an apparent inconsistency between this passage and the Preliminary Remarks, page xi, where the author observes, that "the residuaries by relation are the sons and their descendants, the father and his descendants, *the paternal ancestor in any stage of ascent and his descendants.*" The words which I have underlined seem to comprehend the collaterals, however remote from the deceased.

† Sir W. Jones's Works, vol. iii. p. 537.

inconsistent with the general definition of the term, with which the paragraph commences: "Now the residuary in his own right is every male in whose line of relation to the deceased no female enters; and of this sort there are four classes; the offspring of the deceased and his root, and the offspring of his father and of his nearest grand-father, a preference being given, I mean a preference in the right of inheritance, according to proximity of degree. The offspring of the deceased are his sons *first;* then their sons, in how low a degree soever; then *comes* his root, or his father, then his paternal grand-father, and their paternal grand-fathers; then the offspring of his father, or his brothers; then their sons, how low soever; and then the offspring of his grand-father or his uncles; then their sons how low soever*." There is nothing in the preceding quotation which cannot be reconciled with the definition of "residuary" at its commencement, except the words "nearest grand-father;" and we have fortunately the means of shewing beyond dispute that these are an inadvertence of the translator. In the copy of the text annexed to the translation, the vowel marks are inserted, and if these be correct, it is obvious that the words "nearest" and "grand-father" cannot agree together: and they are so distinct from each other in the Calcutta edition, which contains both the text and the commentary printed together, that the commentator stops at the

* Sir W. Jones's Works, vol. iii. p. 523.

word "grand-father," to make an observation on the sentence that concludes with it, before he suffers the reader to proceed to the next, which begins with the word "nearest*." The passage, as it stands in the Calcutta edition, and stripped of the commentary, a part of which has slipt into the text of Sir William Jones's copy, and may have given rise to the mistake in question, is literally as follows: "and they are four classes: the offspring of the deceased and his root; and the offspring of his father, and the offspring of his grand-father. The nearest is nearest, I mean by this, that the first in the inheritance is the offspring of the deceased, or the sons; then their sons, how low soever; then his root, or the father; then the grand-father, or father's father, how high soever," &c. The reader will observe, that the term grand-father is here taken in its proper comprehensive sense, to signify the lineal male ancestor however remote; and, but for the word nearest, the insertion of which I hope has been satisfactorily explained, there is nothing from which it can be gathered that the term was to be taken in a less comprehensive sense when the descendants of the grand-father are mentioned. It is true, that these are described a little lower down as uncles, but the word in the Arabic, which has been so translated, is one of equal comprehensiveness, being employed to designate not only the father's brothers, but the brother of any male ances-

* Shureefeea, Appendix, No. 149.

tor however remote, provided he be connected with the deceased through males*.

Collateral residuaries among descendants of great grand-father.

It is to be observed, that if the enumeration of residuaries contained in the paragraph quoted from Mr. Macnaghten's work, be complete, all relatives beyond the descendants of the grand-father are excluded, though they should fall within the general definition of the *Sirajiyyah.* In the following extract from the *Koodooree,* a book of very high authority in Arabia, and generally supposed to be the principal source from which the author of the *Hidaya* obtained the text of the law on which his own work is a commentary, the enumeration of residuaries is carried one step farther, to the descendants of the great grand-father. "The nearest residuaries are the sons; then their sons; then the father; then the grand-father; then brothers; then their sons; then the sons of the grand-father, and they are paternal uncles; *then the sons of the father of the grand-father, and they are paternal uncles of the father*†." And to the same effect is the following extract from the *Futawa Sirajiyyah.* It is rather long, but contains a distinct enumeration of the residuaries in the order of their succession, which is sufficient apology for laying it entire before the reader. "The nearest residuaries to the deceased in their own right are sons; then their sons; then the sons of their sons how low soever; then the father; then the grand-

* Sirajiyyah and Shureefeea, Appendix, No. 150.

† Appendix, No. 151.

father, or father's father how high soever; then the full brother; then the half-brother by the same father; then the sons of the full brother; then the sons of the half-brother by the same father; then their sons in this manner; then the father's full brother; then the father's half brother by the same father; then the sons of the father's full brother; then the sons of the father's half-brother by the same father; then their sons after this arrangement; *then the paternal grand-father's full brother; then the paternal grand-father's half brother by the same father; then their sons after this arrangement**."

Collateral residuaries among the descendants of the great great grand-father.

In the extract cited below from the *Futawa Alumgeeree,* a work of perhaps the highest authority in India, as having been compiled under the orders of the Moghul Government in its brightest period, the enumeration of residuaries, after proceeding in nearly the same terms as those of the last quotation, is carried one step higher to the paternal uncles of the grand-father, that is to the descendants of the great great grand-father†. If these works are to be allowed any

* Futawa Sirajiyyah, Appendix, No. 152. In the case of Doe, on the demise of Sheikh Moohummud Bukhsh, v. Shurf-oon-Nissa Begum and Tajun Beebee, tried in the Supreme Court in the sittings after the second term 1831, it was decided in conformity with the above authorities, which were brought to the notice of the Judges, and the *futwa* of Molvee Morad, head Moohummudan officer of the Court, that the plaintiff, who was descended from the great grand-father of the deceased, was entitled to a share of the residue.

† Futawa Alumgeeree, Appendix, No. 153.

weight at all, it is clearly impossible, that the limitation implied in the expression "descendants of the nearest grand-father," can be correct; and there is nothing else, even in Sir William Jones's translation of the passage previously quoted from the *Sirajiyyah*, to restrict the meaning of the definition of the term residuary, with which the paragraph commences, the comprehensiveness of which is worthy of the reader's particular attention. "Now, the residuary in his own right," says the author, "is *every* male in whose line of relation to the deceased no female enters*."

Last of residuaries. The emancipator.

To an English lawyer it may seem of little importance to trace the destination of the residue beyond a series of persons whom he may consider to be inexhaustible. It must however occasionally happen, that the residuary does not appear, or is unable to make good his claim; and the general provision, which the Moohummudan law has made for the appropriation of the remainder of the estate in that event, forms the subject of the chapter on the return. In the special case of emancipated slaves, the surplus does not revert to the sharers on failure of residuaries by descent, but passes to the emancipator, who is thus in consequence termed the last of the residuaries†.

* In the Persian translation of the *Sirajiyyah*, which is probably referred to by the natives of this country, at least as often as the original Arabic, the important word *every* is omitted, though it occurs both in the copy of the original given by Sir William Jones, and in that printed at Calcutta with the *Shureefeea*. The latter was, I presume, collated with other copies, and I am not aware that its accuracy has ever been called in question.

† Sirajiyyah, Appendix, No. 154.

His residuaries.

If the emancipator be dead, *his* residuaries are called to the succession in the order already explained; his sons first, then his son's son how low soever, grandfather, and so on*. When there are legal sharers of the slave's estate and nothing but residue passes to the emancipator, it is hardly out of the ordinary course of the law that his residuaries should be substituted for him in the event of his death, instead of his general heirs. But when, as may sometimes happen, the emancipated slave has no known relatives of any kind, and the whole of his property falls to the emancipator, it appears hard that the legal sharers of the latter should be excluded from all participation. Yet the law is so. Females have been expressly excluded by the prophet himself†; and of legal sharers even the nearest of all, a father, is not allowed to participate with a son according to the concurring judgments of *Aboo Huneefa* and *Moohummud*. The last opinion delivered by *Aboo Yoosuf* was in favor of the father, whom he considered to be entitled to a sixth. But even he agreed with the others in assigning nothing to the grand-father in such circumstances ‡.

I should now perhaps proceed to consider the farther destination of the residue when there are no residuaries of any kind, or of the whole estate upon

* Sirajiyyah and Shureefeea, Appendix, No. 155.

† Sirajiyyah, Appendix, No. 156.

‡ Ibid. and Shureefeea, Appendix, No. 157.

the failure of sharers also. Cases of this description must necessarily be of rare occurrence ; and it seems desirable to place at once before the reader the rules adopted by the Moohummudan lawyers for distributing an estate among sharers and residuaries. I shall, therefore, after the example of the author of the *Sirajiyyah*, first direct the reader's attention to the method of extracting shares, which forms the subject of the following chapter.

CHAPTER VI.

Of the Extractors of Shares.

It will be found, on reverting to the enumeration of shares at the commencement of the fourth chapter, that they may be all divided into two series, each consisting of three terms, of which the intermediate term is half that which precedes, and double of that which follows it. The first series comprehends the shares a half, a fourth, and an eighth, and the second the shares two-thirds, one-third, and one-sixth*. Shares divisible into two series.

Whatever the share may be, if there is only one, nothing more is required, in order to extract it from the general mass of the estate, than to divide the latter by the fraction which represents the share, and the quotient will be the amount required. In this case, therefore, the name of the share itself is said to be the extractor; thus two is the extractor for a half, three for a third, four for a fourth, and so on†. When only one share is to be extracted, the name of the share is the extractor.

When there are two or more shares, but they all fall within the same series, as a sixth and a third, a When there are two or more

---

* Sirajiyyah, Appendix, No. 158.

† Sirajiyyah, Appendix, No. 159.

shares, but all of one series, the name of the smallest share is the extractor.

half, a fourth, and an eighth, the name of any of the shares might serve the purpose of an extractor; yet there would be this inconvenience in assuming the greater share for the purpose, that the smaller must be expressed by a fraction. The rule, therefore, in all such cases is, that the name of the lowest share shall be taken for the extractor. Thus, when the shares are a third and a sixth, the extractor is six*, and when they are a half, a fourth, and an eighth, the extractor is eight; and the estate is divisible into six or eight portions accordingly.

Shares of different series.

If there are shares to be extracted which belong to different series, the extractor must be sufficiently large to admit of being divided by all the shares without a fraction, and it is the smallest number which is so divisible. Thus, when there is a half with one or more of the other series, the extractor is six†, which is the least number divisible by a half, a sixth, a third, and two-thirds, without a fraction. And when there is a fourth with one or more of the other series, the smallest number divisible without a fraction by a fourth, a sixth, a third, and two-thirds, is twelve, which is accordingly the extractor of the case‡. In like manner, when an eighth is found in conjunction with a sixth, a third, or two-thirds, the extractor is twenty-four§; which is the lowest

When there is a half with any of the second series, the extractor is six.

When a fourth, it is twelve.

When an eighth, it is twenty-four.

---

* Sirajiyyah, Appendix, No. 160.

† Ibid, Appendix, No. 161.

‡ Ibid, Appendix, No. 162.

§ Ibid, Appendix, No. 163.

number that can be divided by all these numbers without a fraction.

The estate is of course to be divided, in all the cases mentioned, into as many parcels as there are units in the extractor, and a corresponding number of these parcels set apart for each share. Thus, if a woman die, leaving a husband and two half-sisters by the mother, the share of the former under such circumstances is a half, and of the latter, a third; which presents the concurrence of a half with one of the second series; the estate is accordingly divisible into six parcels, whereof three belong to the husband, and two to the sisters, the remainder being the property of the residuary. In like manner, when there is a husband with two daughters, the share of the former being a fourth, and of the latter, two-thirds; the estate must be divided into twelve parts, three of which belong to the husband, eight to the daughters, and the surplus is residue. Or when a wife, two daughters, and a mother are left, the share of the first being an eighth, of the second, two-thirds, and of the last, a sixth; the estate is to be divided into twenty-four parcels, three of which are the property of the wife, sixteen of the daughters, four of the mother, and the single one remaining passes to the residuary*.

The estate is to be divided into as many parts as there are units in the extractor.

The preceding rules would be always sufficient for extracting the shares, if the estate were in all cases

Mode of reducing the shares

* The preceding illustrations are taken generally from the *Shureefeea*; but as they are only applications of rules, it is unnecessary to quote the authority at length.

when they exceed the amount of the estate.

ample enough to meet the claims of every person entitled to participate in it. But in some cases it is not so; and a method is required for reducing the shares ratably whenever there happens to be a deficiency. Nothing can be more simple and complete than the expedient adopted by the Moohummudan lawyers for this purpose; which consists in raising the extractor of the case, or in other words, the common denominator of the fractions in which the shares are expressed, while their enumerators remain unchanged. Thus, suppose the deceased to have left a husband and two full-sisters, the share of the former being in such circumstances a half, and of the latter, two-thirds, or when reduced to fractions of the same denomination, three-sixths and four-sixths, there is obviously one sixth more than the amount of the estate, and it is distributed over the shares by advancing the common denominator from six to seven, the number indicated by the addition of all the numerators. The husband's share becomes three-sevenths in consequence, and the share of the sisters four-sevenths. That the original ratio between the shares is preserved is obvious from the proportion $\frac{3}{6}\times\frac{4}{7}=\frac{4}{6}\times\frac{3}{7}$.

The increase.

This is called the doctrine of the increase, because the extractor is increased in the manner described*.

The extractors two, three, four, and eight never increased.

The extractors two, three, four, and eight, are never increased†; because in all the cases where they are

---

* Sirajiyyah, Appendix, No. 164.

† Sirajiyyah, Appendix, No. 165.

called into operation, the estate is either exactly commensurate with the claims upon it, or there is a surplus after the sharers have been satisfied. Thus, the only case where the extractor *two* can be required is, either where the estate is to be divided into two equal parts, as between a husband and a full-sister, or into a half and residue, as between a husband and a full-brother. In like manner, the only cases that require the extractor *three* are those which present a third and residue, as when the deceased has left a mother and a full-brother; two-thirds and residue, when there are two daughters and a full-brother; or one-third and two-thirds, as with two half-sisters by the mother, and two full-sisters. The extractor *four* comes into operation only when there is a fourth and residue, as in the case of a husband and a son; a fourth, a half, and residue, where the heirs are a husband, a daughter, and a full-brother; or a fourth, a third, and residue, as in the case of a widow with both parents. And the only occasions which call for the extractor *eight* are where the estate is to be divided into an eighth and residue, as in the case of a widow and a son; or an eighth, a half, and residue, as in the case of a wife, a daughter, and full-brother*.

The extractor six may be increased to ten and all the intermediate numbers.

Of the remaining extractors, six may be increased to ten, inclusive, and all the intermediate numbers both odd and even. Thus, it is increased to *seven* in

* Shureefeea, Appendix, No. 166.

the case already mentioned of a husband and two full-sisters; and also in the case of a husband, a full-sister, and a half-sister, the share of the two first being each a moiety, or three-sixths, and that of the last being one-sixth. It is increased to *eight* when a half, two-thirds, and a sixth meet in the same case, as where the deceased has left a husband, two full-sisters, and a mother; or when two moieties and a thirdare found together, as in the case of a husband, a full-sister, and two half-sisters by the mother. It is increased to *nine*, at the conjunction of a half with two-thirds and one-third, as in the case of a husband, two full-sisters, and two half-sisters by the mother; or of two moieties, a third and a sixth, as in the case of a husband, a full-sister, two half-sisters by the mother, and a mother. And it is increased to *ten* when the deceased has left a husband, two full-sisters, two half-sisters by the mother, and a mother: the share of the first being a half or three-sixths, of the second, two-thirds or four-sixths, of the third one-third or two-sixths, and of the last, one-sixth, making together ten-sixths*.

The extractor twelve may be increased to thirteen, fifteen, and seventeen.

The extractor twelve may be increased to seventeen, and the two intermediate odd numbers, to the exclusion of the even numbers. Thus it is raised to *thirteen* when a fourth, two-thirds, and a sixth meet together, as in the case of a widow, two full-sisters, and a half-sister by the mother. It is raised to *fif-*

* Sirajiyyah and Shureefeea, Appendix, No. 167.

teen when there are parties entitled to a fourth, two-thirds, and one-third, as a wife, two full-sisters, and two half-sisters by the mother; or at the conjunction of a fourth, two-thirds, and two-sixths, as in the case of a widow, two full-sisters, a half-sister by the mother, and a mother. And it is raised to *seventeen* when a fourth, two-thirds, one-third, and a sixth, meet together, as in the case of a wife, two full-sisters, two half-sisters by the mother, and a mother*.

The extractor twenty-four may be increased to twenty-seven.

The extractor twenty-four admits of no more than one increase, which is in the case of a widow, two daughters, and both parents, the share of the first being an eighth or three twenty-fourths, that of the second, two-thirds, or sixteen twenty-fourths, and that of each of the last, one-sixth, or four twenty-fourths, making in the whole twenty-seven parts. This is the case styled *Mimbereea*, because decided by the Khuleef Alee in the pulpit†.

And to thirty-one according to the opinion of *Ibn Musood*.

The only doctor of any sect, who considered that the extractor twenty-four is susceptible of any other increase, was *Ibn Musood,* who was of opinion that it must be raised to thirty-one, when the deceased has left a widow, a mother, two full-sisters, two half-sisters by the mother, and a son who is excluded on account of some one of the impediments mentioned in the second chapter. His dissent from the rest of the learned in the present case arises from the pecu-

---

* Sirajiyyah and Shureefeea, Appendix, No. 168.

† Ibid, Appendix, No. 169.

liarity of his opinions on the subject of disqualification, which, as already noticed at the end of that chapter, he considers to have the effect of reducing the portions of other parties, though the disqualified person himself cannot derive any benefit from the reduction. Thus in the case above cited, where others would consider the son in the same light as if actually dead, and the share of the widow being a fourth, the extractor would be twelve raised to seventeen, he would reduce the share of the widow to an eighth, by which means the extractor must become twenty-four, and be accordingly raised to thirty-one by the shares of the other parties*.

---

* Sirajiyyah and Shureefeea, Appendix, No. 170.

CHAPTER VII.

Of the Arrangement of Estates where several persons are entitled to participate in the same portion.

WHEN there are several persons entitled to the same share, it must be divided among them equally; and if all the shares admit of such division, there is no occasion for any farther operation. Thus, when the deceased has left two daughters, and both his parents, the estate being divisible into six parts, one goes to each parent, and the remaining four are divided among the daughters equally, leaving two to each*. First principle of arrangement.

When there is only one class of sharers, among whom their share cannot be divided without a fraction, and on a comparison of the parcels composing the share, with the individuals who are entitled to it, the numbers are found to be commensurable, divide the number of individuals by the common measure, and multiply all the shares by the quotient. Thus, when the deceased is survived by both his parents and ten daughters, the share of each parent is a sixth, and that of the daughters four-sixths Second principle of arrangement.

* Sirajiyyah and Shureefeea, Appendix, No. 171.

between them. On comparing four, the number of parcels, with ten, the number of persons among whom they are to be distributed, it is found that they are both measured by the number two ; ten is accordingly to be divided by two, and all the shares are to be multiplied by the quotient five. They accordingly become five-thirtieths for each parent, and two-thirtieths for each daughter, making in all thirty parcels exactly*.

Third principle of arrangement.

When, as in the last case, there is only one class of sharers, among whom the parcels constituting their share cannot be divided without a fraction, but the parcels and the individuals entitled to them are incommensurable, the extractor is to be at once multiplied by the number of individuals†, as in the case of a husband, a grand-mother, and three half-sisters by the mother. The extractor being six, the estate is divided into that number of parcels, of which three are the husband's, one the grand-mother's, and the two remaining are to be divided among the three sisters; where it is evident, that they cannot obtain their portions without a fraction, and that there is no common measure of the number of parcels and the number of individuals among whom they are to be divided. The extractor (6) is accordingly to be multiplied by the number of individuals in the class (3), which gives eighteen parcels;

* Sirajiyyah and Shureefeea, Appendix, No. 172.

† Sirajiyyah, Appendix, No. 173.

that is, nine to the husband (or 3×3), three to the grand-mother (or 1×3), and the remaining six to the sisters; each of whom is entitled to two parcels*.

Procedure the same whether the extractor be original or increased.

It is obvious that there can be no difference in the procedure, if, instead of an original extractor, we take a case where the extractor is increased for the reason and in the manner explained in the last chapter. Thus, suppose that the deceased is survived by a husband and five full-sisters, the original extractor, which is six, is here increased to seven, and the estate accordingly divided into so many parcels, of which three are the husband's, and four belong to the sisters; but four parcels cannot be divided among five persons without a fraction, and as there is no common measure of these numbers, the increased extractor must be multiplied by the whole number of the sisters, by which means it is raised to thirty-five, and the parcels increased accordingly; when fifteen (or 3×5) will belong to the husband, and the remaining twenty (or 4×5) become the property of the sisters, the portion of each sister being four parcels†.

The principles of arrangement of two descriptions--difference between them.

The cases already considered being limited to one class of sharers, who cannot receive their portions without a fraction, the principles are said to lie between the shares and sharers, as they depend upon a comparison of the one with the other. But in the four cases that follow, there are supposed to be two

* Shureefeea, Appendix, No. 174.

† Sirajiyyah and Shureefeea, Appendix, No. 175.

or more classes of persons who are so situated ; and it becomes farther necessary to compare the individuals in one class with those in another ; the principles applicable to the case are accordingly said to be between individuals and individuals. They are not intended, however, to supersede the necessity of considering, in the first place, each class of sharers with a reference to the number of parcels allotted to them. On the contrary, it is implied that this is done, before the cases are submitted to the operation of the second set of principles. Thus, if in the case before put of the two parents and ten daughters, we substitute for one of the former three grand-mothers, we shall have two classes amongst whom their portions cannot be distributed without fractions, and the case would properly fall under one of the rules following. But we must nevertheless first reduce the number of the daughters and of the parcels constituting their share, to their lowest terms, and instead of the whole of the former number, or ten, only take that number divided by the common measure ; and it is of the quotient or five that we proceed to make use in the future operation. Having premised thus much, I now proceed to the fourth principle.

Fourth principle of arrangement.

When there are two or more classes of sharers, whose portions cannot be distributed to them without a fraction, but the numbers of individuals in the classes are all equal, it is evident that the parcels will be sufficiently increased, so as to be distributable among all without a fraction, by merely multiplying the extractor by the number of persons contained in one of the classes. Thus, suppose the deceased to have left three daughters, three grand-mothers, and three paternal uncles ; the extractor of the case being six, four parcels belong to the daughters, one parcel to the grand-mothers, and the remaining one as residue to the paternal uncles; but none of the parcels can be divided without a fraction between the persons entitled to them, though the number of individuals in each class is the same. Then multiply the extractor (6) by that number (3), and the result is eighteen parcels, which are divisible among all the parties exactly. Thus, the daughters' four-sixths, become twelve-eighteenths, whereof each of them obtains four parcels, and the one-sixth of the grand-mothers and of the paternal uncles, become three-eighteenths, or one parcel to each*.

If, instead of three, there were six daughters in the last case, we should subject them to the operation of the second rule before proceeding to consider them with reference to the individuals in the other classes †; but the result would be exactly the same ; for the number of daughters and the number of shares divisible among them, having the common measure two, we should divide the former by it, and the quotient would be equal to the number of individuals in the other classes. That the parcels would still be di-

---

* Sirajiyyah and Shureefeea, Appendix, No. 176.

† This is in fact the case put in the Shureefeea, but to simplify the illustration, I have first supposed that the numbers of individuals in the different classes were equal originally.

visible without a fraction is evident; for twelve-eighteenths, which in the last case were distributed among three persons, leaving four parcels to each, would in this be allotted to six, each of whom would be entitled to two parcels.

Fifth principle of arrangement. When there are several classes of sharers, as in the last case, but the numbers of some of them are *aliquot* parts of others, (as 2 of 4 or 8, and 3 of 9 or 12,) it will be obviously sufficient if we multiply the extractor by the largest number; which is accordingly the principle of the case. Thus, when there are four widows, three grand-mothers, and twelve paternal uncles, the extractor of the case being twelve, the shares are three-twelfths to the first, two-twelfths to the second, and the remainder or seven-twelfths to the last. And it is clear, that none of the shares can be divided among the individuals entitled to them without a fraction; but the numbers of the widows and grand-mothers are each an *aliquot* part of the number of uncles. Multiply, therefore, the original extractor (12) by that number, and the result will be one hundred and forty-four parcels, which are divisible exactly among all the parties. The $\frac{3}{12}$ths of the widows will thus become $\frac{36}{144}$ths, giving nine parcels to each; the $\frac{2}{12}$ths of the grand-mothers will become $\frac{24}{144}$ths, or eight parcels to each; and the remaining $\frac{7}{12}$ths of the uncles will become $\frac{84}{144}$ths, or seven parcels to each*.

* Sirajiyyah and Shureefeea, Appendix, No. 177.

When the number of individuals in one of the classes which cannot receive its share without a fraction, is found to be commensurable with the number of individuals in another class in the same predicament, the rule is, to divide one of the numbers by the common measure, and multiply the whole of the other by the quotient; then if the product is found to have a common measure with the number of individuals contained in any other class, repeat the same process between the product and such number; but if there is no such measure, multiply the whole of the product by the number; and so on through all the other classes, until the last; then multiply the original extractor of the case (or the increased extractor if it be increased) by the result of the whole multiplication, and the product will give a number of parcels, which it will be found may be divided among all the parties without a fraction*. Sixth principle of arrangement.

Thus, suppose the deceased to have left four widows, eighteen daughters, fifteen grand-mothers, and six paternal uncles; rather a strong supposition, it must be allowed, but it will serve equally well for the purpose of illustration. The extractor of the case being twenty-four, there are three parcels or one-eighth to the widows, sixteen parcels or two-thirds to the daughters, four parcels or one-sixth to the grand-mothers, and only one parcel as residue for the uncles. According to the principle applicable to all Illustration.

* Sirajiyyah, Appendix, No. 178.

cases, we must first compare the number of individuals in each class with the number of parcels to be divided among them. But on comparing the parcels of the widows (3) with their number (4), we find that there is no common measure between them, and therefore set down *four*. Between the daughters and their shares, there is the common measure two, and we therefore divide their number (18) by two, and set down the quotient *nine*. In like manner, finding no common measure of the grand-mothers and their shares, or the paternal uncles and their shares, we set down the full numbers of the respective classes, *fifteen* and *six*.

We have thus the numbers four, six, nine, and fifteen, as the elements of our operation under the present rule. But between four and six we find the common measure *two*; and therefore, according to the rule, divide one of them (6) by the measure, and multiply the quotient (3) by the other (4), which gives us the product twelve; between which and nine there is the common measure *three*; we accordingly again divide one of these (9) by the measure (3), and multiply the quotient by the other (12), which raises the case to thirty-six. There is still the common measure *three* between that number and fifteen, and repeating the process of division and multiplication, we obtain one hundred and eighty, as the result of the whole; and the original extractor twenty-four, multiplied by that number, gives four thousand three hundred and twenty as the number of parcels into which the estate must be divided.

The common denominator of the fractions which represent the shares having been multiplied by one hundred and eighty, their numerators must be raised to a corresponding height; and the $\frac{3}{24}$ths of the widows will thus become $\frac{540}{4320}$ths, or one hundred and thirty-five parcels to each; the $\frac{16}{24}$ths of the daughters, $\frac{2880}{4320}$ths, or one hundred and sixty parcels to each; the $\frac{4}{24}$ths of the grand-mothers $\frac{720}{4320}$ths, or forty-eight parcels to each; and the single twenty-fourth of the uncles will become $\frac{180}{4320}$ths, or thirty parcels to each*.

When there are two or more sets of persons among whom their shares cannot be divided without a fraction, and there is no common measure of the number of individuals in one class, and the number in any other, the case is obviously already in its lowest terms, and nothing more can be done than to multiply all the numbers into each other, and then multiply the original extractor by the result of the whole. Seventh principle of arrangement. Thus, suppose there are two widows, six grand-mothers, ten daughters, and seven paternal uncles. Illustration. The extractor of the case being twenty-four, the share of the widows is three parcels, which cannot be divided among two without a fraction; and as there is no common measure of three and two, we must take the whole number of the widows for our future operations. The one-sixth of the grand-mothers', constituting four parcels, is in like manner indivisible among six persons without a fraction;

---

* Sirajiyyah and Shureefeea, Appendix, No. 179.

but of four and six there is the common measure two, and we therefore take only half the number of the grand-mothers', or three. The same number also measures the daughters', and the sixteen parcels which constitute their two-thirds, and we accordingly take no more than half of the daughters, or five. As there is only one parcel left to the uncles, it is obvious that they cannot be reduced any farther, and we take their whole number seven. We have thus the numbers two, three, five, and seven to operate with under the present rule; and as there is obviously no common measure of any of them, we multiply the whole together, and the original extractor by the general result. Thus $2\times3\times5\times7=210$, and $210\times24=5040$: which is the smallest number of parcels divisible among all the sharers without a fraction. Of these parcels six hundred and thirty (or 3×210) belong to the widows, giving three hundred and fifteen to each; eight hundred and forty (or 4×210) to the grand-mothers, being one hundred and forty to each; three thousand three hundred and sixty (or 16×210) to the daughters, giving three hundred and thirty-six to each: and two hundred and ten to the paternal uncles, or thirty to each*.

* Sirajiyyah and Shureefeea, Appendix, No. 180.

CHAPTER VIII.

Of the Distribution of Assets.

AFTER the number of parcels into which the estate is to be divided has been ascertained, the actual distribution of the property can never be a matter of much difficulty. When the assets have been converted into money, where that can be accomplished, the rule for determining the portions of the respective heirs is to multiply the amount of the assets by the number of parcels allotted to each heir, and to divide the product by the whole number of parcels into which the estate is divisible*. Thus, take the case of a husband, a mother and two full-sisters, who are to divide an estate between them, the assets of which, when reduced into money, amount to twenty-five deenars. The extractor being six, raised to eight, the share of the husband is three-eighths; that of the mother, one-eighth, and the share of each sister two-eighths. But three multiplied by twenty-five, and the product, or seventy-five, divided by eight, give nine deenars and three-eighths of

Rules for distribution among individuals.

First rule.

---

* Sirajiyyah, Appendix, No. 181.

a deenar, which are accordingly the share of the husband. In like manner $1\times25\div8=3\frac{1}{8}$ deenars, which are the share of the mother; and $2\times25\div8=6\frac{2}{8}$ deenars, which are the share of each sister*; the aggregate of all the shares, or $9\frac{5}{8}+3\frac{1}{8}+6\frac{2}{8}+6\frac{2}{8}$, being obviously twenty-five deenars, the amount of the assets.

Second rule. When a common measure can be found of the number of parcels into which the estate is to be divided, and of the amount of assets, the process may be shortened by dividing each number by the measure, and making use of the quotients in the subsequent operation†. Thus, suppose that the estate in the last case had consisted of twenty-four instead of twenty-five deenars; there would then be a common measure of the amount of assets, and the number of parcels; for twenty-four and eight are both divisible exactly by four. Let them be divided, and the quotients will be six and two. Then $3\times6\div29=$deenars, the share of the husband; $1\times6\div2=3$ deenars, the share of the mother; and $2\times6\div2=6$ deenars, the share of each daughter; the aggregate of the shares, or $9+3+6+6$, being twenty-four deenars, or the whole amount of the estate.

Rules for distribution among classes. The preceding are the rules for distributing the assets among the individual heirs. The rules applicable to classes of sharers are of the same description; but the extractor of the case is substituted for the number of parcels into which the estate can be divided without a fraction.

---

* Shureefeea, Appendix, No. 182.

† Sirajiyyah, Appendix, No. 183.

If there be any common measure of the extractor and the amount of assets, multiply the number of shares allotted to each class, by the quotient of the assets divided by the common measure, and divide the product by the quotient of the extractor and the common measure*. Thus, in the case of a husband, four full-sisters, and two half-sisters by the mother, the extractor being six, increased to nine, the share of the first is three-ninths, of the second four-ninths, and of the third two-ninths. And, if we suppose the assets of the estate to amount to thirty deenars, we shall have the common measure three of the assets and the extractor, which, when divided by it, will be respectively reduced to ten and three. Then $3 \times 10 \div 3 = 10$ deenars, the share of the husband; $4 \times 10 \div 3 = 13\frac{1}{3}$ deenars, the share of the full sisters; and $2 \times 10 \div 3 = 6\frac{2}{3}$ deenars, the share of the half-sisters by the mother; the aggregate, or $10 + 13\frac{1}{3} + 6\frac{2}{3}$, being thirty deenars†. First rule.

When there is no common measure of the extractor, and the amount of assets, we proceed in the same way, only making use of the original numbers in multiplying and dividing‡. Thus, if the estate in the last case were thirty-two deenars, there would no longer be any common measure of the assets, and the extractor nine; we should therefore multiply the parcels in each share by the whole of the former, Second rule.

---

* Sirajiyyah, Appendix, No. 184.

† Shureefeea, Appendix, No. 185.

‡ Sirajiyyah, Appendix, No. 184.

and divide the product by the whole of the latter. So $3\times32\div9=10\frac{6}{9}$ deenars would be the share of the husband; $4\times32\div9=14\frac{2}{9}$ deenars would be the share of the full-sisters; and $2\times32\div9=7\frac{1}{9}$ deenars, the share of the half-sisters by the mother*.

Effect of composition by an heir.

When one of the heirs compounds with the others, for his share of the inheritance, by accepting instead of it a certain sum of money, or some specific article, the case is nevertheless to be arranged on the same principles as if he were to receive his share, in order that the proper ratio may be preserved between the portions of the remaining heirs, which might otherwise be deranged. The remainder of the estate, after deducting the amount of the compromise, is to be divided among the other heirs in proportion to their respective shares. Thus, take the case of a husband, a mother, and a paternal uncle, being the sole heirs of a deceased person, and suppose that the husband relinquishes his share of the estate in lieu of his wife's dower†, which has remained in his hands unpaid up. The extractor of the case being six, the husband's share is three parcels, the share of the mother two, and the one parcel that remains is the property of the uncle. But the husband having compromised his share, the remainder of the assets, after deducting the unpaid dower, is to be divided into

* Shureefeea, Appendix, No. 186.

† Arabice *muhr;* the provision made by a husband on marriage for his wife; usually a sum of money, which if not paid constitutes a debt against him.

three parcels, whereof the mother receives two, and the paternal uncle one*.

Before quitting the subject of the distribution of assets, it may be proper to say a few words on the mode of distribution among creditors. Distribution among creditors.

When the deceased's property, after payment of funeral expenses, is sufficient for the discharge of all his debts, there can be no difficulty in the case, every creditor being paid in full. But if there happens to be a deficiency, the claim of each creditor must be ratably reduced, and the following rule has been adopted for that purpose. Let the claim of each creditor stand in the place of the portion of each heir, and the whole amount of the debts in the place of the number of parcels into which the estate must be divided, so that all the heirs may receive their portions without a fraction; and then proceed to multiply and divide as already directed†. Thus, suppose the assets of an estate to amount to nine deenars, and that the deceased had two creditors, one to whom he was indebted for ten deenars, and the other to whom his debt was five deenars. Here the amount of the debts is fifteen deenars, between which and nine deenars, the amount of the assets, there is evidently the common measure three. And, substituting the debts for the number of parcels in the preceding operations, and the creditors for the heirs, we have ten multiplied by three, (the quotient of nine

Rule.

When the debts and assets are commensurable.

---

* Sirajiyyah, Appendix, No. 187.

† Sirajiyyah and Shureefeea, Appendix, No. 188.

and three,) and divided by five, (the quotient of fifteen and three,) for the portion of the first creditor, which is thus six deenars, and $5 \times 3 \div 5 = 3$ deenars, for the portion of the second*.

When the debts and assets are incommensurable.

But if, instead of nine deenars, we suppose the estate to amount to thirteen deenars, after the payment of funeral and other necessary charges, there is no longer a common measure of the debts and assets, and we are reduced to the necessity of operating with the whole numbers. The share of the first creditor will be accordingly $13 \times 10 \div 15 = 8\frac{2}{3}$ deenars, and of the second $13 \times 5 \div 15 = 4\frac{1}{3}$ deenars†.

* Shureefeea, Appendix, No. 189.

† Ibid, Appendix, No. 190.

CHAPTER IX.

Of the Return.

Disposal of surplus on failure of residuaries.

WE have seen that when there is a surplus after the shares have been satisfied, it passes to a class of persons who are called residuaries. If the term is to be understood as comprehending every male who can establish a connection with the deceased through an unbroken line of males, there seems to be no assignable limit to the persons who may be included under it. It must however occasionally happen that the residuary is so remote from the deceased as to be unable to prove his relationship to him, or even in some instances to be unconscious of it himself. And it may be asked, how is the surplus to be disposed of in such an event when there is no person who claims it. According to both *Malik* and *Shafei*, it escheats to the *Beit-ool-mal*†; but *Aboo Huneefa* was of opinion, in conformity with the general sentiments of the companions of the prophet, that it ought to revert to the sharers*. It may still, however, be inquired, whether the surplus shall be immediately distributed among them, with such portion of the inheritance as

Reverts to the sharers according to Aboo Huneefa.

---

* Sirajiyyah, Appendix, No. 191.

† See *ante*, page 19.

they are entitled to in their own right, or be reserved for some time, to abide the possibility of a residuary subsequently appearing and establishing his claim to it. A few words therefore may not be improper in this place, as to the amount of evidence which may be required from the claimants of the inheritance, both with respect to their own right, and the absence of other heirs.

Evidence in cases of inheritance.

It is not considered enough, that the witnesses for the claimants should state generally that they are heirs; but their relation to the deceased, as father, son, or brother, must also be distinctly explained*. It is further required, that the witnesses should declare their ignorance of the existence of any other heir. And where they have omitted to make such declaration, it is the duty of the judge to postpone his decision for a reasonable time, to allow of the appearance of other heirs. But after the expiration of that time, he is then to order a partition of the property among the present claimants†. Nor is he entitled, according to *Aboo Huneefa*, to require security from them to refund, in case of the appearance of another heir. This appears to have been the practice of some judges in his time, but the precaution is condemned by him as oppressive. Both his disciples, however, considered, that security ought to be taken in such

---

* Futawa Sirajiyyah, Appendix, No. 192. Futawa Kazee Khan, as cited in the Futawa Alumgeeree, Appendix, No. 193.

† Futawa Sirajiyyah, Appendix, No. 194. Zukheera, as cited in the Futawa Alumgeeree, Appendix, No. 195.

cases; but it is only where the witnesses have been allowed to retire without declaring their ignorance of the existence of any other heir than the claimants, that there is any difference of opinion between the master and his disciples*. Where the claimant belongs to the class of persons who may be wholly excluded by the existence of other heirs, as a grandfather, brother, or paternal uncle, the property is not to be surrendered to him, if the witnesses have omitted to disclaim any knowledge of the existence of other heirs. Should the claimant be a husband or wife, the greatest portion to which he or she can possibly be entitled, that is a moiety for the former, and a fourth for the latter, is to be surrendered in such circumstances, according to *Moohummud;* but the least, that is a fourth for the former and an eighth for the latter, in the opinion of *Aboo Yoosuf* †. Having premised these few general observations, we now proceed to trace the destination of the surplus, and the manner of distributing it, in the absence of residuaries, which form the doctrine of what is technically called the Return.

Definition of the return.

"The return," says the author of the *Sirajiyyah,* "is the converse of the increase; and it takes place in what remains above the shares of those entitled to them when there is no legal claimant of it; this surplus is returned to the sharers, according to their

* Hidaya, Appendix, No. 196. The translation of this passage by Mr. Hamilton (vol. ii. p. 651) is very incorrect.

† Futawa Sirajiyyah, Appendix, No. 197.

Fourfold division of cases. rights, except the husband and wife*." The exclusion of the husband and wife has given rise to a four-fold division of the cases in which the return takes place†. Thus, there may be only one class, or there may be two or three classes, of persons who are entitled to participate in it; and in each of these cases there may, or may not be, a person who has no right to participate, in other words a husband or wife.

First case. Rule. In the first case, where there is only one class of sharers, and neither husband nor wife, the rule is to divide the property into as many parcels as there are individuals in the class, and to give a parcel to each. As when the deceased has left two daughters, or two sisters, or two grand-mothers, the estate is to be divided into two parcels, and one given to each, on account of the equality of their rights in the share and in the return ‡.

The return is the converse of the increase. The reader has been already made acquainted with the simple and ingenious expedient of the Moohummudan lawyers for reducing the shares ratably when the estate is insufficient to meet the claims of every person entitled to participate in it. It consists, as has been explained, in raising the extractor of the case, or, in other words, the common denominator of the fractions in which the shares are expressed, while their numerators remain unchanged. The return being

---

* Appendix, No. 191.

† Sirajiyyah, Appendix, No. 198.

‡ Sirajiyyah and Shureefeea, Appendix, No. 198.

the converse of the increase, the operation is to be reversed by reducing the extractor of the case, or the common denominator of the shares, while the numerators are left unaltered. And in both cases, the new extractor, whether increased or reduced, is the aggregate of all the shares. Thus, where the deceased has left a husband and two full-sisters, the extractor of the case being six, is raised to seven, the sum of the three shares of the former, and four of the latter, which become three and four-sevenths respectively. And in the case of a mother and daughter being the sole heirs, the extractor, which is also six, is reduced to five, the aggregate of the one-sixth of the former, and four-sixths of the latter, which become in like manner one fifth and four-fifths respectively.

II. When there are two or three classes of sharers, and neither husband nor wife, arrange the case according to the number of shares; that is, divide the estate into as many parcels as may correspond with the number of shares to which the parties are entitled*. Thus, where the sole heirs of the deceased are a grand-mother and a half-sister by the mother, whose shares are each a sixth, divide the estate into two parcels, the aggregate of their shares, and give one parcel to each†. In like manner, when the heirs are two half-brothers or sisters by the mother, and a mother, the shares being two-sixths and one-sixth, the estate is to be divided into three parcels, whereof Second case. Rule.

* Sirajiyyah, Appendix, No. 199.

† Shureefeea, Appendix, No. 200.

one belongs to the mother, and two to the half-brothers or sisters*. So, where the deceased has left a daughter and a son's daughter, or a daughter and mother, the division is into four parcels, whereof three belong to the daughter, and one to the son's daughter or to the mother†. And in the case of a daughter, son's daughter, and a mother, whose shares are respectively three-sixths, one-sixth, and one-sixth, the estate is to be divided into five parcels, whereof three are the property of the first, and one of each of the others‡.

Third case.

Rule.

III. When there is a husband or wife, and only one class of persons entitled to participate in the return, the estate is in the first place to be divided into the smallest number of parcels, which will admit of the extraction of the share of the person who is not entitled to participate, and the share of such person to be deducted. If the remainder be divisible among the sharers without a fraction, no further operation is necessary. Thus, if the deceased has left a husband and three daughters, the share of the former being a fourth, the smallest number of parcels into which the estate must be divided for its extraction, is four; and when the husband has taken his fourth, the remaining three-fourths are divisible among the daughters without a fraction§. But suppose, that instead of three daughters, there are six; here the

* Shureefeea, Appendix, No. 201.

† Ibid, Appendix, No. 202.

‡ Ibid, Appendix, No. 203.

§ Sirajiyyah and Shureefeea, Appendix, No. 204.

remaining parcels cannot be divided among them without a fraction. The parcels, and the number of individuals entitled to them are, however, commensurable by three; and we, therefore, according to the rule which has been so often explained, divide the number of the individuals by the common measure, and multiply the extractor by the quotient. Thus, six divided by three gives two, which being multiplied by four, the product is eight parcels, and deducting two for the husband, there remain six for the daughters, or one to each*. If there is no common measure of the remaining parcels, and of the number of individuals who are to receive them, we must multiply the extractor by the whole number. Thus, if we substitute five daughters for six, in the last case, the three parcels which remain after the fourth of the husband has been deducted, cannot be divided among them without a fraction, and there is obviously no common measure of three and five. We accordingly multiply the extractor four by five, and the product or twenty is the number of parcels into which the estate is to be divided; one fourth or five parcels being the portion of the husband, and the remaining fifteen being that of the daughters, or three parcels to each†.

Fourth case.

IV. When there is a husband or wife, and two or three classes of persons who are entitled to the re-

* Sirajiyyah and Shureefeea, Appendix, No. 205.

† Ibid, Appendix, No. 206.

Rule. turn, the share of the person who has no right to participate in it is first to be extracted, as in the last case. And if the remaining parcels quadrate with the number of sharers, there is no necessity for any further process than to distribute them among them. It is to be observed, however, that this can occur only in one case, that is, when the share of the person who is not entitled to participate in the return is a fourth, and there are three-fourths to be divided among the sharers. As where the deceased has left a widow, a grand-mother, and two half-sisters by the mother*. The share of a widow being a fourth in such circumstances, four is the smallest number of parcels into which the estate can be divided so as to admit of its being extracted; and the share of the grand-mother being a sixth, while that of the two sisters is exactly double, or one-third, the three remaining parcels are obviously divisible among them without a fraction†.

When the remaining parcels and sharers are commensurable.

If the parcels which remain after deducting the share of the person who is not entitled to participate in the return, do not quadrate with the shares of the persons who are entitled to participate, multiply the extractor of the case by the aggregate of these shares, and the product will be a number of parcels out of which it will be found that all the shares may be extracted without a fraction‡. Thus, where the sole

When they are incommensurable.

* Sirajiyyah, Appendix, No. 207.

† Shureefeea, Appendix, No. 208.

‡ Sirajiyyah, Appendix, No. 209.

heirs of the deceased are a wife, two daughters, and a grand-mother, the share of the first in such circumstances being an eighth, the least number of parcels into which the estate must be divided is eight, and after setting apart one for the widow, seven remain for the daughters and grand-mother. The share of the daughters being two-thirds, and that of the grand-mother a sixth, the aggregate of the shares when reduced to fractions of the same denomination is five, and as seven parcels cannot be distributed among five sharers without a fraction, multiply the extractor eight by five, and the product forty is the number of parcels into which the estate must be divided. Of these one-eighth or five parcels belong to the widow, and of the remaining thirty-five, four-fifths or twenty eight parcels are the property of the daughters, and one-fifth or seven parcels that of the grand-mother.

If instead of one wife and one grand-mother, as in the preceding illustration, we suppose that there are several of each, and also enlarge the number of daughters, the process will be the same so far as relates to the doctrine of the return, but the case must be further subjected to the operation of some of the rules mentioned in chapter seventh. Thus, if the deceased had left four widows, nine daughters, and six grand-mothers, the shares would be the same as in the last case, though divisible among a greater number of individuals. The portion of the widow being five-fortieths, that of the daughters twenty-eight, and the portion of the grand-mothers seven, we first, according to the second rule, consider if there be any common measure of the classes, and the individuals composing them. But there is no common measure of five and four, nor of twenty-eight and nine, nor of seven and six, and we are obliged to operate with the whole numbers. We next compare the individuals in the different classes with each other, and find the common measure two of the number of widows and the number of grand-mothers. Dividing six by two, and multiplying the quotient by four, according to the first rule, we have the product twelve, which we proceed under the same rule to compare with the number of daughters, and find that the numbers are both measured by three. By dividing and multiplying as before, we obtain the product thirty-six, which (following the same rule and) multiplying by forty, the extractor of the case, the result is fourteen hundred and forty parcels, into which the estate must be divided before the portions of the respective individuals can be extracted without a fraction. Having multiplied the denominators of the fractions which represent the shares by thirty-six, we must of course increase the numerators in the same *ratio*, and have thus $5 \times 36 = 180$ parcels for the portion of the widows, or 45 to each; $28 \times 36 = 1008$ parcels for the daughters, or 112 to each; and $7 \times 36 = 252$ parcels, for the portion of the grand-mothers, or 42 to each*.

---

* Sirajiyyah and Shureefeea, Appendix, No. 210.

CHAPTER X.

Of vested Inheritances.

Rule for increasing the number of parcels when some of the heirs die before a division of the estate has taken place.

WHEN some of the portions have become inheritances by the death of the parties entitled to them, before the estate has been actually divided, the number of parcels must be enlarged so as to include the representatives of the deceased heir. The procedure will be exactly the same as that which has been explained in the seventh chapter, if we substitute for the original shares in that chapter the arrangement of the estate of the first deceased, that is, the number of parcels into which it must be divided, so as to give the individuals of each class their portions without a fraction, and substitute for this arrangement the arrangement of the estate of the deceased heir, that is, the number of parcels into which it must be divided, so as to give his representatives their portions without a fraction.

Illustration.

Thus, take the case of a woman who has died, leaving a husband, a daughter, and a mother. And suppose, that all the heirs also die before the inheritance has been divided; the husband first, leaving a widow and both parents; then the daughter, leaving two sons, a daughter, and a grand-mother, who, it is to be observed, is the mother of the deceased; and last, the mother, leaving a husband and two brothers. Here we must first ascertain the portions of the original heirs, and as they present the concurrence of a fourth, a half, and a sixth, we must divide the estate into twelve parcels, whereof three are the husband's, six the daughter's, and two the mother's, leaving one to the residuary. But there happens to be no residuary, and the surplus reverting to the daughter and mother, the case must be arranged on the principles of the return. After the share of the husband has been extracted, there remain three-fourths, which cannot be divided among the four shares of the daughter and mother; that is, the three-sixths of the former and the one-sixth of the latter, without a fraction; and the extractor of the husband's share is accordingly to be multiplied by the aggregate of the shares of the daughter and mother. The number of parcels into which the original inheritance must be divided is thus raised to sixteen, whereof four are the husband's, nine the daughter's, and three belong to the mother.

Continued. Having arranged the original inheritance, we proceed in the same way to arrange each of the secondary inheritances, and if we find that the number of parcels which fall to the share of the original heir can be divided among his representatives without a fraction, there is no occasion for any farther procedure. Thus, the representatives of the husband being his widow and both parents, the share of the first is a fourth, and the remaining three-fourths are to be distributed to the others in the proportion of two parts to the father and one to the mother. The four parcels reserved for the husband in the primary inheritance are therefore obviously divisible among his representatives without a fraction, his father's portion being accordingly two-sixteenths of the whole, his mother's one-sixteenth, and his widow's the same*.

But if the portion of the original heir cannot be divided among his representatives without a fraction, we first consider whether there be any common measure of the number of parcels which fall to the original heir, and of the number into which his own inheritance must be divided; and if there be such common measure, we divide the latter number by it, and multiply the quotient by the whole number of parcels into which the first inheritance was divided†. Thus, in the case of the daughter who has died, leaving two sons, a daughter, and a grand-mother, the secondary inheritance being divisible into six parts, that is, two for each son, one for the daughter, and one for the mother, there is the common measure three of that number, and of the nine parcels to which the original heir was entitled in the primary inheritance. We accordingly divide six by three, and multiply the quotient by sixteen, which gives the product thirty-two, as the number of parcels to Continued.

* Sirajiyyah and Shureefeea, Appendix, No. 211.

† Sirajiyyah, Appendix, No. 212.

which the original estate must be raised, so as to include the shares of the representatives of the daughters. Raising all the shares in proportion, the representatives of the husband shall receive $\frac{8}{32}$dths among them, or $\frac{4}{32}$dths to his father, and $\frac{2}{32}$dths to each of his mother and widow; while the nine-sixteenths of the daughter will become $\frac{18}{32}$dths, whereof three parcels shall belong to her mother, and the remaining fifteen be divided among her children in the usual ratio of two portions to the males and one portion to the females, thus making the share of each son $\frac{6}{32}$dths, and that of the daughter $\frac{3}{32}$dths*.

If there be no common measure of the number of parcels which fall to the original heir, and of the number into which his own inheritance is divided, we multiply the whole of the latter into the full amount of parcels into which the first inheritance is divisible†. Thus, in the case of the mother who has died leaving a husband and two brothers, the first inheritance having been already raised to thirty-two parcels, her three-sixteenths become $\frac{6}{32}$dths, to which the three that she became entitled to as grand-mother to the daughter must be added, thus making in all $\frac{9}{32}$dths as the portion to be divided among her representatives. Her own succession is divisible into four parts, and there is obviously no common measure of nine and four; thirty-two is accordingly to be multiplied by four, and the product, or one hundred and

---

* Shureefeea, Appendix, No. 213.

† Sirajiyyah, Appendix, No. 214.

twenty-eight, is the number of parcels into which the original inheritance must be divided, so as to give the representatives of the mother their shares without a fraction. Again, raising the shares of all the other parties in proportion, the representatives of the first deceased will receive $\frac{32}{128}$ths among them, or sixteen parcels to his father, and eight to each of his mother and widow; the representatives of the second deceased will receive $\frac{72}{128}$ths among them, or twenty-four parcels to each son, twelve to the daughter, and the same to the mother; while the $\frac{9}{32}$dths of the grand-mother will become $\frac{36}{128}$ths, whereof eighteen parcels shall belong to her husband, and the remaining parcels shall be divided equally among her brethren, thus, giving nine to each. The sum of 32, 72, and 36 is 140; but from that number twelve is to be deducted, being the share of the grand-mother as mother to the daughter, which is included both in seventy-two and thirty-six; and the remainder will be one hundred and twenty-eight, being the whole number of parcels into which the inheritance is divisible*.

---

* Shureefeea, Appendix, No. 215.

CHAPTER XI.

Of Distant Kindred.

THE distant kindred are defined to be "all relatives who are neither sharers nor residuaries," and, on failure of these classes, they are entitled to the inheritance, according to the report of most of the prophet's companions. *Zeid* the son of *Thabit*, however, was of opinion that the property ought rather to be given to the *Beit-ool-Mal*; in which respect he has been followed by *Malik* and *Shafei*. But *Aboo Huneefa* and his followers have adopted the more general opinion*; for which there is the further sanction of a text of the *Kooran*, though it does not occur in the chapter on inheritance. **Definition.**

Of the distant kindred there are four classes. The first class comprehends the children of daughters, and of son's daughters, how low soever, and whether male or female. The second are the excluded or false grand-fathers, how high soever, as the maternal **Four classes of distant kindred.**

---

* Sirajiyyah, Appendix, No. 216.

grand-father and his father, and the excluded or false grand-mothers, how high soever, as the mother of the maternal grand-father, and the mother of the maternal grand-father's mother. The third class are the children of sisters, whether male or female, and the daughters of brothers, how low soever, and whether the sister or brother from whom they are descended was connected with the deceased through both parents, or only through one; also the sons of half-brothers by the mother, how low soever*. And the fourth class are the paternal aunts of the deceased, that is, the sisters of his father, whether of the whole or half-blood; his paternal uncles by the mother, that is, the half-brothers of his father by the same mother; his maternal uncles, and aunts of whatever description; and the children of all these persons, how low soever, and of whichever sex†.

Order of succession.

There are contrary reports of *Aboo Huneefa's* opinion respecting the order in which the several classes of the distant kindred are to be called to the

---

* Sirajiyyah and Shureefeea, Appendix, No. 217.

† Ibid, Appendix, No. 218. The author of the Sirajiyyah concludes his general summary of the classes by observing, "that all "who are related to the deceased through them are among the "distant kindred." But the summary is still imperfect, as the commentator remarks; not extending to many persons who are also included among them. The reader will find hereafter that the distant kindred are in fact as unlimited as I have endeavoured to shew the residuaries to be.

succession. But the more generally received, and that according to which cases are decided, is that they are called in the order in which they are above enumerated*. The rules for the preference of individuals are nearly the same for all the classes, and occupy a larger space in the *Shureefeea* than they appear to me to deserve ; considering how rarely it can happen that a person should die without leaving either a sharer or some known residuary to inherit his property, in which case only there is room for the succession of the distant kindred. All that I propose in this place is a full exposition of the rules, as they are applicable to the first class, to which I shall refer the other classes as far as possible, noticing however at some length where there is any difference in their mode of application.

§ *First class of distant kindred.*

Of the first class of the distant kindred the nearer to the deceased are preferred to the more remote. Thus, the daughter of a daughter will take the whole inheritance, though alone, before daughters of a son's daughter†. When the claimants are equal in degree, that is, both the same number of steps from the deceased, the child of an heir is preferred to the child of a distant kinsman or kinswoman ; as the daughter of First rule. Second rule.

* Sirajiyyah, Appendix, No. 219.

† Ibid, Appendix, No. 220.

a son's daughter to the son of a daughter's daughter*. If the claimants are not only equidistant from the deceased, but also on an equal footing as to descent, all or none of them being the offspring of heirs, respect is to be had to their sex, according to *Aboo Yoosuf*, and the property to be divided among them in the proportion of two parts to a male and one to a female, whether they claim from ancestors of the same or different sexes. *Moohummud* assents to this doctrine, when the ancestors are of the same sex, but otherwise he refers to *their* sex as the criterion for determining the rights of their descendants, giving to the branches the inheritance of the roots†. Thus, when the deceased has left the son of a daughter, and the daughter of a daughter as his sole heirs, his property is to be divided into three parts, according to *Aboo Yoosuf,* by reason of the sex of the claimants, two-thirds being the portion of the son, and one-third that of the daughter; while it is to be distributed in the same way according to *Moohummud,* the persons through whom their right is derived, being of the same sex. But if we carry the heirs in the last case a step farther down, and suppose that the deceased has left the daughter of a daughter's son and the son of a daughter's daughter, the opinions

Third rule.

Difference of opinion between *Aboo Yoosuf* and *Moohummud.*

---

* Sirajiyyah, Appendix, No. 221. By the child of an heir is here meant the child of a sharer, as the author of the *Shureefeea* observes in a subsequent part of his work.

† Sirajiyyah, Appendix, No. 222.

will no longer coincide; for while *Aboo Yoosuf*, looking only to the sex of the claimants, would still distribute the property in the same way, *Moohummud*, having respect to the sex of the ancestors in the second generation, where they first differ, would divide the property into three portions at that stage, by which means two parts would descend in the next generation to the daughter as the representative of her father, and one part to the son as the representative of his mother*. The opinion of *Moohummud*, which has certainly the appearance of being more complex than that of *Aboo Yoosuf*, was at first entertained by the latter doctor himself, though he subsequently saw reason to depart from it, and it is conformable to the more general report of *Aboo Huneefa's* judgment. For which reason, and because it is also considered to be more agreeable to the general principle of his doctrine respecting the succession of the distant kindred, it has been adopted by his followers as the rule of decision†. It seems also to be fairly deducible from an admitted decision of the companions of the prophet in the case of a paternal and a maternal aunt, two-thirds having been awarded to the former and one-third to the latter; which *Moohummud* very justly observes cannot be reconciled with *Aboo Yoosuf's* principle of looking only to the sex of the claimants; for accord-

Moohummud's opinion preferred.

* Sirajiyyah and Shureefeea, Appendix, No. 223.

† Shureefeea, Appendix, No. 224.

ing to that the property ought to have been distributed in moieties*.

Further illustration of his opinion.

In the case already put, the branches were equal in number to the roots, and there was a difference of sex among the latter only at one stage. To illustrate the doctrine of *Moohummud* more fully, we must vary the case, and let us first suppose that the deceased has left distant kindred at a low stage of descent, and that the sex of the persons through whom they are connected with him is different at several of the intermediate stages. In this case, *Moohummud's* rule is to divide the property at the stage where the difference of sex first appears, on the principle of two parts to the males and one part to the females. He then separates all the males and females at that stage into two classes; and collecting the portions of all the males into one fund, he divides it among their descendants at the next stage, where a difference of sex appears, on the same principle of giving two parts to the males and one part to the females. The portions of the females are divided in the same way among their descendants; and the process continued with both classes, until he arrives at the actual claimants, who receive the portions of their immediate predecessors†. Thus, to take a case in the *Shureefeea*, let us suppose, however extravagant the supposition, that the deceased has left twelve descendants in the sixth stage of

* Shureefeea, Appendix, No. 225.

† Sirajiyyah, Appendix, No. 226.

descent, of different sexes themselves, and also connected with him through persons of different sexes, according to the following scheme:

Deceased.

S.	S.	S.	D.	D.	D.	D.	D.	D.	D.	D.	D.
D.	D.	D.	D.	D.	D.	D.	D.	D.	D.	D.	D.
S.	D.	D.	S.	S.	S.	D.	D.	D.	D.	D.	D.
D.	D.	D.	S.	D.	D.	S.	S.	S.	D.	D.	D.
D.	S.	D.	D.	D.	D.	D.	S.	D.	S.	D.	D.
D.	D.	D.	D.	D.	S.	D	D.	S.	D.	S.	D.

Here there are twelve claimants, of whom three are males and nine females, all being in the same degree, and none of them the child of an heir. According to *Aboo Yoosuf*, as each son is equivalent to two daughters, the estate is to be divided into fifteen parcels, whereof the sons shall have two each, leaving nine, or one each, to the daughters. But according to *Moohummud*, the division is into sixty parcels, as we shall see on arranging the scheme upon his principles. Thus, there being three sons and nine daughters in the first stage, the property must be there separated into fifteen parcels, or six to the sons and nine to the daughters. Then following the portions of the sons, we find that there is no difference of sex among their descendants in the second stage, but that in the third, a son occurs with two daughters. The six parts of the sons are therefore here to be divided, the son taking half or three parts, which are transmitted to his descendant in the lowest line as his representative, and the two daughters the remaining three parts. These three parts undergo a fresh division at the next stage where a difference of sex appears, two parts being the property of the son, and transmissible to his daughter, and the remaining third being the right of the daughter, and transmissible to her descendant in the same way. Thus, the shares of the first three claimants, commencing at the left hand, are three and two-fifteenths, and one-fifteenth, of the whole property. The portions of the nine daughters in the first stage being also collected into one fund, pass through the second generation, which is entirely composed of females, without undergoing any alteration ; but in the third, we find three sons and six daughters ; and the nine parts are to be distributed among twelve persons, each son being equal to two daughters. This cannot be done without enlarging the number of parcels into which the whole inheritance is to be divided ; and, as we have the common measure three of fifteen and twelve, we divide the latter by it, according to the rule so often explained, and multiply the quotient four into fifteen, which raises the number of parcels to sixty, and the nine-fifteenths of the daughter's become accordingly thirty-six sixtieths. Of these the three males in the third generation take half or eighteen, which are again to be divided into two equal parts at the next stage, by reason of the occurrence of a son with two daughters: the moiety or nine parts of the son passing to his representative in the lowest line; and the nine parts reserved for the two daughters passing without farther alteration through the fifth stage, and being divisible at the next or lowest, by reason of the occurrence of a son and daughter, the former taking six parts and the latter three. The shares of the six females in the third generation being the same as those of the three males, or eighteen parcels, are divided into two lots at the fourth stage, twelve parcels being appropriated to the three sons, and six to the daughters. The twelve parcels undergo a fresh division in the fifth stage, by reason of the occurrence of a son with two daughters; the former taking the half or six, which pass to his representative in the last line; and the latter the remaining six, which are subject to a still farther division by reason of the occurrence of a male and female in the lowest stage, the male receiving four parcels and the female two. The six parcels of the three last females in the fourth line are in like manner divided into two parts at the fifth stage; the son taking three parcels, which descend to his daughter; and the remaining three being divisible in the last stage between a son and a daughter, the former takes two parcels and the latter one parcel. Reducing the portions of the three first claimants to the left of the scheme from fifteenths to sixtieths, and raising the numerators of their shares proportionably, the shares of all the claimants will be as follows:—taking them in the order in which they stand, viz. 12, 8, 4, 9, 3, 6, 2, 6, 4, 3, 2, 1; which are accordingly their portions upon the principles of *Moohummud**.

* Shureefeea, Appendix, No. 227.

In all the cases put hitherto, the branches were equal in number to the roots, each ancestor having only one descendant among the claimants, and in each of the intermediate lines. Let us now suppose, that some of the roots have several branches, and we shall find, that in these circumstances the doctrine of *Moohummud* is subject to some modification. Thus, suppose that there are five claimants, descended in the fourth degree from three ancestors, as in the following scheme:

Deceased.

daughter	daughter	daughter
son	daughter	daughter
daughter	son	daughter
dr. dr.	daughter	son son

According to *Aboo Yoosuf* the property ought to be divided into seven parcels, agreeably to the number of branches or claimants, the two sons being equivalent to four daughters; each daughter would accordingly reserve one share, and each son two shares. *Moohummud* also would divide the property into seven parcels; but on different principles, and he would distribute them differently; his rule in such circumstances being to consider the sex in the roots, but the number of parcels in the branches. Thus, the difference of sex first appears in the second stage, where there is a son with two daughters. The portion of the son being equal to that of both daughters, the estate ought to be divided into four parts, whereof two would go to the son, and one to each of the daughters. But the son has two branches that is two daughters among the claimants, and the sex being taken from the root, and only the number from the branches, the single son becomes equivalent to two, and his shares are accordingly raised to four. Of the second daughter there is only one branch; but of the third there are two branches, namely, two sons in the line of the claimants; and the sex being considered in the root at the first stage where the difference appears, and the number in the branches, the single daughter in the second stage is equivalent to two daughters, and her share accordingly doubled. The estate is thus divided at the second stage into two lots; one containing four parcels for the son, and the other three parcels for the daughters. The portion of the son passes without division, till it reaches his two grand-daughters, who are each entitled to two parts; while the three parts of the daughters undergo a new division in the third stage, where there is a son and daughter; but the daughter having two branches, her share is doubled, becoming the same as the son's: so that, one-seventh and a half of a seventh compose the share of each, and pass to their respective representatives. The daughter being represented by two sons, her portion must be farther divided into two parts, and it will be found, that the whole estate must be arranged into twenty-eight parcels, in order that the claimants may receive their shares without a fraction*. The portions of all, taking them in the order in which they stand, and beginning from the

* Sirajiyyah and Shureefeea, Appendix, No. 228.

left, will accordingly be as follows, viz. 8, 8, 6, 3, 3, which added together are twenty-eight parcels.

Claimants deriving right through both parents

It may happen that some of the distant kindred of the first class are descended from the deceased through both parents. Thus, suppose a person to have left a great grand-son and two great grand-daughters, who are neither sharers nor residuaries, and the last of whom are related to him by both sides, as in this scheme*; viz.

Deceased.

daughter	daughter	daughter
daughter	son ———	——— daughter
son	2 daughters	

According to *Aboo Yoosuf*, the property is in this case to be divided into three equal parts; for the females being doubly related are considered equivalent to two on either side, and the property of the deceased is in the same situation as if he had left four great grand-daughters and one great grand-son, two-thirds of the estate passing to the former and one-third to the latter†. *Moohummud*, on the other hand, would divide the property into twenty-eight parcels, giving twenty-two to the daughters, and only six to the son. This is easily explained upon his principle of considering the sex in the roots, but the number of parcels in the branches. The difference of sex appearing first in the second stage, where there

* Sirajiyyah, Appendix, No. 229.

† Sirajiyyah and Shureefeea, Appendix, No. 230.

is a son with two daughters, and one of the daughters and the son having each two branches, they are to be considered in the same light as if they were two sons and two daughters; but the share of one son is equivalent to that of two daughters, and there is also another daughter, by which means, the number of parcels is swelled to seven, whereof the son would take four and the daughters three. Arranging the shares of the males and the shares of the females into separate lots, the four parcels of the son would descend to his daughters, giving two to each, and the three parcels of the daughters pass in like manner to their descendants, that is, the same two daughters and the son. The portion of the latter being equivalent to that of two females, the three parcels must be divided into four parts, which cannot be accomplished without a fraction, and there is no common measure of three and four; we must therefore multiply seven by four, and the product or twenty-eight will be divisible among all the claimants without a fraction. The four parcels of the male in the second stage will thus become sixteen, giving eight to each of the great grand-daughters; and the three parcels of the females in the same stage will become twelve, of which the half or six parcels will pass to the great grand-son, and the remaining six to the great grand-daughters, which with the other sixteen parcels, will make their shares twenty-two, or eleven to each*.

* Sirajiyyah and Shureefeea, Appendix, No. 231.

§ *Second class of distant kindred.*

There is little differenco between the distant kindred of the first and second classes, except that they recede from the deceased in opposite directions.

How preferred.

The rules for the succession of both are nearly the same. Thus in the second, like the first class, proximity to the deceased forms the principal ground of preference, the nearer taking precedence of the more remote by whatever side related*. The maternal grand-father is accordingly preferred to all the others, as being the only false ancestor in the stage immediately preceding the parents of the deceased, and the father of the paternal grand-mother is in like manner preferred to the father of the paternal grand-mother's mother†. When the claimants are in the same degree of proximity to the deceased, he whose right is derived through an heir is entitled to preference, according to some of the followers of *Aboo Huneefa*‡. Thus, among those who hold this opinion, the father of the mother's mother, who is a true grand-mother, and therefore an heir, is preferred to the father of the mother's father, who is himself only a false grand-father, and therefore not an heir§. But others reject this distinction, dividing the pro-

---

* Sirajiyyah, Appendix, No. 232.
† Shureefeea, Appendix, No. 233.
‡ Sirajiyyah, Appendix, No. 234.
§ Shureefeea, Appendix, No. 235.

perty at once according to the next rule, and giving, in the case put, two-thirds to the father of the grandfather, and the other third to the father of the grandmother*. When none of the claimants can shew a ground of preference, either by proximity, or relationship through an heir, the property is to be divided according to the difference of sex, on the principle of two parts to males and one part to females; but it is only when the claimants are all on the same side, and their relationship to the deceased continued through persons of the same sex, that the difference is to be considered in the persons of the claimants themselves. When they are connected through persons of different sexes, the property is to be divided at the stage where the difference first appears, and distributed in the manner already explained. If the difference appears at the earliest stage, that is, if some of the claimants are related to the deceased by the father's side and some by the mother's, the property is to be divided *ab initio* into three parts, whereof two are to be distributed among the distant kindred on the paternal side, and one among those of the maternal†.

§ *Third class of distant kindred.*

The third class of distant kindred comprises, as already mentioned, the children of sisters and the daughters of brothers absolutely, with the sons of

* Sirajiyyah and Shureefeea, Appendix, No. 236.

† Sirajiyyah, Appendix, No. 237.

half-brothers by the mother; and the rules for their succession are similar to those which have been explained for the first class. That is, the nearest to the deceased is first entitled to the inheritance, and of claimants equal in proximity, the child of a residuary* is preferred to the child of a distant kinsman or kinswoman. Thus, when the claimants are the daughter of a brother's son, and the son of a sister's daughter, whether the brother and sister were related to the deceased through both parents or by the father only, or one by both parents, and the other by the father, the daughter of the brother's son shall take the whole property, because her father ranks among residuaries, while the parent of the other claimant, that is the sister's daughter, is no more than a distant kinswoman†.

The child of a residuary preferred among claimants of equal degree.

Issue of half brothers and sisters by the same mother.

If the brother and sister, in the last case, from whom the claimants are descended, had been related to the deceased by the mother's side only, the property would be distributed differently, both according to *Aboo Yoosuf* and *Moohummud*; though they are not exactly agreed as to the precise mode of distribution. The former would divide the property among the claimants, according to the common rule of giving two parts to the male and one part to the

* In the first class, the preference is given to the child of a sharer; but neither can the child of a residuary be in the same degree with the child of a distant kinsman in the first class, nor the child of a sharer be in the same degree with the child of a distant kinsman in the third class. (*Shureefeea*, *p.* 159.)

† Sirajiyyah, Appendix, No. 238.

female. It is true, that though this be the general principle, there is a special exception with respect to the persons through whom their rights are derived; brothers and sisters by the mother only succeeding equally, without any regard to difference of sex, upon the express authority of the *Kooran*. But this exception is not to be extended by analogy to cases where the similarity is not complete in all respects; and as the children of half-brothers and sisters by the mother are not in circumstances precisely similar to their parents, having no right for instance to inherit as sharers, they are subject to the operation of the general rule. *Moohummud*, however, disputes the justness of this reasoning, because the sole right of the children arises in consequence of the propinquity of their parents to the deceased; and he accordingly declares, that the property ought in this case to be divided equally between the claimants, without any preference of the male over the female sex. It is to be observed, that the general current of tradition is in favor of his opinion*.

Mode of distribution among claimants of the full and half blood.

When the claimants are equal in degree, and none or all of them the children of residuaries, or some the children of residuaries and some of sharers, respect is to be had, according to *Aboo Yoosuf*, to the strength of propinquity. So that the descendant of a full brother would be preferred to the descendant of a brother by the father only, and the latter be preferred to one descended from a brother of the deceas-

---

* Sirajiyyah, Appendix, No. 239. See *ante*, page 70.

ed by the mother only*. *Moohummud*, however, first divides the property among the brothers and sisters, with reference to the sides of their relationship to the deceased, and the number of their branches, and then distributes what may fall to the share of each sex among the branches, in the manner explained for distant kindred of the first class. Thus, suppose the deceased to be survived by three nieces, the daughters of different kinds of brothers, and by three nephews and three nieces, the children of different kinds of sisters, after the following scheme:

Full br.	full sr.	br. by fr.	sr. by fr.	br. by mr.	sr. by mr.
daughter,	s. d.	dr.	s. d.	daughter,	s. d.

According to *Aboo Yoosuf*, the whole property is to be divided among the descendants of the full brother and sister, in the proportion of two parts to the male and one part to each of the females, respect being had to the sex of the claimants, and the strength of their propinquity to the deceased. On failure of descendants of the whole blood, the property would pass to the descendants of the half-brother and sister by the father, and be distributed among them in the same way. And on failure of them, it would be distributed in like manner among the descendants of the half brother and sister by the mother†. According to *Moohummud*, on the other hand, one-third of the property is to

* Sirajiyyah and Shureefeea, Appendix, No. 240.

† Sirajiyyah, Appendix, No. 241.

be allotted to the descendants of the half-brother and sister by the mother, and divided equally among them, on account of the equality of their roots. The sister having two branches, viz. a son and a daughter, is accounted the same as two sisters, and her portion is therefore two-thirds of the third, which accordingly pass to her descendants, among whom they are equally divided; and the remaining third of that third, being the portion of the brother who has only one branch, goes to his daughter. Two-thirds of the whole property still remain, which belong to the descendants of the full-brothers and sisters, who it may be remembered entirely exclude half-brothers and sisters by the father. The sister here has also two branches, by which means her portion is doubled, and raised to an equality with that of her brother; the two-thirds are accordingly to be divided into moieties, whereof one moiety, that is a third of the whole property, passes to the daughter of the full-brother, and the remaining moiety, or third of the whole, is to be divided among the children of the full-sister in the proportion of two parts to the son and one part to the daughter. The whole estate will thus be arranged by a separation into nine lots; whereof three, passing to the children of the half-brother and sister by the mother, will be divided among them equally, giving one lot to each; and of the remaining six lots, which belong to the children of the full-brother and sister, three will pass to the daughter of the brother, two to the son of the sister, and one lot to her daughter*.

If instead of brother's daughters, as in the last case, the deceased were to leave descendants of different kinds of brothers through their sons, as if, for instance, he were survived by the daughter of a full-brother's son, the daughter of the son of a half-brother by the father, and the daughter of the son of a half brother by the mother, the first would take the whole property, by the general agreement of the learned, as being the child of a residuary, and having also the strength of propinquity†.

Case. Some commentators have in this place adduced a case, to illustrate the mode of appreciating the sides of relationship, and the branches in the roots. Thus, suppose the deceased to have left the son of a half-brother by the father, two daughters of the son of a half-sister by the father, who are also the children of a full sister's daughter, and the daughter of the son of a half-sister by the mother; as in the following scheme:

h. B by F.	h. S by F.	Full sister.	h. S by M.
daughter,	son,—	—daughter,	son.
son,	two daughters,		daughter.

According to *Aboo Yoosuf*, the whole property ought here to go to the grand-daughters of the full-

* Sirajiyyah and Shureefeea, Appendix, No. 242.
† Sirajiyyah, Appendix, No. 243.

sister by strength of propinquity. But *Moohummud* would divide the property in the roots, that is, the brother and sisters, having respect to the sides and number of the branches. Thus, the property would be originally divisible into six parts, by reason of the occurrence of a sixth, which is the share of the half-sister by the mother; the full sister having two branches is accounted the same as two full-sisters, whose share being two-thirds of the property, four parts would be allotted to her, and the remaining sixth pass to the half-brother by the father, as residuary, when his sister would also participate with him; but she has two branches in the present case, and her portion would be accordingly raised to an equality with her brother's, and the sixth be divided between them in moieties; when the case would be raised to twelve. The single sixth of the half-brother and sister by the father would thus become two-twelfths, one of which would be allotted to each. But it will be found, that the twelfth of the sister must again be divided between two persons, namely, her grand-daughters, and the case must be further raised to twenty-four, or four times the original number of parcels into which it was to be arranged. The one sixth of the half-sister by the mother, which passes to her grand-daughter, will thus become four twenty-fourths; the four parts of the full-sister will become sixteen twenty-fourths, and pass to her grand-daughters, who will also have two twenty-fourths as the descendants of the half-sister by the father; while the remaining two will pass to the grandson of the half-brother by the father*.

§ *Fourth class of distant kindred.*

The fourth class of the distant kindred are the paternal aunts of the deceased, his paternal uncles by the mother, that is, the half brothers of his father by the same mother, and his maternal uncles and aunts without distinction†. The descendants of this class being treated of in a separate section, there is no room here for preference by proximity, as all the claimants must be equidistant from the deceased. When they all happen to be related to him by the same side, as paternal aunts, and paternal uncles who were related to his father by the mother only, or maternal uncles and aunts, preference is given to strength of propinquity, that is, the person related by both parents is preferred, whether male or female, to one connected by the father only, and the latter is preferred to one connected only through the mother. When there are male and female claimants, and all upon a footing of equality as to strength of propinquity, all being related by both parents, or by father only, or mother only, the portion of the male is double that of the female, according to the general rule. When the claimants are of different sides, some being related by the father and some by the mother, there is no longer any room

How preferred.

* Shureefeea, Appendix, No. 244.

† Ibid, Appendix, No. 245.

for preference according to strength of propinquity, two-thirds of the property being allotted to the relatives by the father, and one-third to those by the mother, and divided among them respectively in the same way as if they were all of the same side*.

§ *Children of the fourth class.*

The succession of the children of the fourth class of distant kindred is regulated in a great measure in the same way as the succession of the distant kindred of the first class. That is, the first entitled to the inheritance is the nearest to the deceased, on whatever side related; and among equidistant relatives, provided they are all on the same side, the preference is determined by strength of propinquity. When the claimants are not only equidistant, but also on a footing of equality as to the strength of their propinquity, the child of a residuary is preferred to one who is not so. Thus, where the claimants are the daughter of a paternal uncle, and the son of a paternal aunt, both uncle and aunt being of the full-blood to the father of the deceased, the former will take the whole estate, as being the offspring of a residuary. But if the aunt had been of the full-blood, and the uncle only of the half-blood, the son of the former would be preferred, by reason of the strength of propinquity, according to the most probable traditions, and agreeably to the analogy of a maternal aunt by the father, who though

The child of a residuary preferred among claimants equal in degree & strength of propinquity.

* Sirajiyyah, Appendix, No. 246.

the child of a false grand-father, who is only a distant kinsman, is preferred to the maternal aunt by the mother, though she is the child of the maternal grand-mother, who is a sharer. Some, however, maintain, that the daughter of the paternal uncle by the father ought to have the preference in the supposed case, by reason of her being the child of a residuary*.

When the claimants, though equidistant, are not related by the same side to the deceased, there is no longer any dependance on the strength of propinquity, nor the fact of one of them being the child of a residuary. This is both agreeable to the more generally received traditions, and to the analogy of the case of a paternal aunt of the full-blood, who, though the mistress of two propinquities, and also the child of an heir on both sides, (her father being a true grand-father to the deceased, and therefore a residuary, and her mother his true grand-mother and consequently a sharer) does not exclude a maternal aunt by the father alone. No regard being had to either of the circumstances above-mentioned, two-thirds of the property pass to the relatives on the father's side, and one-third to those connected by the mother's. In distributing the portions of the former class, respect is first to be had to the strength of propinquity, and then to the offspring of residuaries. For the latter class, the rule is the same, as far as possible, but all the relatives being connected through a female, there cannot be any residuary among them.

Among claimants of both sides, a double portion to the relatives by the father.

---

* Sirajiyyah, Appendix, No. 247.

According to *Aboo Yoosuf*, the portion of each class is to be divided among the individuals composing it, with reference to their own sex and number; while in the opinion of *Moohummud*, the number of the branches is to be taken into account at the first stage where the difference of sex appears, as explained for the distant kindred of the first class*. Thus, let us Case.
suppose that the deceased has left four grand-sons and four grand-daughters of paternal and maternal uncles and aunts of the half blood, that is, related to his father or mother through one parent only, according to the following scheme:

p. a. by f. p. a. by f. p. u. by f. m. a. by f. m. a. by m. m. u. by f.

daughter, son,——daughter, daughter, son,——dr.

2 sons, 2 daughters, 2 daughters, 2 sons.

Here the property is first to be divided into three parts, whereof two parts go to the relatives by the side of the father, and one part to those by the side of the mother. Among the former the two daughters are equivalent to four, according to *Aboo Yoosuf*; that is, to two on each side: but four daughters (How arranged according to *Aboo Yoosuf*.) being equivalent to two sons, and there being also two other sons, the whole of the two-thirds which fall to the relatives by the father, will be divisible into four parts, which obviously cannot be done without a fraction. There is however a common measure of the number of parcels (two), and the individuals among whom they are to be distributed (four), and the former will accordingly be raised to

* Sirajiyyah, Appendix, No. 248.

four sixths, in the manner so often explained. In the same way, the two sons on the side of the mother, being doubly related, are equivalent to four, and there being two daughters, who are equivalent to one son, the number of claimants among whom the remaining third is to be divided, is five. Here there is no common measure of the parcel and parties entitled to it, and the number of the latter must accordingly be preserved entire. On comparing five with two (the measure of the relatives by the father), as directed in chapter seventh, we find that there is no common divisor of the numbers, which must accordingly be multiplied together; and the product (ten) being multiplied by three, the original divisor of the case, the whole number of the parcels will be raised to thirty, whereof twenty will pass to the claimants on the father's side, or ten to the two sons, and ten to the two daughters ; and the remaining ten to the claimants by the mother's side, or eight to the sons and two to the daughters*.

According to Moohummud.

With respect to the opinion of *Moohummud*, I shall content myself with stating the general result of his principles in the above case, without following their application at each step, which would be fatiguing the reader's attention unnecessarily, after the full explanation that has been given of them in treating of the distant kindred of the first class. According to *Moohummud*, the property ought to

* Shureefeea, Appendix, No. 249.

be divided into thirty-six parcels; of these, two-thirds or twenty-four parcels would pass to the relatives by the father's side; of whom the two daughters would receive nine each, (that is, six in virtue of their descent from the paternal uncle by the father, and three as descendants from the paternal aunt by the father;) and each of the two sons three parcels. The relatives by the side of the mother would take the other third or remaining twelve parcels, whereof the two sons would have each five parcels, (that is, three by virtue of their descent from the maternal uncle by the father, and two as descendants of the maternal aunt by the father;) while only two parcels would be left for the daughters, or one to each. On reckoning up all the shares, it will be found that they amount to thirty-six exactly. Thus, $9+9+3+3=24$; $5+5+1+1=12$; and $24+12=36$*.

If there be none of the persons mentioned in the preceding section in existence, the estate will revert to the maternal uncles and aunts of the deceased's parents, the paternal uncles of his mother, and such of the paternal uncles of his father as were related to him by the mother only. In default of all these, it passes to their children. Failing whom, it will revert to the same description of uncles and aunts of the parents of the deceased's parents; and then to their children. And so on through the more remote branches without any limit; the succession

* Shureefeea, Appendix, No. 250.

being regulated in the same way as that of the distant kindred of the fourth class and their children*.

---

* The authority for the last paragraph was omitted at the proper place in the Appendix, and has been added at the end as No. 286. The distant kindred are of small importance compared to the residuaries, and it is worthy of remark, that the author of the *Sirajiyyah*, after observing that the estate will pass, on failure of the uncles and aunts of the deceased and their children, to the uncles and aunts of his parents and their children, subjoins the words "as in the case of residuaries." Here we have his own authority that he did not mean to restrict his definition of the term "residuaries" to the descendants of the *nearest* or immediate grandfather, as has been apparently supposed by his learned translator. And it may be fairly inferred from the generality of that definition, that there is in truth no limit whatever to the residuaries in the collateral any more than in the direct line; an inference which is confirmed by the analogy of the distant kindred; for whose unlimited succession in the former as well as in the latter line, we have the express authority of the *Shureefeea*.

CHAPTER XII.

Of Posthumous Children, Missing Persons, Captives, and persons perishing by a common accident.

The author of the *Sirajiyyah* has annexed to his chapter on the Distant Kindred, which is the last in his treatise, a few supplementary sections on subjects closely connected with the Law of Inheritance, if they do not strictly form a part of it. The first of these sections, which treats of hermaphrodites, I shall pass over entirely, referring the reader who is curious respecting the notions entertained by Moohummudan lawyers on the obscure question of doubtful sex, to the third volume of Sir William Jones's Works, quarto edition, and Mr. Hamilton's translation of the *Hidaya*, vol. iv. p. 559, where the subject is treated at all the length which it probably deserves. The matter of another of the sections has been introduced, with some additional observations drawn from other sources, in the second chapter under the head of the third impediment to inheritance. And of the remaining sections I propose to give some account in this place. The most important, which treats of posthumous children, I shall consider at some length. For the others a shorter notice will be sufficient.

§ *Of Posthumous Children.*

Different nations have entertained different opinions respecting the longest and shortest periods of gestation in the human species, though all mankind are agreed in fixing the ordinary term at about nine calendar months. The instances of any considerable protraction of this period are probably very rare; but a slight excess is by no means unfrequent. And we know that the usual period has been anticipated in many well authenticated cases by so long as two months. There seems to be nothing, therefore, to warrant us in assigning any positive limit beyond which gestation can never be protracted, nor to enable us to determine the shortest possible time required by nature for the formation of a perfect *fœtus*. There is at the same time an obvious convenience in possessing a rule of law for determining how far questions of this kind may be entertained; and such a rule is accordingly found in the codes of several nations. By the Roman law, ten and six months respectively were prescribed for the *maximum* and *minimum* of gestation; and both the law of Scotland and the Code Napoleon have adopted its provisions in this respect. The law of England is perhaps not fixed on the subject, but the decisions of the courts would probably be regulated in a doubtful case, pretty much, though not strictly, by the same rule. With respect to the shortest period of gestation, the Moohummudan law is the same as the Roman, and upon

Shortest period of gestation.

this point the doctors of all sects seem to be agreed*. But there is less unanimity regarding the longest period, though the notions entertained by all on the subject will probably excite the smile of an European physiologist. They form, however, a part of the Moohummudan code, and cannot well be entirely disregarded by our courts of justice, without altering the law which they are bound to administer in some cases, and assuming in so far the functions of the legislature.

Longest period of gestation.

According to *Shafei*, the period of gestation may be extended to four years†; and two cases, apparently well authenticated, of persons who are said to have remained so long in their mothers' wombs are cited in support of his opinion. With respect to these cases the author of the *Shureefeea* pertinently observes, that the parties could neither have known the fact themselves, nor have well been informed of it by others, since none but God himself can tell what takes place in the womb. Moreover, the protraction might have been occasioned by an unusual rigidity of the mouth of the *uterus*, induced by disease, and so rare an occurrence cannot be drawn into a precedent‡. The opinion of *Aboo Huneefa* seems to rest on less questionable grounds. He assigned two years as the longest period of gestation, on the authority of *Ayesha*, one of the Prophet's

---

* Sirrajiyyah and Shureefea, Appendix, No. 251.

† Appendix, No. 251.

‡ Shureefeea, Appendix, No. 252.

widows, who expressly declared, that "a child re-"mains no longer than two years in the womb of "its mother, even so much as the turn of a wheel." And this she delivered, not as her own opinion, but as a saying of the Prophet himself. It is therefore entitled to the same implicit respect as any other of the traditions, and is accordingly so observed by all the sect of *Aboo Huneefa**.

Disbelieving entirely in all reports of extraordinary protraction, we may be apt to suppose that, notwithstanding the latitude allowed by the Moohummudan law, the only difference which can exist between its practice and that of European nations is, that questions of pregnancy may be entertained in the former as worthy of investigation, which would be entirely rejected in the latter. If our notions on the subject be correct, and the investigation be fairly conducted, the practical result ought to be nearly the same. The issue of an investigation, however, must depend in some degree on the spirit in which it is pursued; and we should not be surprized if a much less degree of evidence would satisfy a Moohummudan lawyer upon a point of this nature, than would be required to command the belief of an English jury. There are still facts, such as the external symptoms of pregnancy, which cannot be entirely disregarded; and it can hardly be supposed, if a woman should fail to exhibit any of these signs

---

* Shureefeea, Appendix, No. 253.

at the usual time, reckoning from her husband's death, that any child which she might ultimately produce within two years from that period would still be pronounced legitimate even by a Moohummudan lawyer. His law allows that the usual period of gestation may in some cases be protracted so long; but it does not allow, so far as I have been able to discover, that pregnancy may possibly exist without any of the symptoms by which it is usually distinguished. There would thus be still a fact in most cases to be accounted for, as contrary to Moohummudan experience as to our own. It seems therefore probable, that the only instances where any real difficulty can occur, are those rare cases of disease which occasionally perplex even the most skilful of the medical faculty in Europe.

Distinction between cases involving the child's paternity, and those which do not.

The law has so strong an inclination to favor the paternity of children, that there is a marked distinction, in the application of the rules respecting pregnancy to the subject of inheritance, between cases where the paternity of the *fœtus* is involved, and those where the question is merely whether it shall be entitled to a portion of the succession or not. Thus, if the pregnant woman be the widow of the person whose succession is in dispute, the child shall inherit, if born within two years from such person's decease, unless the woman has acknowledged the completion of her *iddut*, which would be tantamount to an admission that she was either not pregnant at the death of her husband, or had been intermediately delivered of another child*. While if she were the widow of a relative of the deceased, as of his father or son for instance, it is necessary that she should be delivered within six months from his death, in order that her child may participate in his inheritance†. The reason assigned by the commentator for this distinction, is the necessity of finding a legal descent for the infant in the first instance; while in the second, his paternity being already established, and the question reduced to one of mere inheritance, it is necessary to establish his existence in the womb at the death of the party from whom he claims to inherit, and that can be predicated with certainty only when he is born at or within the shortest period of gestation, reckoning from that event‡.

Evidence of life.

When a child is born alive, he acquires a vested interest, which passes to his representatives in the event of his death. If that should occur immediately after delivery, it may be a question of some difficulty to determine, whether the infant was actually born alive or not. The Moohummudan law has provided for cases of this kind, with a minuteness which is perhaps unknown to other systems of jurisprudence. If the infant exhibits any of the signs by which life is usually indicated, as a sound, sneezing, weeping, laughing, or the motion of a limb,

* See Note to page 4.

† Sirajiyyah, Appendix, No. 254.

‡ Shureefeea, Appendix, No. 255.

it is to be accounted alive*. And if it should die in the birth, the vestiture of interest wil: depend on the fact of the greater or smaller portion of the body being delivered before death. In cases of natural labor, where the head is presented, the breast is to be considered, that is, the infant shall inherit if the whole breast be delivered while he yet discovers signs of life; but if the feet are first delivered, the navel is to be taken into consideration, and his right of inheritance will depend on so much of his body being protruded while he is yet alive†.

Portion to be reserved for an infant in the womb.

According to *Aboo Huneefa*, of the portions of four sons, and four daughters, whichever is the greater in the particular circumstances of the case, is to be reserved for an infant in the womb, and the remainder of the property to be immediately divided among the other heirs. By one report of *Moohummud's* opinion, the larger of the portions of three sons and of three daughters, but by another, the portion of two sons, ought to be reserved. *Aboo Yoosuf*, on the other hand, according to the more generally received accounts of his sentiments, considered, that no more than the share of one son, or the share of one daughter, can be properly reserved for an infant in the womb; security however being taken from the other heirs to refund in case of there proving to be more than one child. And the reasonableness of this opinion has recommended it to the

* Shureefeea, Appendix, No. 256.

† Sirajiyyah, Appendix, No. 257.

approbation of the learned, by whom it has been generally adopted, as the rule of decision*.

Arrangement of cases of pregnancy.

In arranging cases of pregnancy, the property must be divided into so many parcels as will allow of all the heirs' receiving their portions without a fraction, whether the infant should prove to be male or female; and the following rule has been laid down for that purpose.

Rule.

First, arrange the case on either supposition; then compare the number of parcels upon one supposition with the number of parcels upon the other; and if the numbers be commensurable, divide one of them by the measure, and multiply the quotient by the other. Otherwise, multiply the whole of the one number by the whole of the other. The product in either case will be a number of parcels which can be divided among the heirs exactly, whether the infant be male or female†.

This being ascertained, we are next to take the portion of each heir on the supposition of the infant's being a male, and multiply it either by the whole number of parcels required on the supposition of the infant's being a female, or by the quotient of that number when divided by the common measure if there happens to be one. We are then to proceed in the same way with the portion of each heir, on the supposition of the infant being a female‡. And of the products of the two operations, that which hap-

* Sirajiyyah, Appendix, No. 258.

† Sirajiyyah and Shureefeea, Appendix, No. 259.

‡ Sirajiyyah and Shureefeea, Appendix, No. 260.

pens to be the less, is to be surrendered to the particular heir, and the difference reserved till the birth of the infant*.

Illustration.

Thus, suppose, that the deceased has left a daughter, both parents, and a pregnant widow. If the infant be a male, the property must be divided into twenty-four parcels, by reason of the concurrence of an eighth with two-sixths. The widow's portion will accordingly be three parcels, eight will fall to the parents, and the remaining thirteen will belong to the daughter and the unborn son. Again, on the supposition of the infant's being a female, we should have the concurrence of two-thirds, an eighth, and two-sixths, and the number of parcels would be raised to twenty-seven; whereof eleven would be taken by the widow and parents as before, while sixteen would belong to the daughter and the unborn child. The property must accordingly be divided upon both suppositions into twenty-four and twenty-seven parcels. But of these numbers there is the common measure three, and, dividing one of them by it, and multiplying the other by the quotient, we have two hundred and sixteen for the number of parcels required to meet either supposition. Then taking the portion of each heir on the supposition of the infant being a male, and multiplying such portion by the quotient of the number of parcels on the supposition of the infant's being a female, when divided by the common measure of the parcels on

* Sirajiyyah, Appendix, No. 261.

both suppositions, we have 3×9=27 parcels, for the share of the widow, on the first supposition; and 4×9=36 parcels, for the share of each parent, on the same supposition. Reversing the operation for the contingency of the infant's proving to be a female; we have 3×8=24 parcels for the share of the widow, and 4×8=32 parcels for the portion of each parent. It is obvious, that the shares are larger on the last supposition; and the difference, or 27—24+2(36—32)= 11 parcels, must be reserved from the portions of the widow and parents, to abide the event of the delivery*.

Illustration continued.

The estate being originally divisible into twenty-four parcels, on the supposition of the infant's being a son, and eleven of these being absorbed by the shares of the widow and parents, there remain thirteen for the daughter and the unborn child. If with *Aboo Huneefa* we reserve the portions of four sons, to await the birth of the child, the daughter can receive in the mean time only a ninth part of the remaining thirteen parcels, which multiplied by nine, as in the cases of the widow and parents, will give $\frac{13}{216}$ths, as the amount immediately claimable by her†. But, according to the more reasonable opinion of *Aboo Yoosuf*, she would be immediately entitled to $\frac{39}{216}$ths, being one-third of the remainder, after deducting the portions of the other heirs; the other two-thirds being reserved for the infant in the womb. If the birth should be female,

* Sirajiyyah and Shureefeea, Appendix, No. 262.

† Sirajiyyah, Appendix, No. 263.

whether one or more, the whole of what was reserved is to be divided among the daughters, because the very contingency has happened with respect to which the portions were reserved, the widow and both parents having received all that they were entitled to, on the supposition of the infant being female. The daughter, who was born before her father's death, having already received a certain part of her share, is entitled to no more of the reserved portion than is sufficient to put her on a footing of equality with her posthumous sister or sisters. If the widow be delivered of a son or sons, the amounts deducted from the portions of the sharers must be restored to them, and the remainder will then be divided among the children, according to the general rule of a double share to the male, whatever the daughter may have already received being deducted from her share. If the infant be still-born, the portions reserved from the shares of the widow and parents must in like manner be restored, and the amount received by the daughter must be made up to a full half of the whole estate, the surplus being the property of the father as the residuary*.

It seems hardly necessary to observe, that an heir, whose portion cannot be affected by any condition of the infant, is entitled to have the whole of it immediately surrendered to him; and that, on the other hand, where the heir would be entirely excluded in one condition of the infant, no part

* Sirajiyyah and Shureefeea, Appendix, No. 264.

of his share can be delivered to him until its birth. Thus, where the heirs are a grand-mother and a pregnant widow, the former is at once entitled to her sixth, which is subject neither to increase nor diminution, whether the child be male or female, or be born alive or dead*. And where the heirs are a pregnant widow, a brother, and a paternal uncle, neither of the two last is entitled to anything until the birth of the child, because they would be wholly excluded if it should prove to be a son†.

§ *Of Missing Persons.*

Definition. A person is said to be missing when he is absent, and there is no certain intelligence whether he be alive or dead‡. In these circumstances, he is not to be considered dead so long as there are any of his contemporaries alive. This is agreeable to the general current of the traditions§; though according to one report, *Aboo Huneefa* extended the time to a hundred and twenty years, reckoning from the birth of the person missing, while *Moohummud* fixed it at a hundred and ten years, and *Aboo Yoosuf* at a hundred and five years, reckoning from the same period‖. But these reports are not found in books of good authority, and seem to be generally rejected¶. There is however another opinion, which

* Shureefeea, Appendix, No. 265.

† Ibid, Appendix, No. 266.

‡ Ibid, Appendix, No. 267.

§ Sirajiyyah, Appendix, No. 268.

‖ Ibid, Appendix, No. 269.

¶ Shureefeea, Appendix, No. 270.

assigns ninety years, as being usually the extreme limit of human existence in the present age of the world; and, according to the *Imam Timurtashee*, judicial decisions are given in conformity to this opinion*. But the author of the *Hidaya* says, that it is more agreeable to the analogy of the law, that there should be no fixed period, though it is more convenient to limit it to ninety years†. The writer quoted in the *Futawa Alumgeeree* declares, with the *Imam Timurtashee*, and perhaps on his sole authority, that the *Futwa* is according to this opinion; but he remarks, that the most general tradition is in favor of the other, which refers to the missing person's contemporaries‡. There is some difference as to the persons who shall be considered his contemporaries for this purpose; but by the most correct opinion they are contemporaries in his city. It may be remarked, that this is according to the *Imam Timurtashee*, on whose authority, as already observed, the exact period of ninety years has been assumed for determining the death of the missing person §. So that much reliance, it would appear, cannot be placed upon any of the opinions cited; and if a case of the kind were to occur in our courts, the judges would perhaps consider themselves at liberty to exercise their own discretion, taking into

---

* Sirajiyyah and Shureefeea, Appendix, No. 271.

† Hidaya, Appendix, 272.

‡ Futawa Alumgeeree, Appendix, No. 273.

§ Shureefeea, Appendix, No. 274.

consideration the health and age of the party missing, and all other circumstances which might have the effect of shortening or prolonging his days. Some of the followers of *Aboo Huneefa* have asserted the right of the *Imam* to exercise his discretion in each particular case; a course which is farther recommended by the practice of *Shafei**.

Rule. A missing person is considered alive with respect to his own estate, so that no one can inherit from him, but dead as to the property of others, so that he does not inherit from any one†. Any share in a succession which may open to him before a judicial declaration of his death, is to be reserved to await the possibility of his return‡. Should he return, it is of course to be transferred to him, and all his other property restored, which it is the duty of the judge to place in the meantime under the custody of a proper officer. If he should never return, the principle of accounting him alive as to his own property, but dead as to that of others, comes into operation; for it is only such of his heirs as are alive at the time of the Judicial declaration of his death, who are entitled to participate in his estate, while the portions reserved for him from the estates of others revert to their other heirs§.

---

* Sirajiyyah and Shureefeea, Appendix, No. 275.

† Ibid, Appendix, No. 276.

‡ Sirajiyyah, Appendix, No. 277.

§ Sirajiyyah, Appendix, No. 278.

An estate, where one of the heirs is missing, is to be arranged first on the supposition, that he is alive, and will return to claim his share, and then upon the supposition of his being dead. The rest of the operation is the same as has been already explained under the head of pregnancy*. Thus, suppose that the deceased has left a husband and two full-sisters, all of whom are present, claiming their shares, and a full-brother, who is missing. Then, upon the supposition of the brother being dead, the husband and sisters being the sole heirs, the share of the former would be a half and of the latter two-thirds, the extractor of the case being six originally, but increased to seven. On the supposition of his being alive, while the husband's share would still remain the same or a half, the sisters would have only a fourth; for on that supposition the estate would be originally divided into two parts, the husband taking one, and the brother with his sisters the other; but the share of the brother being equivalent to that of two sisters, the whole of the estate would be divided into eight parts, whereof the husband's would be four, the brother's two, and the sisters' one each. In these circumstances, it is obviously for the advantage of the sisters that their missing brother should prove to be dead, while it is for the benefit of the husband that he should be alive, and accordingly no more than one-fourth of the estate can be immediately surrendered to the sis-

Arrangement of an estate when one of the heirs is missing.

* Sirajiyyah, Appendix, No. 279.

ters, and only three-sevenths to the husband, the remainder being reserved to abide the event of the missing person's return, or the judicial declaration of his death. To resolve the case, the estate must be arranged into fifty-six parcels, or the product of the parcels, on the supposition of the missing person's being alive, which was shewn to be eight, multiplied by the number of parcels on the supposition of his death, which is seven. Eight and seven being incommensurable, the number of parcels cannot be reduced by any of the processes so often alluded to. The husband's share on the supposition of the missing person's being alive (four parcels) being multiplied by the number of parcels on the supposition of death, or seven, the product is twenty-eight. In like manner his share on the supposition of death (three) being multiplied by the number of parcels on the supposition of life (eight), the product is twenty-four; which being the smaller, is surrendered to him, and the difference between the products, or four parcels, must be reserved to await the return or death of the missing person. The shares of the sisters being subjected to the same operation, the results are fourteen parcels for the supposition of life, aud thirty-two parcels for that of death; and the difference (or eighteen parcels) must be reserved. The whole of what is immediately payable to the present heirs being thus 24+14=38 parcels, the amount to be reserved for the missing son is eighteen out of the fifty-six. If he be alive, four of these are to be restored to the husband, to make up twenty-eight parcels, the half of fifty-six, and the remaining fourteen added to the fourteen already paid to the sisters, make up the other half; but as the brother is entitled to a double portion, the whole fourteen are surrendered to him. If he should prove to be dead, the whole of the reserved eighteen parcels are to be delivered to the sisters, to complete with what they have already received (14+18=32) thirty-two parcels, which it will be found are four-sevenths of fifty-six*.

§ *Of Captives.*

A CAPTIVE is with respect to inheritance on the same footing as all Moohummudans, so long as he abides in the faith. If he abandons the faith, his condition is like that of other apostates. And if it be unknown whether he has apostatized or not, or be alive or dead, the rules respecting him are the same as those applicable to missing persons†. Rule.

Should the heirs of a captive lay claim to his property, on the ground of his apostasy, they must prove the fact by two credible Moohummudan male witnesses. And if they are able to do so, it is incumbent on the *Kazee* to decree a division of the captive's property among them, the apostasy being in these circumstances a civil death‡.

---

* Shureefeea, Appendix, No. 280.
† Sirajiyyah, Appendix, No. 281.
‡ Shureefeea, Appendix, No. 282.

§ *Of Persons perishing by a common accident.*

Rule. WHEN relatives perish together, as by the sinking of a boat, the fall of a house, or in a common conflagration, and the exact times of their respective deaths cannot be ascertained, it is to be presumed, that they all died at the same moment, and the property of each shall pass to his living heirs, without any portion of it vesting in his companions in misfortune*. According to one account, *Alee* and *Ibn Musood* were of opinion, that the relatives ought all to be considered as having succeeded to the property possessed by each other at the time of the accident, but not to the portion derived by inheritance from a fellow-sufferer†. The reason of the exception is obvious, as without it a man might in some circumstances be made heir to himself.

Illustration. To illustrate these different opinions, let us suppose, that two brothers perish together, each leaving a wife, a daughter and an emancipator, as his heirs, and an estate to the value of ninety deenars. According to the more general opinion, the mothers would each take a sixth, or fifteen deenars, the daughters a half, or forty-five deenars, and the emancipators the remainder, or each thirty deenars. According to the other opinion, the mothers and daughters would receive fifteen and forty-five deenars respective-

---

* Sirajiyyah and Shureefeea, Appendix, No. 283.

† Sirajiyyah, Appendix, No. 284.

ly as before ; but the remaining thirty of each estate would be presumed to have vested in the other brother, and would accordingly pass to his heirs. Thus, the remainder of the elder brother's property would be divided among the mother, daughter, and emancipator of the younger ; giving a sixth, or five deenars to his mother, a half or fifteen deenars to his daughters, and the surplus or ten to his emancipator. The same thing would take place with respect to the remainder of the younger brother's estate, which would be divided in like manner among the mother, daughter, and emancipator of the elder. The mothers of each brother would thus get in the whole twenty deenars, the daughters sixty, and the emancipators no more than ten*.

Both opinions are supported by ingenious reasons, and the second is further recommended by its giving a larger portion of the estates to the nearer relatives ; but there is only one tradition in favour of it, and the other is the more approved, and appears to be generally adopted by the followers of *Aboo Huneefa*†.

---

* Shureefeea, Appendix, No. 285.

† Appendix, Nos. 283 and 285.

INDEX.

كما يجب بدلا عن مال ملكه او استهلكه كان ذلك
بالحقيقة من دين الصحة اذ قد علم وجوبه بغير اقراره
فلـــذلك ساواه في الحكم * شريفية صفحه ٦

٧ فان كان الكل دين الصحة اعني ما كان ثابتا بالبينة
او بالاقرار في زمان الصحة او كان الكل دين المرض
اعني ما كان ثابتا باقراره في مرضه فانه يصرف الباقي
اليهم على حسب مقادير ديونهم فان اجتمع الدينان
معا يقدم دين الصحة لكونه اقوي * شريفية صفحه ٦

٨ ومن مات وعليه سلم او دين سواه الى اجل حل
ما عليه والاصل ان موت من عليه الدين يبطل الاجل
لان الاجل من حقه وقد بطل حقه لموته وموت من
له الدين لا يبطل الاجل لان الاجل من حق المطلوب
وهو حي وليس لورثته ان يطالبوه قبل الاجل * الجوهرة
النيرة في باب المرابحة والتوليـــــــة

٩ ومقتضي عبارة الكتاب تقديم الوصية على الارث
في مقدار ثلث الباقي بعد الدين سواء كانت الوصية
مطلقة او معينة وهو الصحيح * شريفيـة صفحه ٧

١٠ ومن اوصى بثلث دراهمه او بثلث غنمه فهلك ثلثا

ذلک وبقی ثلثه وهو يخرج من ثلث مابقی من ماله
فله جميع ما بقي * الهـــداية صفحه ١٠١٩

١١ ولواوصى بثلث ثيابه فهلک ثلثاها وبقي ثلثها وهو يخرج
من ثلث ما بقی من ما بقی من ماله لم يستحق الا ثلث
ما بقی من الثيا ب قالوا هذا اذا كانت الثياب من
اجناس مختلفة ولوكانت من جنس واحد فهو بمنزلة
الدراهم وكذلک المكيل والموزون بمنزلتها لانه يجري
فيه الجمع جبرا بالقسمة * الهداية صفحه ١٠٢٠

١٢ ولهذا منع من التبرع والمحاباة الا بقدر الثلث
بخلاف النكاح لانه من الحوائج الاصلية وهو بمهر
المثل * الهـــــــــداية صفحه ٦٦٣

١٣ واقرار المريض لوارثه باطل الا ان يصدقه بقية الورثه
وكذا هبته له ووصيته له لا يجوز الا ان يجيزه بقية الورثة وهذا
اذا اتصل المرض بالموت فانه يبطل بالموت لقوله عم لا وصية
لوارث ولا اقرار له بالدين * الجوهرة النيرة في كتاب الاقرار

١۴ ولو اقر المريض لوارثه لا يصح الا ان يصدقه فيه بقية
ورثته * الهـــــداية صفحه ٦٦۴

١٥ اذا طلق الرجل امرأته في مرض موته طلاقا بائنا

فمات وهي في العدة ورثته وان مات بعد انقضاء العدة
فلا ميراث لها * الهــــداية صفحه ٢٦٠

١٦ قيد بالكبير لان الورثة اذا كانوا صغارا جاز للوصي
ان يبيع من تركة الميت العروض والضياع والعقار على
جواب السلف كما ذكرنا من قبل سواء كانوا حاضرين
او غيبا وقال المتأخرون انما يجوز للوصي بيع عقار الصغير اذا
كان على الميت دين لا وفاء له الا من ثمن العقار او يكون
للصغير حاجة الى ثمن العقار او يرغب المشتري في شرائه
بضعف القيمة * عناية فى الجـــلد الثاني صفحة ٦٣

١٧ فان قلت قد علم حكم المسئلة اذا كانت الورثة كبارا
بعبارة الكتاب واذا كانوا صغارا بمفهومه فما حكمها اذا
كانوا صغارا وكبارا قلت حكمها ان الكبار ان كانوا غيبا
وخلت التركة عن دين ووصية فالوصي يبيع المنقول
بالاجماع ويبيع حصة الصغار من العقار واما بيع حصة
الكبار منه فعلى الخلاف الذي مر وان اشتغلت بدين
مستغرق يبيع المنقول والعقار جميعا وبغير مستغرق يبيع
بقدر الدين من المنقول والعقار جميعا وفى الزيادة الخلاف
وان كانوا حضورا او كانت التركة خالية عن الدين

يبيع حصة الصغار من العقار بالاجماع وفي بيع حصة
الكبار الخلاف وان كانت مشغولة بدين مستغرق يبيع
الكل وبغير مستغرق بقدر الدين والزيادة على
الخلاف * عناية المجلد الثاني صفحه ٦١٣

١٨ رجل اوصى الى رجل واوصى لرجل آخر بثلث
ماله وله ورثة صغارا وكبار غيب فقاسم الوصى الموصى له
نائبا عن الورثة واعطاه الثلث وامسك الثلثين للورثة
فالقسمة نافذة على الورثة فى المنقول والعقار ان كانوا
صغارا وفى المنقول ان كانوا كبارا حتى لو هلك حصة
الورثة في يده لم يرجع الورثة على الموصى له بشيء
واما اذا كان الوارث كبيرا حاضرا وصاحب الوصية
غائبا فقاسم الوصي مع الوارث عن الموصى له فاعطى
الورثة حقهم وامسك الثلث للموصى له لم ينفذ القسمة على
الموصى له صغيرا كان او كبيرا حاضرا او غائبا فى المنقول
والعقار جميعا حتى لو هلك في يد الوصي ما افرزه كان له
ان يرجع على الورثة بثلث ما في ايديهم والفرق بين
المنقول والعقار ان الورثة اذا كانوا صغارا كان للوصي بيع
نصيب الصغار من المنقول والعقار جميعا اما اذا كانوا كبارا

فليس له بيع العقار عليهم وله ولاية بيع المنقول فكذا القسمة
لانها نوع بيع * عناية الجلد الثاني صفحه ٦٠٩

١٩ وبيع الوصي على الكبير الغائب جائز في كل شيئ
الا فى العقار لان الاب يلي ماسواه ولايليه فكذا وصيه
فيه وكان القياس ان لا يملك الوصي غير العقار ايضا
لانه لا يملكه الاب على الكبير الا انا استحسناه لما انه حفظ
لتسارع الفساد اليه وحفظ الثمن ايسر وهو يملك الحفظ
اما العقار فمحصن بنفسه * الهداية صفحه ١٠٤٨

٢٠ لوكان للكبير الغائب مال نقلي لامن تركة الاب
لم يملك الوصى بيع ذلك * فتاوى سراجية صفحه ٤٦١

٢١ وصى الاخ والعم والام فيما ورث الصغير والكبير
الغائب من هولاء بمنزلة وصى الاب فى الكبير
الغائب * فتاوى سراجيه صفحه ٤٦١

٢٢ وقال ابويوسف ومحمد رح وصى الاخ فى الصغير
والكبير الغائب بمنزلة وصى الاب فى الكبير الغائب
وكذا وصى الام ووصى العم وهذا الجواب في تركة
هولاء لان وصيهم قائم مقامهم وهم يملكون ما يكون
من باب الحفظ فكذا وصيهم * الهداية صفحه ١٠٤٨

٢٣ وهذا الجواب في تركة هؤلاء يعنى الاخ والام والعم
وانما قيد بتركة هؤلاء لان وصي هؤلاء فيما ترک الاب
ليس كوصى الاب في الكبير الغائب فان وصى الام لا يملک
على الصغير بيع ما ورثه الصغير عن ابيه العقار والمنقول
في ذلک سواء لانه قائم مقام الام والام حال حياتها لا تملک
بيع ما ورثه الصغير المنقول والعقار المشغول بالدين والخالى
عنه فكذلک وصيها واما ما ورثه الصغير من الام فلوصيها فيه
بيع المنقول دون العقار لان له ولاية الحفظ وبيع المنقول
من الحفظ دون العقار * عناية الجلد الثانى صفحه ٦١٤
٢٤ وقيد بالغيبة لانهم اذا كانوا حضورا ليس للوصي
التصرف فى التركة اصلا لكن يتقاضى ديون الميت ويقبض
حقوقه ويدفع الى الورثة الا اذا كان على الميت ديون
او اوصى بوصية ولم يقض الورثة الديون ولم ينفذوا
الوصية من مالهم فانه يبيع التركة كلها ان كان الدين
محيطا وبمقدار الدين ان لم يحط وله بيع مازاد على
الدين ايضا عند ابي حنيفة رح خلافا لهما رحمهم الله تعالى
وينفذ الوصية بمقدار الثلث ولو باع لتنفيذها شيئا من
التركة جاز بمقدارها بالاجماع وفى الزيادة الخلاف

المذكور فى الدين * عناية الجلد الثانى صفحه ٦١٣

٢٥ ولوكان فى التركة وصية مرسلة الوصي يملك البيع بقدر ما ينفذ الوصية عند الكل * الفتاوى العالمگيرية فى كتاب الوصايا

٢٦ ولكن هذا المذكور حكم المسئلة اذا لم يكن على التركة دين فان كان وهو مستغرق فله ان يبيع الجميع لانه لا يمكنه قضاء الديون الا بالبيع فكان مامورا بالبيع من جهة الموصى وان كان غير مستغرق يبيع بقدر الدين من المنقول والعقار والزيادة عليه من المنقول بالاتفاق ومن العقار ايضا عند ابي حنيفة رح خلافا لهما رحمهما الله قالا في منع بيع الزيادة ان جوازه للحاجة ولا حاجة الى بيع الزيادة فلا يجوز واستحسن ابو حنيفة رحمه الله تعالى فقال الولاية ههنا بسبب الوصاية وهي لا تتجزى فمتى ثبت له الولاية في بيع البعض ثبت فى الباقي ولان في بيع البعض اضرار التعيب الباقي فكان في بيع الكل توفير المنفعة عليهم وللوصي ولاية ذلك في نصيب الكبير الا يرى انه يملك الحفظ وبيع المنقولات حال غيبته لما فيه من المنفعة * عناية الجلد الثاني صفحه ٦١٣

٢٧ وان كان على الميت دين ان كان محيطا بالتركة بيع
كل التركة بالاجماع وان لم يكن محيطا بيع بقدر الدين
وفيما زاد على الدين بيع عنده خلافا لهما كذا في الكافي *
الفتاوى العالمگيرية في كتاب الوصايا

٢٨ وصي باع عقار اليقضي بثمنه دين الميت وفي يده من المال
ما يفوء لقضاء الدين جاز هذا البيع كذا في خزانة المفتيين *
الفتاوى العالمگيرية في كتاب الوصايا

٢٩ ومن اوصى الى اثنين لم يكن لاحدهما ان يتصرف
عند ابي حنيفة ومحمد رح دون صاحبه الا في اشياء معدودة
الا في شراء الكفن وتجهيزه وطعام الصغار وكسوتهم ورد
الوديعة بعينها ورد المغصوب والمشترى شراء فاسدا وحفظ
الاموال وقضاء الديون وتنفيذ وصية بعينها وعتق عبد
بعينه والخصومة في حق الميت وقبول الهبة وقبول بيع
ما يخشى عليه التوي والتلف وجمع الاموال الضائعة *
الهـــــــــــداية صفحه ١٠٤٣

٣٠ ولو اوصى الى كل واحد على الانفراد قيل
ينفرد كل واحد منهما بالتصرف بمنزلة الوكيلين اذا
وكل واحد على الانفراد * الهداية صفحه ١٠٤٥

٣١ ولومات احد الوصيين لا تنتقل ولا ينه الى الآخر حتى
انه ليس له ان يتصرف ما لم ينصب القاضي وصيا آخر
اوالوصى الذي مات اوصى الى الحي او الى رجل
آخر وعن ابي حنيفة انه اذا اوصى الى الحي لا يجوز له
ان يتصرف مالم ينصب القاضي وصيا آخر لان الميت
لم يرض براي احد هما وانما رضي براي اثنين * الجوهرة
النيرة في كتاب الوصايا

٣٢ واذا مات الوصي واوصى الى آخر فهو وصي في تركته
وتركة الميت الاول عندنا وقال الشافعي لا يكون وصيا
فى تركة الميت الاول لانه رضي برائه لا براىٔ غيره ولنا انه لما
استعان به في ذلک مع علمه انه تعتريه المينة قبل تتميم
مقصوده صار راضيا با يصا به الى غيره * الجوهرة النيرة
في كتاب الوصايا

---

٣٣ فيبدأ با صحاب الفرائض وهم اللذين لهم سهام مقدرة
في كتاب الله تعالى اوسنة رسوله عليه السلام او الاجماع *
سراجية مع شريفيه صفحه ٨

٣٤ ثم بالعصبات من جهة النسب والعصبة مطلقا كل من
ياخذ من التركة ما ابقته اصحاب الفرائض وعند الانفراد

يحرز جميع المال * سراجيـــــــة صفحه ٩

٣٥ ثم الرد على ذوى الفروض النسبية * دون ذوى الفروض
السببية بقدر حقوقهم * سراجية وشريفيـة صفحه ١٠

٣٦ ثم ذوى الارحام * سراجيـــــــة صفحه ١٠

٣٧ ثم مولى الموالات * وصورة مولى الموالات شخص
مجهول النسب قال لآخر انت مولاي ترثني اذا مت
وتعقل عني اذا جنيت وقال الآخر قبلت فعندنا يصح هذا
العقد ويصير القابل وارثا عاقلا واذا كان الآخر ايضا مجهول
النسب وقال للاول مثل ذلك وقبله فورث كل منهما
صاحبه وعقل عنه وللمجهول ان يرجع عن عقد الموالات
مالم يعقل عنه مولاه * سراجية وشريفيـة صفحه ١٠

٣٨ ثم المقر له بالنسب على الغير بحيث لم يثبت نسبه
باقراره من ذلك الغير اذا مات المقر على اقراره *
سراجيـــــــــة صفحه ١١

٣٩ واعتبرت فيه قيود الاول ان يكون الاقرار بنسبه من المقر
متضمنا لاقراره بنسبه على غيره كما اذا اقر لمجهول
النسب بانه اخوه فانه يتضمن اقراره على ابيه بانه ابنه *
شريفيـــــــــة صفحه ١١

٤٠ الثاني ان يكون ذلک الاقرار بحيث لا يثبت به نسبه من ذلک الغير کما اذا لم يصدقه ابوه في هـــذا النسب * شريفيـــــــــة صفحه ١١

٤١ الثالث ان يموت المقر علي اقراره * شريفية صفحه ١١

٤٢ ثم الموصى له بجميع المال لان منعه عما زاد علي الثلث کان لاجل الورثة فاذا لم يوجد منهم احد فله عندنا ما عين له کملا * سراجيـــة وشريفية صفحه ١٢

٤٣ ثم بيت المال * سراجيـــــــــة صفحه ١٢

الباب الثاني في موانع الارث

٤٤ المانع من الارث اربعة الرق وافرا کان اوناقصا والقتل الذي يتعلق به وجوب القصاص اوالکفارة واختلاف الدينين واختلاف الدارين * سراجية صفحه ١٣ و١٥ و١٧

٤٥ وذلک لان الرقيق مطلقا لا يملک المال بسائر اسباب الملک فلا يملکه ايضا بالارث ولان جميع ما في يده من المال فهو لمولاه فلو ورثناه من اقربائه لوقع الملک لسيده فيکون توريثا للاجنبي بلاسبب وانه باطل اجماعا * شريفيـــــــة صفحه ١٣

٤٦ واذاكان العبد بين شريكين فاعتق احدهما نصيبه
عتق فان كان موسرا فشريكه بالخيار ان شاء اعتق وان
شاء ضمن شريكه قيمة نصيبه وان شاء استسعى العبدفان
ضمن رجع المعتق على العبد والولاء للمعتق وان اعتق
اواستسعى فالولاء بينهما وان كان المعتق معسرا فالشريك
بالخيار ان شاء اعتق وان شاء استسعى العبد والولاء بينهما
فى الوجهين وهذا عند ابي حنيفة رح وقالا ليس له الا
الضمان مع اليسار والسعاية مع الاعسار ولا يرجع المعتق
على العبد والولاء للمعتق * الهداية صفحه ٣٢٦

٤٧ معتق البعض عند ابي حنيفة رح بمنزلة المملوك مابقي
عليه درهم في فكاك رقبته فلا يرث ولا يحجب احدا عن
ميراثه وعندهما هو حر فيرث ويحجب * شريفية صفحه ١٣

٤٨ والقتل الذي يتعلق به وجوب القصاص
اوالكفارة * سراجية صفحه ١٣

٤٩ اما القتل الذي يتعلق به وجوب القصاص فهو القتل
عمدا وذلك بان يتعمد ضربه بسلاح او مايجري مجراه
في تفريق الاجزاء كالمحدد من الخشب او الحجر وموجبه
الاثم والقصاص ولاكفارة فيه وعند ابي يوسف ومحمد رح

اذا تعمد ضربه بما يقتل به غالبا وان لم يكن محددا كحجر عظيم فهو ايضا عمد * شريفية صفحه ١٣

٤٠ واما القتل الذي يتعلق به وجوب الكفارة فهو ما شبه عمد كان يتعمد ضربه بما لا يقتل به غالبا وموجبه على القولين معا الدية على العاقلة والاثم والكفارة * شريفية صفحه ١٣

٤١ واما خطاء كان رمى الى صيد فاصاب انسانا او انقلب في النوم عليه فقتله او وطئته دابة وهو راكبها او سقط من سطح عليه او سقط حجر من يده فمات موجبه الكفارة والدية على العاقلة ولا اثم فيه * شريفية صفحه ١٣

٤٢ واما اذا كان القتل بالتسبيب دون المباشرة كحافر البير او واضع الحجر في غير ملكه ففيه الدية على العاقلة ولا قصاص فيه ولا كفارة * شريفية صفحه ١٤

٤٣ فان قلت أليس اذا قتل الاب ابنه عمدا لم يثبت به قصاص ولا كفارة ايضا مع انه محروم اتفاقا قلت هو موجب في اصله للقصاص الا انه سقط بقوله عليه السلام لا يقتل الوالد بولده ولا السيد بعبده * شريفية صفحه ١٤

٤٤ فلا يرث الكافر من المسلم اجماعا ولا المسلم من الكافر * شريفية صفحه ١٥

٥٥ ثم ان الكفار يتوارثون فيما بينهم وان اختلف نحلهم
لان الكفر ملـــــة واحدة * شريفية صفحه ١٦

٥٦ وقال ابن ابي ليلى اليهود والنصارى يتوارثون فيما
بينهم ولا توارث بينهما وبين المجوس واستدل بانهما قد اتفقا
على التوحيد والاقرار بنبوة موسى عليه السلام وانزال التورية
فهما على ملة واحدة بخلاف المجوسي حيث ينكرون
التوحيد ويثبتون آلهين يزدان واهرمن ولا يعترفون بنبي
ولا كتاب منزل فهم اهل ملة اخرى * شريفية صفحه ١٦

٥٧ وذهب بعض الفقهاء الى عدم التوارث بين اليهود
والنصارى ايضا لاختلاف اعتقادهما في عيسى عليه السلام
والانجيل فهما اهل ملتين شتى كالمسلمين مع النصارى *
شريفيـــــــــــة صفحه ١٧

٥٨ بخلاف اهل الاهواء فانهـم معترفون بالانبيـــاء
والكتب ويختلفون في تاويل الكتاب والسنة وذلك
لا يوجب اختلاف المـــلة * شريفية صفحه ١٧

٥٩ واما المرتد فلا يرث من احد لا من مسلم ولا من مرتد
مثلـــــــــه * سراجية صفحه ٢٠٣

٦٠ لانه جان بارتداده فلا يستحق الصلة الشرعية التي

هی الارث بل یحرم عقوبة کالقاتل بغیر حق وایضا المرتد
لاملة له لان ما انتقل الیه لا یقر علیه وتعتبر فی المیراث
الملـــــــــــــة * شریفیة صفحه ٢٠٢

٦١ الا انه لامیراث منها لزوجها لا نها بنفس الردة قد
بانت منه * شریفیـــــــــــة صفحه ٢٠٢

٦٢ ویرثها زوجها المسلم ان ارتدت وهي مریضة لقصدها
ابطال حقه وان کانت صحیحة لا یرثها لانها لا تقتل فلم
یتعلق حقه بمالها بالردة بخلاف المرتد * الهدایة صفحه ٤٤٤

٦٣ وترثه امراته المسلمة اذا مات اوقتل علی ردته وهي
فی العدة لانه یصیر فارا وان کان صحیحا وقت الردة *
الهـــــــــــدایة صفحه ٤٤٤

٦٤ ویحبس ثلثة ایام فان اسلم والا قتل هذا اذا استمهل
فاما اذا لم یستمهل قتل من ساعته ولا فرق في ذلک
بین الحر والعبد کذا فی السراج الوهاج * الفتاوی
العالمگیریة في جلـــــــــــد الثاني صفحه ٣٤٧

٦٥ وما باعه اواشتریه اواعتقه اووهبه اورهنه اوتصرف فیه
من امواله في حال ردته فهو موقوف فان اسلم صحت
عقوده وان مات اوقتل اولحق بدار الحرب بطلت وهذا

عندابي حنيفة رح وقال ابو يوسف ومحمد رح يجوز
ماصنع في الوجهين * الهـــــداية صفحه ۴۴٥

٦٦ اذامات المرتداوقتل اولحق بدار الحرب وحكم
القاضي بلحاقه بدار الحرب فما اكتسبه في حال اسلامه
فهولورثته المسلمين وما اكتسبه في حال ردته يوضع في
بيت المال عندابي حنيفة رحمه الله وعندهما رح الكسبان
جميعالورثته المسلمين * سراجـــيه صفحه ٢٠٠

٦٧ واماالمرتدة فلا تقتل ولكن تحبس حتى تسلم *
الهـــــــــداية صفحه ۴۴۳

٦٨ وكسب المرتدة جميعالورثتها المسلمين بلاخلاف
بين اصحابنا رح * سراجيـــة صفحه ٢٠١

٦٩ وبخلاف المرأة لانهاليست حربية ولهذالاتقتل *
الهـــــــــداية صفحه ۴۴٦

٧٠ فان كان احد الزوجين مسلمافالولد على دينه وكذلك
ان اسلم احدهما وله ولد صغير صار ولده مسلما باسلامه *
الهـــــــــداية صفحه ٢٢٢

٧١ ان ثبت الاسلام على وجه ولم يثبت على وجه آخر
فانه يثبت ويعلوكالمولود بين المسلم والكافر فانه يحكم

باسلام الولد او ان المراد العلو بحسب الحجة او بحسب القهر والغلبة اى النصرة فى العاقبة للمسلمين * شريفية صفحه ۱٦

۷۲ واختلاف الدارين اما حقيقة كالحربي والذمي اوحكما كالمستأمن والذمي اوالحربيين من دارين مختلفين * سراجيـــــــــة صفحه ۱۷

۷۳ فاذا مات الحربي فى دار الحرب ولـه اب وابن ذمي في دار الاسلام اومات الذمي في دار الاسلام وله اب وابن في دار الحرب لم يرث احدهما من الآخر لان الذمي من اهل دار الاسلام والحربي من اهل دار الحرب * شريفيـــــــــة صفحه ۱۷

۷٤ اما المثـال الاول فظاهر لان الحربي اذا دخل دار الاسلام بامان فهو والذمي في دار واحدة حقيقة لكنهما في دارين مختلفين حكما لان المستأمن من اهل دار الحرب حكما* شريفيـــــــــة صفحه ۱۷

۷٥ والدار انما تختلف باختلاف المنعة والملك لانقطاع العصمة فيمابينهم * سراجيـــــــــة صفحه ۱۸

۷٦ وذلك لان دار الاسلام دار احكام فلا تختلف الدار فيما بين المسلمين باختلاف المنعة والملك لان حكم

الاسلام يجمعهم * شريفية صفحه ١٩

٧٧ واما اذا كان بينهما تناصر وتعاون على اعدائهما كانت الدار واحدة والوراثة ثابتة * شريفية صفحه ١٩

٧٨ كان يكون مثلا احد الملكين في الهند وله دار ومنعة والآخر في الترك وله دار ومنعة اخرى وانقطعت العصمة فيما بينهم حتى يستحل كلا منهما قتال الآخر واذا ظفر رجل من عسكر احدهما برجل من عسكر الآخر قتله فهاتان الداران مختلفتان فتنقطع باختلافهما الوراثة لانها تبتني على العصمة والولاية * شريفية صفحه ١٩

٧٩ والمحروم عن الميراث بالكلية لا يحجب عندنا غيره اصلا لا حجب حرمان ولا حجب نقصان وهو قول عامة الصحابة رضي الله عنهم * سراجية وشريفية صفحه ٦٥

٨٠ وعند ابن مسعود رض يحجب حجب النقصان كالكافر والقاتل والرقيق * سراجية صفحه ٦٦

٨١ روي ان امرأة مسلمة تركت زوجا مسلما واخوين من امها مسلمين وابنا كافرا فقضى فيها علي وزيد بن ثابت رض بان للزوج النصف ولاخويها الثلث وما بقي فهو للعصبة * شريفية صفحه ٦٦

الباب الثالث في ثبوت النسب

٨٢ ولد الزنا يثبت نسبه من الام دون الزاني * فتاوى سراجية صفحه ٤٦١

٨٣ واذا زنا الرجل بامرأة فجاءت بولد فادعاه الزاني لم يثبت نسبه منه واما الام فالنسب منها بالولادة * الجوهرة النيرة في كتاب الاقرار

٨٤ والفرق هو ان الاصل ان كل من ادعى امرا لا يمكن اثباته بالبينة كان القول فيه قوله من غير بينة وكل من يدعي امرا يمكنه اثباته بالبينة لا يقبل قوله فيه الا بالبينة والمرأة يمكنها اثبات النسب بالبينة لان انفصال الولد منها مما يشاهد فلا بد لها من بينة والرجل لا يمكنه اقامة البينة على الاعلاق لخفاء فيه فلا يحتاج اليها * عناية في جلد الاول صفحه ٥٨٨

٨٥ وفى الينابيع الزنا الموجب للحد الوطى الحرام الخالي عن حقيقة الملك وحقيقة النكاح وملك اليمين وعن شبهة الملك وشبهة النكاح وشبهة الاشتباه واما الوطى فى الملك كوطى جاريته المجوسية وجاريته التي هي اخته من

الرضاعة ووطي المملوكة بعضها وان كان حراما فليس بزنا وكذا وطي امرأته الحائض والنفسا والمتزوجة بغير شهودا ويتزوج امة بغير اذن مولاها اويتزوج العبد بغير اذن سيده اووطي جارية ابنه اومكاتبه والجارية من المغنم في دار الحرب اوبعد ما اخرجت قبل القسمة اوتزوج مجوسية اوخمسا في عقد واحد اوجمع بين اختين اوتزوج امة على حرة اوتزوج لمحارمه فوطئها وقال علمت انها حرام فانه لا يحد عند ابي حنيفة رحمه الله وقال ابويوسف ومحمد رح يحد في كل وطي حرام على التابيد كوطي محارمه والترويج لا يوجب شبهة فيه وماليس بحرام على التابيد فعقد النكاح يوجب شبهة فيه كالنكاح بغير شهود وفي عدة الغير وشبه ذلك وشبهة الاشتباه ان يقول ظننت انها تحل لي فانه لا يحد * الجوهرة النيرة في كتاب الحدود

٨٦ الوطي الموجب للحد هو الزنا وانه في عرف الشرع واللسان وطي الرجل المرأة في القبل في غير الملك وشبهة الملك لانه فعل محظور والحرمة على الاطلاق عند التعري عن الملك وشبهته يؤيد ذلك قوله عم ادرأوا الحدود

بالشبهات ثم الشبهة نوعان شبهة فى الفعل وتسمى شبهة اشتباه وشبهة في المحل ويسمى شبهة حكمية فالاولى يتحقق في حق من اشتبه عليه لان معناه ان من يظن غير الدليل دليلا ولابد من الظن لتحقق الاشتباه والثانية يتحقق لقيام الدليل النافي للحرمة في ذاته ولا يتوقف على ظن الجاني واعتقاده فالحد يسقط بالنوعين لاطلاق الحديث والنسب يثبت فى الثانية اذا ادعى الولد ولايثبت فى الاولى وان ادعاه لان الفعل تمحض زنا فى الاولى وانما يسقط الحد لامر راجع اليه وهو اشتباه الامر عليه ولم تمحض في الثانية * الهـــــــداية صفحه ٣٧٣

٨٧ الوطى الموجب للحد هو الزنا كذا فى الكافي فان تمحض حراما يجب الحد وان تمكنت فيه الشبهة لا يجب الحد كذا في فتاوى قاضيخان والشبهة ما يشبه الثابت وليس بثابت وهي انواع شبهة فى الفعل وتسمى شبهة اشتباه وهي ان يظن غير دليل الحل دليلا وهو يتحقق في حق من اشتبه عليه دون من لم يشتبه عليه ولا بد من الظن ليتحقق الاشتباه فان ادعى انه ظن انها حلال له لم يحد وان لم يدع حد وشبهة فى المحل وتسمى شبهة حكمية

وذالقيام دليل الحل فى المحل وامتنع عمله لمانع فتعتبر
شبهة في حق الكل ولا يتوقف ثبوتها على ظن الجاني
ودعواه الحل فالحد يسقط بالنوعين والنسب يثبت فى الثاني
ان ادعى الولد ولا يثبت فى الاول وان ادعاه *
فتاوى عالمگيرية الجلـــد الثاني صفحه ٢٠٨

٨٨ والشبهة فى المحل في ستة مواضع جارية ابنه والمطلقة
طلاقا بائنا بالكنايات والجارية المبيعة في حق البائع قبل
التسليم والممهورة في حق الزوج قبل القبض والمشتركة
بينه وبين غيره والمرهونة في حق المرتهن في رواية كتاب
الرهن ففي هذه المواضع لا يجب الحد وان قال علمت
انها علي حرام * الهـــداية صفحه ٣٧٤

٨٩ والشبهة في المحل في وطى امة ولده وولد ولده كذا
فى الكافي سواء كان ولده حيا او ميتا هكذا فى العتابية
ثم ان حبلت وولدت يثبت النسب من الاب ولا يجب
العقر وان لم تحبل فعلى الاب العقر ولا يثبت الملك له فيها
والجد كالاب لكن لا يثبت نسبه عند قيام الاب وفي وطى
المعتدة بالكنايات ووطى الامة المبيعة في حق البائع قبل
التسليم كذا فى الكافي وكذا في وطى جارية مكاتبه او عبده

المأذون له وعليه دين يحيط بماله ورقبته ووطى الجارية المهورة قبل التسليم في حق الزوج ووطى الجارية المشتركة بينه وبين غيره هكذا في التبيين * فتاوى عالمگيرية فى الجلـــــــد الثاني صفحه ٢٠٩

٩٠ واذا تزوج الرجل امرأة فجاءت بالولد لاقل من ستة اشهر منذ يوم تزوجها لم يثبت نسبه وان جاءت به لستة اشهر فصاعدا يثبت نسبه منه اعترف به الزوج او سكت * فتاوى عالمگيرية فى الجلـــــــد الاول صفحه ٧٢٣

٩١ ولو زنى بامرأة فحملت ثم تزوجها فولدت ان جاءت به لستة اشهر فصاعدا ثبت نسبه وان جاءت به لاقل من ستة اشهر لم يثبت نسبه الا ان يدعيه ولم يقل انه من الزنا اما ان قال انه مني من الزنا لا يثبت نسبه ولا يرث منه كذا فى الينابيع * فتاوى عالمگيرية فى الجلد الاول صفحه ٧٢٧

٩٢ واذا باع جارية فجاءت بولد فادعاه البائع فان جاءت به لاقل من ستة اشهر من يوم باع فهو ابن للبائع وامه ام ولد له وتفسخ البيع فيها ويرد الثمن وان ادعاه المشتري مع دعوة البائع او بعده فدعوة البائع اولى وان جاءت به لاكثر من سنتين من وقت البيع لم يصح دعوة البائع

الا اذا صدقه المشتري وان جاءت به لاكثر من ستة اشهر
من وقت البيع ولا قل من سنتين لم تقبل دعوة البائع فيه
الا ان يصدقه المشتري * الهـــداية صفحة ٦٤٩

٩٣ قال اصحابنا لثبوت النسب ثلث مراتب احدٰها
النكاح الصحيح وما هو في معناه من النكاح الفاسد والحكم
فيه انه يثبت النسب من غير دعوة ولا ينتفي بمجرد النفي
وانما ينتفي باللعان فان كانا ممن لا لعان بينهما لا ينتفي
نسب الولد كذا في المحيط والثانية ام الولد والحكم فيها
ان يثبت النسب من غير دعوة وينتفي بمجرد النفي كذا
في الظهيرية وذكر في النهاية معزيا الى المبسوط انما
يملك نفيه ما لم يقض القاضي به اولم يتطاول ذلك فاما
اذا قضى به فقد لزمه على وجه لا يملك ابطاله وكذا
بعد التطاول كذا في التبيين في باب الاستيلاد قالوا انما
يثبت نسب ولد ام الولد بدون الدعوة ان كان يحل
للمولى وطيها اما اذا كان لا يحل فلا يثبت النسب بدون
الدعوة كام ولد كاتبها مولاها وامة مشتركة بين اثنين
استولدها ثم جاءت بولد بعد ذلك لا يثبت النسب بدون
الدعوة كذا في الظهيرية وكذا لو حرم وطئها عليه بعد ذلك

بوطی ابیه اوابنه او بوطئه امها او بنتها لم یثبت نسب ما تلده بعد ذلک الا بالدعوة کذا فی الاختیار شرح المختار الثالثة الامة اذا جاءت بولدلا یثبت النسب بدون الدعوة عندنا کذا فی الظهیریة * فتاوی عالمگیریة في المجلد الاول صفحه ٧٢٢

٩٤ ولصحة الاقرار بالولد ثلث شرائط ان یکون یولد مثله لمثله کیلا یکون مکذبا فی الظاهر وان لا یکون الولد ثابت النسب اذ لو کان لا متنع ثبوته من غیره وان یصدق المقربه في اقراره اذا کان یعبر عن نفسه لانه في ید نفسه بخلاف الصغیر الذي لا یعبر عن نفسه علی ما مر في باب دعوی النسب ولا یمتنع الاقراربه بسبب المرض لان النسب من الحوائج الاصلیة وهو یلزمه خاصة لیس فیه تحمیله علی الغیر فیثبت واذا ثبت کان کالوارث المعروف فیشارک ورثته * عنایة في المجلد الاول صفحه ٦١٤

٩٥ ثم المقران کان امرأة لا بد ان یکون سنها اکبر منه بتسع سنین ونصف وان کان رجلا فلا بد ان یکون سنه اکبر منه باثنی عشر سنة ونصف * الجوهرة النیرة في کتاب الاقرار

٩٦ ولیس له نسب معروف لان من له نسب معروف

قد تعلق به حق من ثبت نسبه فلا يملك نقله منه وشرط
ان يولد مثله لمثله لكي لا يكون مكذبا فى الظاهر * الجوهرة
النيرة في كتاب الاقرار

٩٧ صدقه الغلام هذا اذا كان يعبر عن نفسه وكان عاقلا
اما الصغير فلا يحتاج الى تصديقه وسواء صدقه في حيوة
المقرا وبعد موته * الجوهرة النيرة في كتاب الاقرار

٩٨ ومن اقر بغلام يولد مثله لمثله وليس له نسب معروف
انه ابنه وصدقه الغلام ثبت نسبه وان كان مريضا
ويشارك الورثة فى الميراث لان اقراره بالبنوة معنى
الزمه نفسه ولم يحمله على غيره فلزمه * الجوهرة النيرة
في كتاب الاقرار

٩٩ ويجوز اقرار الرجل بالوالدين والولد والزوجة والمولى
لانه ليس فيه تحميل النسب على الغير ويعتبر تصديق
كل واحد منهم بذلك وان كان الولد لا يولد مثله لمثله
لا يصح دعواه سواء اصدقه الابن اولم يصدقه اقام البينة
اولم يقم لاستحاله ذلك * الجوهرة النيرة في كتاب الاقرار

١٠٠ ويجوز اقرار الرجل بالوالدين هذا بيان اما يجوز
الاقرار به ومالا يجوز اقرار الراجل بالوالدين والولد والزوجة

والمولى يعني مولى العتاقة سواء كان اعلى او اسفل جائز سواء كان اقراره بهولاء في حال الصحة او المرض لانه اقر بما يلزمه وليس فيه تحميل النسب على الغير فتحقق المقتضي وانتفى المانع فوجب القول بجوازه * عناية في المجلـــــــد الاول صفحه ٦١٤

١٠١ ويقبل اقرار المراة بالوالدين والزوج والمولى لان ذلك معنى يلزمه نفسها ولا تحمله على غيرها * الجوهرة النيرة في كتاب الاقرار .

١٠٢ ويقبل اقرار المرأة بالوالدين والزوج والمولى لما بيناه انه اقرار بما يلزمه الخ وقال في المبسوط واقرار المرأة يصح بثلثة نفر بالاب والزوج ومولى العتاقة والامر في ذلك ماذكرنا * عناية في المجلـــــد الاول صفحة ٦١٤

١٠٣ ولا يقبل بالولد لان فيه تحميل النسب على الغير وهو الزوج لان النسب منه قال الله تعالى ادعوهم لآبائهم وعليه الاجماع الا ان يصدقها الزوج لان الحق له او تشهد القابلة بالولادة اذا الفرض أن الفراش قائم فيحتاج الى تعيين الولد وشهادتها في ذلك مقبولة * عناية في المجلـــــد الاول صفحه ٦١٥

١٠٤ ولا يقبل اقرارها بالولد الا ان يصدقها الزوج اويشهد بولادتها قابلة يريد به اذا كانت مزوجة اوفي عدة من تزوج اما اذا لم يعرف لها زوج ثبت نسبه منها وان لم يقبل اقرارها بالولد لانها تحمله على غيرها فلا يصدق فان صدقها الزوج قبل اقرارها وكذا اذا شهدت بولادتها قابلة لان الولادة تثبت بشهادة امرأة واحدة عندنا واذا ثبتت الولادة منها ثبت نسبه فالحاصل انه يجوز اقرار المرأة بثلثة الزوج والمولى والاب لا غير فيظهر بهذا ان بالوالدين وقع سهوا لانه يقع التناقض لانه لوصح الاقرار بالام وذلك يتوقف على تصديقها فيكون تصديقها بمنزلة اقرارها بالولد وقد ذكر بعد هذا ان اقرار المرأة بالولد لا يقبل * الجوهرة النيرة في كتاب الاقرار

١٠٥ ويصح التصديق في النسب بعد موت المقر لانه مما يبقى بعد الموت وكذا تصديق الزوجة بالزوجية بعد موت الزوج المقر بالاتفاق لان حكم النكاح باق وهو العدة فانها واجبة بعد الموت وهي من آثار النكاح الا يرى انها تغسله بعد الموت لقيام النكاح وكذا تصديق الزوج بعد موتها لان الارث من احكام النكاح وهو مما يبقى بعد النكاح كالعدة

وهذا عندهما * عناية في الجلد الاول وصفحه ٦١٤

١٠٦ ولوان الغلام انما صدقه بعد موته صح تصديقه وثبت نسبه منه لان النسب لا يبطل بالموت وكذا لواقر بزوجة ثم ماتت فصدقته بعد موته جاز لان حقوق النكاح باقية بعد الموت وهي العدة ولو كانت هي المقرة بالزوج ثم ماتت فصدقها بعد موتها لم يصح تصديقه عند ابي حنيفة لان النكاح زال بالموت وزالت احكامه فلم يجز التصديق وقال ابو يوسف ومحمد يصح تصديقه لان الميراث ثابت وهو من احكام النكاح * الجوهرة النيرة في كتاب الاقرار

١٠٧ الزنا يثبت بالبينة والاقرار فالبينة ان تشهد اربعة من الشهود على رجل وامرأة بالزنا * الهداية صفحه ٣٦٨

١٠٨ ولا ينعقد نكاح المسلمين الا بحضور شاهدين حرين عاقلين بالغين مسلمين رجلين او رجل وامرأتين عدولا كانوا او غير عدول او محدودين في القذف * الهداية صفحه ١٩٠

١٠٩ ومنها الشهادة قال عامة العلماء انها شرط جواز النكاح هكذا في البدائع وشرط في الشاهد اربعة امور الحرية والعقل والبلوغ والاسلام فلا ينعقد بحضرة العبيد ولا فرق بين

القن والمدبر والمكاتب ولا بحضرة المجانين والصبيان
ولا بحضرة الكفار في نكاح المسلمين هكذا في البحر الرايق *
فتاوى عالمگيرية الجلد الاول صفحه ٣٧٧

١١٠ ويصح بشهادة الفاسقين والاعميين كذا في فتاوى
قاضيخان وكذا بشهادة المحدودين في القذف وان لم يتوبا
كذا في البحر الرائق وكذا يصح بشهادة المحدود في الزنا هكذا
في الخلاصة * فتاوى عالمگيرية الجلد الاول صفحه ٣٧٧

١١١ ولا يجوز للشاهد ان يشهد بشيء لم يعاينه الا النسب
والموت والنكاح والدخول وولاية القاضي فانه يسعه
ان يشهد بهذه الاشياء اذا اخبره بها من يثق به وهذا
استحسان ويشترط ان يخبره بذلك رجلان عدلان او رجل
وامراتان ممن يثق بهم ويقع في قلبه صدقهم ويشترط ايضا
ان يكون الاخبار بلفظ الشهادة كذا ذكره الخصاف وقيل
في الموت يكتفي باخبار واحد اما رجل واما امرأة واحدة لانه
قل ما يشاهد حاله غير الواحد اذ الانسان يهابه ويكرهه
ولا كذلك النكاح والنسب وينبغي ان يطلق اداء الشهادة
ولا يفسرها اما اذا فسرها للقاضي بان قال اني اشهد بالتسامع
لم تقبل شهادته * الجوهرة النيرة في كتاب الشهادات

١١٢ وينبغي ان يطلق اداء الشهادة ولا يفسر اما اذا فسر القاضي ان يشهد بالتسامع لم يقبل شهادته كما ان معاينة اليد فى الاملاك مطلق للشهادة ثم اذا فسر لا تقبل كذا هذا ولو راى انسانا جلس مجلس القضاء يدخل عليه الخصوم حل له ان يشهد على كونه قاضيا فكذا اذا راى رجلا وامراة يسكنان بيتا وينبسط كل واحد منهما الى آخر انبساط الازواج كما اذا راى عينا في يد غيره * الهداية صفحه ٤٨٩

١١٣ واذا رأى رجلا وامرأة يسكنان بيتا وينبسط كل واحد منهما الى الآخر انبساط الازواج جاز له ان يشهد بانها امرأته فان سأله القاضي هل كنت حاضرا فقال لا تقبل شهادته لانه يحل له ان يشهد بالتسامع كما نشهد بامهات المؤمنين ازواج النبى صلى الله عليه وسلم فعلى الرؤية اولى وقيل لا تقبل لانه لما قال لم يعاين العقد تبين للقاضى انه يشهد به بالتسامع ولو قال اشهد لانى سمعت لا تقبل فكذا هذا * عناية الجلد الاول صفحه ٤٠٢

الباب الرابع في معرفة الفروض ومستحقيها

١١٤ الفروض المقدرة في كتاب الله تعالى ستة النصف

والربع والثمن والثلثان والثلث والسدس واصحاب هذه السهام
اثني عشر نفرا اربعة من الرجال وهم الاب والجد الصحيح
والاخ لام والزوج وثمان من النساء الزوجة والبنت وبنت
الابن وان سفلت والاخت لاب وام والاخت لاب
والاخت لام والام والجدة الصحيحة وهي التي لا يدخل
في نسبتها الى الميت جد فاسد * سراجية صفحه ١٩ و٢٠ و٢١

١١٥ والورثة فيه فريقان فريق لا يحجبون بحال البتة وهم ستة الابن والاب
والزوج والبنت والام والزوجة وفريق يرثون بحال ويحجبون بحال
اخرى وهم غير هؤلاء الستة من الورثة سواء كانوا عصبات
اوذوي فروض وهذا مبني على اصلين احدهما ان كل من
يدلي الى الميت بشخص لا يرث مع وجود ذلك الشخص سوى
اولاد الام فانهم يرثون معها لانعدام استحقاقها جميع التركة
والثاني الاقرب فالاقرب * سراجية وشريفية صفحه ٦٣ و٦٤

١١٦ واما للزوج فحالتان النصف عند عدم الولد وولد
الابن وان سفل والربع مع الولد او ولد الابن وان سفل *
سراجيــــــــة صفحه ٢٤

١١٧ للزوجات حالتان الربع للواحدة فصاعدة عند عدم
لولد او ولد الابن وان سفل والثمن مع الولد او ولد الابن

وان سفل * سراجيـــــــــــــــة صفحه ٢٤

١١٨ واما البنات الصلب فاحوال ثلث النصف للواحدة
والثلثان للاثنتين فصاعدة ومع الابن للذكر مثل حظ
الانثيين وهو يعصبهن * سراجيـــــــــة صفحه ٢٥

١١٩ لقوله تعالى يوصيكم الله في اولادكم للذكر مثل حظ الانثيين
فانه لما لم يبين نصيب البنات عند الاجتماع مع الابن دل
على انه يعصبهن وان المال يقسم بينهن وبين الابن على
ما ذكرنا من القسمة بطريق العصوبة * شريفية صفحه ٢٦

١٢٠ وبنات الابن كبنات الصلب ولهن احوال ست النصف
للواحدة والثلثان للاثنتين فصاعدة عند عدم بنات الصلب *
سراجيـــــــــــــــة صفحه ٢٦

١٢١ هذه حالة ثالثة من الثلث الاولى فان بنات الابن
اذا كان بحذائهن غلام سواء كان اخاهن اوابن عمهن
فانه يعصبهن كما ان الابن الصلبي يعصب البنات الصلبية
وذلك لان الذكر من اولاد الابن يعصب الاناث اللاتى
في درجته اذا لم يكن للميت ولد صلبى بالاتفاق في
استحقاق جميع المال فكذا يعصبها في استحقاق الباقي
من الثلثين مع الصلبيتين واليه ذهب عامة الصحابة وعليه

جمهور العلماء * شريفيــــــــــة صفحه ٢٧

١٢٢ ولا يرثن مع الصلبيين الا ان يكون بحذائهن
او اسفل منهن غلام فيعصبهن والباقي بينهم للذكر مثل
حظ الانثيين * سراجيــــــــــة صفحه ١٧

١٢٣ ولهن السدس مع الواحدة الصلبية تكملة للثلثين *
سراجيــــــــــة صفحه ٢٦

١٢٤ ولنا ان هذه الانثى لو كانت في درجة الذكر لصارت به عصبة
وانما كانت اقرب منه كانت بذلك اولى * شريفية صفحه ٢٨

١٢٥ ولا شيء للسفليات الا ان يكون معهن غلام فيعصبهن من كانت
بحذائه ومن كانت فوقه ممن لم يكن ذات سهم اما انها تاخذ
سهمها ولا تصير به عصبة * سراجية وشريفية صفحه ٣٠

١٢٦ اما الاب فله احوال ثلث الفرض المطلق وهو السدس
وذلك مع الابن او ابن الابن وان سفل والفرض والتعصيب
معا وذلك مع الابنة او ابنة الابن وان سفلت والتعصيب
المحض وذلك عند عدم الولد وولد الابن وان سفل *
سراجيــــــــــة صفحه ٢٢

١٢٧ والجد الصحيح هو الذي لا تدخل في نسبته الى الميت ام *
سراجيــــــــــة صفحه ٢٣

١٢٨ ويسقط الجد بالاب لان الاب اصل في قرابة الجد الى الميت * سراجيــــــــــــة صفحه ٢٣

---

١٢٩ والجد الصحيح كالاب الا في اربع مسائل الاولى ان ام الاب لا ترث معه وترث مع الجد والثانية ان الميت اذا ترك الابوين واحد الزوجين فللام ثلث ما بقي بعد نصيب احد الزوجين ولو كان مكان الاب جد فللام ثلث جميع المال الا عند ابى يوسف رح فان لها ثلث الباقي ايضا * سراجية وشريفيـــــــــــة صفحه ٢٢

١٣٠ واما للام فاحوال ثلث السدس مع الولد او ولد الابن وان سفل او الاثنين من الاخوة والاخوات فصاعدا من اي جهة كانا وثلث الكل عند عدم هؤلاء المذكورين وثلث ما بقي بعد فرض احد الزوجين وذلک في مسئلتين زوج وابوين او زوجة وابوين * سراجية صفحه ٣٧ و ٣٩

١٣١ ولنا انه تعالى قال فان لم يكن له ولد وورثه ابواه فلامه الثلث فان كان له اخوة فلامه السدس والمراد من صدر الكلام ان لامه الثلث والباقي للاب فكذا الحال في آخره كانه قيل فان كان له اخوة وورثه ابواه فلامه السدس ولابيه البـــــــاقي * شريفية صفحه ٣٧

١٣٢ وللجدة السدس لام كانت اولاب واحدة كانت او اكثر اذا كن ثابتات متحاذيات في الدرجة * سراجية صفحه ٤٢

١٣٣ ويسقطن كلهن بالام اما الاميات فلوجود الادلائها بالام واتحاد السبب الذي هو الامومة واما الابويات فلاتحاد السبب وحده وتسقط الابويات دون الاميات ايضا بالاب * سراجيــــــة وشريفية صفحه ٤٣

١٣٤ والقربى من اي جهة كانت تحجب البعدى من اي جهة كانت وارثة كانت القربى او محجوبة كام الاب عند وجوده فانها محجوبة به ومع ذلک تحجب ام ام الام ففي هذه الصورة اعني ان يخلف الميت الاب وام الاب وام ام الام يكون المال كله للاب عندنا لان البعدى محجوبة بالقربى والقربى محجوبة بالاب * سراجيــــــة وشريفية صفحه ٢٥ و ٢٦

١٣٥ واذا كانت الجدة ذات قرابة واحدة كام ام الاب والاخرى ذات قرابتين او اكثر كام ام الام وهي ايضا ام اب الاب * سراجيــــــة صفحه ٤٦

١٣٦ يقسم السدس بينهما عند ابي يوسف رح انصافا باعتبار الابدان وعند محمد رح اثلاثا باعتبار الجهات * سراجيــــــة صفحه ٤٧

١٣٧ قال الامام السرخسي رح لارواية عن ابی حنيفة رح في صورة تعدد قرابة احدى الجدتين وذكر فی فرائض الحسن ابن عبدالرحمن ابن عبدالرزاق الشاشی من اصحاب الشافعي رح ان قول ابي حنيفة ومالک والشافعي كقول ابی یوسف رح * شريفيــــة صفحه ٤٨

١٣٨ واماللاخوات لاب وام فاحوال خمس النصف للواحدة والثلثان للاثنتين فصاعدة ومع الاخ لاب وام للذكر مثل حظ الانثيين يصرن عصبة به لاستوائهم فی القرابة الی الميت * سراجيـــــــــــــــــة صفحه ٣٢

١٣٩ وبنوالاعيان والعلات كلهم يسقطون بالابن وابن الابن وان سفل وبالاب بالاتفاق وبالجد عند ابي حنيفة رح * سراجيــــــــــــــــة صفحه ٣٤

١٤٠ ولهن الباقی مع البنات اوبنات الابن لقوله عليه السلام اجعلوا الاخوات مع البنات عصبة * سراجية صفحه ٣٣

١٤١ والاخوات لاب كالاخوات لاب وام ولهن احوال سبع النصف للواحدة والثلثان للاثنتين فصاعدة عند عدم الاخوات لاب وام ولهن السدس مع الاخت لاب وام تكملة للثلثين ولا يرثن مع الاختين لاب وام الا ان يكون

معهن اخ لاب فيعصبهن والباقي بينهم للذكر مثل حظ الانثيين * سراجيــــــــــة صفحه ۳۴ و ۳۵

۱۴۲ والسادسة ان يصرن عصبة مع البنات او بنات الابن لما ذكرنا * سراجيــــــــــة صفحه ۳۵

۱۴۳ واما لاولاد الام فاحوال ثلث السدس للواحد والثلث للاثنين فصاعدا ذكورهم واناثهم في القسمة والاستحقاق سواء ويسقطون بالولد وولد الابن وان سفل وبالاب وبالجد بالاتفاق * سراجيــــــــــة صفحه ۲۳ و ۲۴

الباب الخامس فى العصبات

۱۴۴ العصبات النسبية ثلث عصبة بنفسه وعصبة بغيره وعصبة مع غيره * سراجيــــــــــة صفحه ۴۹

۱۴۵ اما العصبة بنفسه فكل ذكر لاتدخل في نسبته الى الميت انثى وهم اربعة اصناف جزء الميت واصله وجزء ابيه وجزء جده * سراجيــــــــــة صفحه ۴۹

۱۴۶ الاقرب فالاقرب اعني به اولاهم بالميراث جزء الميت اى البنون ثم بنوهم وان سفلوا ثم اصله اى الاب ثم الجد اى اب الاب وان علا ثم جزء ابيه اى الاخوة ثم بنوهم

وان سفلوا ثم جزء جده ای الاعمام ثم بنوهم وان سفلوا *

سراجیــــــــــــــــــــــــــــة صفحه ۴۹ و ۵۰

۱۴۷ ثم یرجحون بقوة القرابة اعني به ان ذا القرابتین اولی

من ذي قرابة واحدة * سراجیــــــــــــــة صفحه ۵۱

۱۴۸ کالاخ لاب وام والاخت لاب وام اذا صارت عصبة

مع البنت اولی من الاخ لاب والاخت لاب *

سراجیــــــــــــــــــــــــــــه صفحه ۵۱

۱۴۹ الرابع جزء جده فیقدم في هذه الاصناف والمدرجین فیها

الاقرب فالاقرب * شریفیه وسراجیــــــــــــة صفحه ۴۹

۱۵۰ وکذلک الحکم في اعمام المیت ثم فی اعمام ابیه ثم في اعمام جده

اي یعتبر بین هولاء الاصناف من الاعمام قرب الدرجة اولا

وقوة القرابة ثانیا فعم المیت مقدم علی عم ابیه المقدم علی

عم جده وذلک لقرب الدرجة وفي کل واحد من هذه الاصناف

یقدم ذو القرابتین علی ذي قرابة واحدة مع التساوي

فی الدرجة فعم المیت لاب وام اولی من عمه لاب وکذا

الحال في عم ابیه وعم جده وهکذا الحکم في فروع هذه

الاصناف یعتبر اولا قرب الدرجة وثانیا قوة القرابة فابن

عم المیت مقدم علی ابن ابن عمه وابن عم المیت لاب وام

مقدم على ابن عمه لاب * سراجية وشريفية صفحه ۵۱

۱۵۱ وا قرب العصبات البنون ثم بنوهم ثم الاب ثم الجد ثم الاخوة ثم بنوهم ثم بنو الجد وهم الاعمام ثم بنوابى الجد وهم اعمام الاب * قدوري

۱۵۲ اقرب العصبات بنفسها الى الميت بنوالصلب ثم بنوهم ثم بنوا بنيهم وان سفلوا ثم الاب ثم الجداي اب الاب وان علا ثم الاخ لاب وام ثم الاخ لاب ثم بنوا الاخ لاب وام ثم بنو الاخ لاب ثم بنوهم هكذا ثم العم لاب وام ثم العم لاب ثم بنوالعم لاب وام ثم بنوالعم لاب ثم بنوهم على هذا الترتيب ثم عم الاب لاب وام ثم عم الاب لاب ثم بنوهم على هذا الترتيب فافهم * فتاوى سراجيـــــــــــــــــة صفحه ۵٦٨

۱۵۳ فاقرب العصبات الابن ثم ابن الابن وان سفل ثم الاب ثم الجداب الاب وان علا ثم الاخ لاب وام ثم الاخ لاب ثم ابن الاخ لاب وام ثم ابن الاخ لاب ثم العم لاب وام ثم العم لاب ثم ابن العم لاب وام ثم ابن العم لاب ثم عم الاب لاب وام ثم عم الاب لاب ثم ابن عم الاب لاب وام ثم ابن عم الاب لاب ثم عم الجد هكذا

فی المبسوط * فتاوی عالمگیریة

۱۲۴ وآخر العصبات مولی العتاقة * سراجیة صفحه ۴۳

۱۲۵ ثم عصبته ای عصبة مولی العتاقة علی الترتیب الذی ذکرناه
فی العصبات فتکون عصباته النسبیة مقدمة علی عصباته
السببیة اعنی معتق المعتق والمراد بعصباته النسبیة ما هی
عصبة بنفسه فقط کما ستعرفه والترتیب بین هؤلاء العصبات
ما مر فیکون ابن المعتق اولی عصباته ثم ابن ابنه وان سفل
ثم ابوه ثم جده وان علا الی آخر ما فصل هناک * سراجیة
وشریفیة صفحه ۴۴

۱۲۶ ولا شیئ منه للاناث من ورثة المعتق لقوله علیه السلام
لیس للنساء من الولاء * سراجیة صفحه ۴۵

۱۲۷ ولو ترک ای المعتق ابا المعتق وابنه کان عند ابی یوسف رح
سدس الولاء للاب والباقی للابن هذا قوله الاخیر وهو احدی
الروایتین عن ابن مسعود رض وبه قال شریح والنخعی
وعند ابی حنیفة ومحمد رح الولاء کله للابن * سراجیة
وشریفیة صفحه ۴۷

الباب السادس في مخارج الفروض وفى العول

۱۵۸ اعلم ان الفروض الستة المذكورة فى كتاب الله تعالى نوعان الاول النصف والربع والثمن والثانى الثلثان والثلث والسدس على التضعيف والتنصيف * سراجية صفحه ٦٨

۱۵۹ فاذا جاء فى المسائل من هذه الفروض أحاد أحاد فمخرج كل فرض سميه الا النصف وهو من اثنين كالربع من اربعة والثمن من ثمانية والثلث من ثلثة * سراجية صفحه ٦٩

۱٦۰ واذا جاء مثنى اوثلث وهما من نوع واحد فكل عدد يكون مخرجا لجزء فذلك العدد ايضا مخرج لضعف ذلك الجزء ولضعف ضعفه كالستة هي مخرج للسدس ولضعفه ولضعف ضعفه * سراجية صفحه ۷۰

۱٦۱ واذا اختلط النصف بكل الثاني اوببعضه فهومن ستة * سراجية صفحه ۷۱

۱٦۲ واذا اختلط الربع بكل الثاني اوببعضه فهومن اثنى عشر * سراجية صفحه ۷۲

۱٦۳ واذا اختلط الثمن بكل الثانى اوببعضه فهومن اربعة وعشرين * سراجية صفحه ۷۲ و۷۳

۱۶۴ العول ان يزاد على المخرج شيئ من اجزائه اذاضاق
عن فرض * سراجيـــــــــــــة صفحه ۷۴

۱۶۵ اعلم ان مجموع المخارج سبعة اربعة منها لاتعول وهي
الاثنان والثلثة والاربعة والثمانية * سراجية صفحه ۷۵ و۷۶

۱۶۶ فلا عول فى الاثنين لان المسئلة انما تكون من اثنين
اذا كان فيها نصفان كزوج واخت لاب وام او نصف
ومابقي كزوج واخ لاب وام ولافى الثلثة لان المخارج منها
اما ثلث ومابقي كام واخ لاب وام واماثلثان ومابقي
كبنتين واخ لاب وام واما ثلث وثلثان كاختين لام واختين
لاب وام ولافى الاربعة لان مايخرج منهاامار بع ومابقي
كزوج وابن اوربع ونصف ومابقي كزوج وبنت
واخ لاب وام او ربع وثلث مابقي ومابقي كزوجة وابوين
ولا فى الثمانية لان المخارج منها اما ثمن ومابقي كزوجة
وابن اوثمن ونصف ومابقي كزوجة وبنت واخ لاب
وام فلا عول في شيئ من مسائل هذه المخارج الاربعة *
شريفيـــــــــــــة صفحه ۷۶

---

۱۶۷ وثلثة منها قد تعول اما الستة فانها تعول الى عشرة وترا وشفعا

اي تعول بسدسها الى سبعة فيما اذا اجتمع نصف وثلثان

كزوج واختين لاب وام اواجتمع نصفان وسدس كزوج واخت لاب وام واخت لام اواخت لاب وتعول بثلثها الى ثمانية اذا اجتمع نصف وثلثان وسدس كزوج واختين لاب وام اواجتمع نصفان وثلث كزوج واخت لاب وام واختين لام وتعول بنصفها الى تسعة اذا اجتمع نصف وثلثان وثلث كزوج واختين لاب وام واختين لام اواجتمع نصفان وثلث وسدس كزوج واخت لاب وام واختين لام وام وتعول بثلثيها الى عشرة اذا اجتمع نصف وثلثان وثلث وسدس كزوج واختين لاب وام واختين لام وام* سراجية وشريفية صفحه ٧٦

---

١٦٨ واما اثنا عشر فهي تعول الى سبعة عشر وترا لا شفعا اي تعول بنصف سدسها الى ثلثة عشر اذا اجتمع ربع وثلثان وسدس كزوجة واختين لاب وام واخت لام وتعول بربعها الى خمسة عشر اذا اجتمع ربع وثلثان وثلث كزوجة اواختين لاب وام واختين لام اواجتمع ربع وثلثان وسدسان كزوجة واختين لاب وام واخت لام وام وتعول بربعها وسدسها الى سبعة عشر اذا اجتمع ربع وثلثان وثلث وسدس كزوجة واختين لاب وام واختين لام وام* سراجية

وشريفيــــــــــــــــة صفحه ۷۷

۱٦۹ واما اربعة وعشرون فانها تعول الى سبعة وعشرين عولا واحدا

كما في المسئلة المنبرية وهي امرأة وبنتان وابوان وانما سميت منبرية لانها سئلت عن علي رض وهو على المنبر في الكوفة فاجاب عنها بديهة فقال السائل متعنتا اليس للزوجة الثمن فقال صار ثمنها تسعا ومضى في خطبته فتعجبوا من فطنته * سراجية وشريفيــــــــة صفحه ۷۷

۱۷۰ ولا يزاد عول اربعة وعشرين على هذا العدد الذي هو سبعة وعشرون الا عند ابن مسعود رض فان عنده تعول اربعة وعشرون الى احدى وثلثين بزيادة سدسها وثمنها عليها

كامرأة وام واختين لاب وام واختين لام وابن محروم اذ عنده يحجب هذا الابن الزوجة من الربع الى الثمن فالمسئلة عنده من اربعة وعشرين لاختلاط الثمن من النوع الاول بكل النوع الثاني وانما عالت الى احدى وثلثين اذ للزوجة الثمن وهو ثلثة وللام السدس وهو اربعة وللاختين لاب وام الثلثان اعني ستة عشر وللاختين لام الثلث وهو ثمانية فالمجموع احد وثلثون وعند غيره هذه المسئلة من اثنى عشر وتعول الى سبعة عشر * سراجية وشريفية صفحه ۷۸

الباب السابع في التصحيح

۱۷۱ يحتاج في تصحيح المسائل الى سبعة اصول ثلثة منها بين السهام و الروٴس واربعة منها بين الروٴس والروٴس اما الثلثة فاحدها ان كانت سهام كل فريق منقسمة عليهم بلا كسر فلا حاجة الى الضرب كابوين وبنتين فان المسئلة حينئذ من ستة فلكل واحد من الابوين سدسها وهو واحد وللبنتين الثلثان اعني اربعة فلكل واحد منهما اثنان فاستقامت السهام على روٴس الورثة بلا انكسار * سراجية و شريفية صفحه ۸۴

۱۷۲ والثاني ان ينكسر على طائفة واحدة نصيبهم ولكن بين سهامهم وروٴسهم موافقة فيضرب وفق عدد روٴس من انكسرت عليهم السهام في اصل المسئلة وعولها ان كانت عائلة كابوين وعشر بنات او زوج وابوين وست بنات فالاول مثال ماليس فيها عول اذا اصل المسئلة من ستة السدسان وهما اثنان للابوين ويستقيمان عليهما والثلثان وهما اربعة للبنات العشر ولا تستقيم عليهن لكن بين الاربعة والعشرة موافقة بالنصف فان العدد العاد لهما هو الاثنان فرددنا عدد الروٴس اعنى العشرة الى نصفها وهو خمسة وضربناها في الستة التي هي اصل

المسئلة صار الحاصل ثلثين فتصح منه المسئلة اذ كان
للابوين من اصل المسئلة سهمان وقد ضربناهما فى
المضروب الذي هو خمسة صار عشرة فلكل منهما خمسة
وكانت للبنات منه اربعة وقد ضربناها ايضا في خمسة
فصار عشرين فلكل واحدة منهن اثنان *
سراجية وشريفية صفحه ۸۵

۱۷۳ والثالث ان لاتكون بين سهامهم وروؤسهم موافقة
فيضرب حينئذ كل عدد روؤس من انكسرت عليهم السهام
في اصل المسئلة * سراجية صفحه ۸۶

۱۷۴ ومثال غير العائلة زوج وجدة وثلث اخوات لام
فالمسئلة من ستة للزوج منها نصفها وهو ثلثة وللجدة سدسها
وهو واحد وللاخوات ثلثها وهو اثنان ولا يستقيمان على
عدد روؤسهن وليست بين عددي روؤسهن وسهامهن
موافقة بكسر بل بينهما مباينة فضربنا كل عدد روؤس
الاخوات في اصل المسئلة صار الحاصل ثمانية عشر فتصح
المسئلة منها اذ قد كانت للزوج ثلثة ضربناها في المضروب
الذي هو ثلثة صار تسعة وضربنا نصيب الجدة في المضروب
ايضا فكان ثلثة وضربنا نصيب الاخوات لام فى المضروب

صارستةفاعطيناكل واحدةمنهن اثنين *شريفية صفحه ٨٧

١٧٥ كزوج وخمس اخوات لاب وام فاصل المسئلة
من ستة النصف وهوثلثة للزوج وثلثان وهواربعة
للاخوات فقد عالت المسئلة الي سبعة وانكسرت
سهام الاخوات عليهن فقط وبين عددي سهامهن
وروسهن اعني الاربعة والخمسة مباينة فضربنا كل عدد
روسهن وهوخمسة في اصل المسئلة مع عولها وهوسبعة
فصار الحاصل خمسة وثلثين فمنها تصح المسئة اذ كانت
للزوج ثلثة وقد ضربناهافي المضروب وهوخمسة فصار
خمسة عشروكانت للاخوات الخمس اربعة وقد ضربناها
ايضافي الخمسة فصارعشرين فلكل واحدةمنهن اربعة *
سراجية وشريفية صفحه ٨٦

١٧٦ واماالاربعة فاحدها ان يكون الكسرعلي طائفتين او اكثر
ولكن بين اعداد روس سهم مماثلة فالحكم فيها ان يضرب احد
الاعداد في اصل المسئلة مثل ست بنات وثلث جدات
وثلثة اعمام المسئلة من ستة للبنات الست الثلثان وهو
اربعة لا تستقيم عليهن لكن بين الاربعة وعدد روسهن
موافقة بالنصف فاخذنانصف عدد روسهن هوثلثة وللجدات

الثلث السدس وهو واحد ولا يستقيم عليهن ولا موافقة
بين الواحد وعدد رؤسهن فاخذنا جميع عدد رؤسهن وهو ايضا
ثلثة وللاعمام الثلثة الباقي وهو واحد ايضا وبينه وبين عدد
رؤسهم مباينة فاخذنا جميع عدد رؤسهم ثم نسبنا هذه
الاعداد الماخوذة بعضها الى بعض فوجدناها مماثلة
فضربنا احدها وهو ثلثة في اصل المسئلة اعنى الستة فصارت
ثمانية عشر فمنها تستقيم المسئلة اذ قد كانت للبنات
اربعة ضربناها فى المضروب الذي هو ثلثة فصار اثنى عشر
فلكل واحدة منهن اثنان وللجدات واحد ضربناه ايضا في
ثلثة فصار ثلثة فلكل واحدة واحد وللاعمام واحد ايضا
ضربناه فى الثلثة ايضا واعطينا كل واحد منهم واحدا *
سراجية وشريفية صفحه ٨٨

---

١٧٧ والثاني ان يكون بعض الاعداد متداخلا في البعض فالحكم

فيها ان يضرب اكثر الاعداد في اصل المسئلة كاربع زوجات

وثلث جدات واثنا عشر عما اصل المسئلة من اثنى عشر
للجدات الثلث السدس وهو اثنان فلا يستقيم عليهن وبين
رؤسهن وسهامهن مباينة فاخذنا مجموع عدد رؤسهن
وهو ثلثة وللزوجات الاربع الربع وهو ثلثة فلا استقامة وبين

عددي رؤسهن وسها مهن مباينة فاخذنا عدد رؤسهن
وهوا ربعة وللاعمام الباقي وهو سبعة فلا تستقيم على اثنى
عشر بل بينهما تباين فاخذنا عدد الرؤس باسره ثم طلبنا
النسبة بين اعداد الرؤس الماخوذة فوجدنا الثلثة والاربعة
متداخلين في اثنى عشر الذي هواكثر اعداد الرؤس
فضربناه في اصل المسئلة وهوايضا اثنا عشر فصار مائة واربعة
واربعين فتصح منها المسئلة اذ كان للجدات من اصل
المسئلة اثنان وقد ضربناهما فى المضروب الذي هواثناعشر
فصار اربعة وعشرين فلكل واحدة منهن ثمانية وللزوجات
من اصل المسئلة ثلثة ضربناها فى المضروب المذكور
صار ستة وثلثين فلكل واحدة منهن تسعة وللاعمام سبعة
ضربناها في اثنا عشر ايضا فحصلت اربعة وثمانون فلكل واحد
منهم سبعة * سراجية وشريفيــــــــــــة صفحه ٨٩

١٧٨ والثالث ان يوافق بعض الاعداد بعضا فالحكم فيها
ان يضرب وفق احد الاعداد في جميع الثاني ثم ما بلغ
في وفق الثالث ان وافق الثالث والا فالمبلغ في جميع الثالث
ثم فى الرابع كذالك ثم المبلغ في اصل المسئلة *
سراجيــــــــــــــــــــــــة صفحة ٩٠

١٧٩ كاربع زوجات وثماني عشر بنتا وخمس عشر جدة وستة اعمام

اصل المسئلة اربعة وعشرون للزوجات الاربع الثمن وهو ثلثة فلا تستقيم عليهن وبين عددي سهامهن ورؤسهن مباينة فحفظنا جميع عدد رؤسهن وللبنات الثماني عشر الثلثان وهو ستة عشر فلا تستقيم عليهن وبين عددي رؤسهن وسهامهن موافقة بالنصف فاخذنا نصف عدد رؤسهن وهو تسعة وحفظناها وللجدات الخمس عشر السدس وهو اربعة فلا تستقيم عليهن وبين عددي رؤسهن وسهامهن مباينة فحفظنا جميع عدد رؤسهن وللاعمام الستة الباقي وهو واحد ولايستقيم عليهم وبينه وبين عدد رؤسهم مباينة فحفظنا عدد رؤسهم فحصل لنا من اعداد الرؤس المحفوظة اربعة وستة وتسعة وخمسة عشر ثم طلبنا بينهما اي بين الاربعة والستة التوافق فوجدنا الاربعة موافقة للستة بالنصف فرددنا احدهما الي نصفها وضربناه في الاخرى صار المبلغ اثنى عشر وهو موافق للتسعة بالثلث فضربنا ثلث احدهما في جميع الآخر صار المبلغ ستة وثلثين وبين هذا المبلغ الثاني وبين خمسة عشر موافقة بالثلث ايضا فضربنا ثلث خمسة عشر وهو خمسة في ستة وثلثين

فحصلت مائة وثمانون ثم ضربنا هذا المبلغ الثالث في اصل المسئلة اعني اربعة وعشرين صار الحاصل اربعة آلاف وثلثمائة وعشرين فمنها تصح المسئلة اذ كانت للزوجات من اصل المسئلة ثلثة ضربناها في المضروب وهو مائة وثمانون فحصل خمس مائة واربعون فلكل من الزوجات الاربع مائة وخمسة وثلثون وكانت للبنات الثماني عشر ستة عشر وقد ضربناها في ذلك المضروب ايضا فصار الفين وثمان مائة وثمانين فلكل واحدة منهن مائة وستون وكانت للجدات الخمس عشر اربعة وقد ضربناها في المضروب المذكور فصار سبعمائة وعشرين فلكل منهن ثمانية واربعون وكان للاعمام الستة واحد فضربناه في المضروب فكان مائة وثمانين فلكل واحد منهم ثلثون *

سراجية وشريفية ———————— صفحة ٩١

والرابع ان تكون الاعداد متباينة لا يوافق بعضها بعضا فالحكم ١٨٠

فيها ان يضرب احد الاعداد في جميع الثاني ثم ما بلغ في جميع

الثالث ثم ما بلغ في جميع الرابع ثم ما اجتمع في اصل المسئلة

كامراتين وست جدات وعشر بنات وسبعة اعمام

اصل المسئلة اربعة وعشرون فللزوجتين الثمن وهو ثلثة

لاتستقيم عليهما وبين رؤسهما وسهامهما مباينة فاخذنا عدد رؤسهما وهواثنان وللجدات الست السدس وهوا ربعة فلا تستقيم عليهن وبين عددي رؤسهن وسهامهن موافقة بالنصف فأخذنا نصف عدد رؤسهن وهو ثلثة وللبنات العشر الثلثان وهو ستة عشر فلاتستقيم عليهن وبين رؤسهن وسهامهن موافقة بالنصف فأخذنا نصف عدد رؤسهن وهوخمسة وللاعمام السبعة الباقي وهو واحد ولا يستقيم عليهم وبينه وبين عدد رؤسهم مباينة فاخذنا عدد رؤسهم وهوسبعة فصار معنامن الاعداد الماخوذة للرؤس اثنان وثلثة وخمسة وسبعة وهذه كلها اعداد مباينة فضربنا الاثنين فى الثلثة صار ستة ثم ضربناهذا المبلغ في خمسة فصار ثلثين ثم ضربنا الثلثين فى السبعة فحصلت مائتان وعشرة ثم ضربناهذا المبلغ في اصل المسئلة وهوا ربعة وعشرون فصار المجموع خمسة آلاف واربعين ومنها تستقيم المسئلة على جميع الطوائف اذ كانت للزوجتين من اصل المسئلة ثلثة فضربناها فى المضروب الذي هو مائتان وعشرة فحصلت ست مائة وثلثون فلكل واحدة منهما ثلثمائة وخمسة عشر وكانت للجدات الست اربعة

وقد ضربناها فى ذلك المضروب فصار ثمانمائة واربعين فلكل واحدة منهن مائة واربعون وكانت للبنات العشر ستة عشر ضربناها فى المضروب المذكور فبلغ ثلثة آلاف وثلثمائة وستين فلكل واحدة منهن ثلثمائة وستة وثلثون وكان للاعمام السبعة واحد ضربناه في ذلك المضروب فكان مائتين وعشرة فلكل منهم ثلثون ومجموع هذه الانصباء خمسة آلاف واربعون *سراجية وشريفية صفحه ٩٢

الباب الثامن في قسمة التركات

١٨١ واذا لم تكن بينهما مماثلة فاضرب سهام كل وارث من التصحيح في جميع التركة ثم اقسم المبلغ على التصحيح سراجية ———————— صفحه ٩٨

١٨٢ مثلا اذا خلفت زوجا واما واختين لاب وام كانت المسئلة من ستة وتعول الى ثمانية فللزوج منها ثلثة وللام واحد ولكل من الاختين سهمان فان فرضنا ان جميع التركة خمسة وعشرون دينارا كانت بينهما وبين التصحيح الذي هو ثمانية مباينة فاذا اردت ان تعرف نصيب كل وارث من هذه التركة فاضرب نصيب الزوج

من التصحيح وهو ثلثة في كل التركة تحصل خمسة
وسبعون ثم هذا المبلغ على التصحيح اعني ثمانية تخرج
تسعة دنانير وثلثة اثمان دينار فهذه نصيب الزوج من
تلك التركة واضرب نصيب الام من التصحيح وهو
واحد في جميع التركة فيكون الحاصل خمسة وعشرين
فاذا قسمتها على الثمانية خرجت ثلثة دنانير وثمن دينار
فهي نصيب الام من التركة واضرب نصيب كل اخت
من التصحيح وهواثنان في كل التركة يحصل خمسون
فاذا قسمت هذا الحاصل على الثمانية خرجت ستة
دنانير وربع دينار فهي نصيب كل اخت من التركة *
شريفية ——— صفحه ٩٨

١٨٣ واذا كانت بين التركة والتصحيح موافقة فاضرب
سهام كل وارث من التصحيح في وفق التركة ثم اقسم
المبلغ على وفق التصحيح فالخارج نصيب ذلك الوارث
في الوجهين * سراجية ——— صفحة ٩٨

١٨٤ اما المعرفة نصيب كل فريق منهم فاضرب ما كان لكل
فريق من اصل المسئلة في وفق التركة ثم اقسم المبلغ
على وفق المسئلة ان كانت بين التركة والمسئلة موافقة

وان كانت بينهما مباينة فاضرب في كل التركة ثم اقسم الحاصل علي جميع المسئلة فالخارج نصيب ذلك الفريق في الوجهين * سراجيـــــــة صفحه ١٠٠

١٨٥ مثال الموافقة زوج واربع اخوات لاب وام واختان لام فاصل المسئلة من ستة وتعول الي تسعة فلو فرضنا التركة ثلثين كان بين التركة والتصحيح توافق بالثلث فاذا ضربنا نصيب الزوج من اصل المسئلة وهو ثلثة في وفق التركة وهو عشرة حصل ثلثون فاذا قسمنا هذا الحاصل علي ثلث المسئلة وهو ثلثة ايضا خرجت عشرة فهي نصيب الزوج واذا ضربنا نصيب الاخوات لاب وام من اصل المسئلة وهو اربعة في ثلث التركة صار اربعين فاذا قسمناها علي ثلث المسئلة كان الخارج وهو ثلثة عشر نصيب هولاء الاخوات فاذا ضربنا نصيب الاختين لام وهو اثنان في ثلث التركة حصل عشرون فاذا قسمناه علي ثلث المسئلة كان الخارج وهو ستة وثلثان نصيب هاتين الاختين * شريفيـــــــة صفحه ١٠٠

١٨٦ ومثال المباينة ان تفرض التركة في المسئلة المذكورة اثنين وثلثين فتكون بينهما وبين التصحيح وهو تسعة مباينة

فاذا ضربنا نصيب الزوج وهو ثلثة في كل التركة حصلت ستة وتسعون فاذا قسمنا هذا المبلغ على جميع المسئلة وهو تسعة كان الخارج وهو عشرة وثلثان نصيب الزوج من تلك التركة فاذا ضربنا نصيب الاخوات لاب وام وهو اربعة في كل التركة حصلت ماية وثمانية وعشرون فاذا قسمنا هذا الحاصل على التسعة كان الخارج وهو اربعة عشر وتسعان نصيب الاخوات من الابوين من التركة المذكورة واذا ضربنا نصيب الاختين لام في جميع التركة بلغت اربعة وستين فاذا قسمنا هذا المبلغ على تسعة كان الخارج وهو سبعة وتسع نصيبهما من التركة المفروضة *

شريفية صفحة ١٠١

١٨٧ من صالح على شيء معلوم من التركة فاطرح سهامه من التصحيح ثم اقسم باقي التركة على سهام الباقين كزوج وام وعم فصالح الزوج على مافى ذمته من المهر وخرج من البين فيقسم باقى التركة بين الام والعم اثلاثا بقدر سهامهما وحينئذ يكون سهمان للام وسهم للعم *

سراجية صفحة ١٠٣

---

١٨٨ واما في قضاء الديون فدين كل غريم بمنزلة سهام كل وارث

في العمل ومجموع الديون بمنزلة التصحيح اعلم ان الباقي
من التركة بعد التجهيز والتكفين ان وفى بالديون فلا
اشكال لان كل غريم يأخذ دينه كملا وان لم يف بها
مع تعدد الغرماء فالطريق في معرفة نصيب كل غريم
من تلك التركة القاصرة ان يجعل دين كل واحد منهم
بمنزلة سهام كل وارث من تصحيح المسئلة ويجعل
مجموع الديون بمنزلة مجموع التصحيح ويعمل ههنا مامر
في تعيين نصيب كل وارث * سراجية وشريفية صفحه ١٠٢

فان مات شخص وترك تسعة دنانير وكانت عليه ١٨٩
لواحد عشرة دنانير ولآخر خمسة دنانير وجمعنا الدينين
صار المجموع خمسة عشر وهي بمنزلة التصحيح وبين التسعة
والخمسة عشر موافقة بالثلث فاذا ضربنا دين من له عشرة
دنانير على الميت في ثلث التسعة حصل ثلثون فاذا قسمنا
هذا الحاصل على وفق التصحيح وهو خمسة كان الخارج
وهو ستة نصيب من كانت له عشرة فاذا ضربنا دين من له
خمسة دنانير عليه في وفق التركة اعني ثلثة حصلت خمسة
عشر فاذا قسمناه هذا المبلغ على ثلث التصحيح كان الخارج وهو
ثلثة نصيب من كانت له خمسة * شريفية صفحه ١٠٢

١٩٠ ولوفرضنا ان التركة فى الصورة المذكورة ثلثة عشر كانت
بين التصحيح والتركة مباينة فحينئذ يضرب دين صاحب
العشرة في كل التركة فتحصل ماية وثلثون فاذا قسمنا هذا
المبلغ على كل التصحيح وهو خمسة عشر كان الخارج وهو
ثمانية وثلثون نصيب من كانت له عشرة ويضرب ايضا
دين صاحب الخمسة في جميع التركة فيبلغ خمسة ستين
فاذا قسمنا هذا المبلغ على خمسة عشر خرجت اربعة وثلث
وهو نصيب من كانت له خمسة * شريفية صفحه ١٠٢

الباب التاسع فى الرد

١٩١ الرد ضد العول ما فضل عن فرض ذوى الفروض
ولا مستحق له يرد على ذوى الفروض بقدر حقوقهم الا
على الزوجين وهو قول عامة الصحابة رض وبه اخذ
اصحابنا رح وقال زيد ابن ثابت الفاضل لبيت المال وبه
اخذ مالك والشافعي رح * سراجيــــة صفحه ١٠٥

١٩٢ شهد انه وارث لا وارث له غيره لم تقبل حتى يبينا
فيقولا انه اخوه او ابوه او ابنه او عمه ونحو ذلك فلو ذكرا انه
ابنه او ابوه او امه لا يحتاجان الى قولهما انه وارثه ولو

ذکرا انه اخوه يجب ان يقولا انه اخوه لاب وام اولاب اولام*
فتاوی سراجية صفحه ٤٨٠

١٩٣ رجل ادعی انه وارث فلان الميت واقام شاهدين فشهدا انه وارث فلان الميت لا وارث له سواه فان القاضي يسألهما عن السبب ولا يقضی قبل السؤال لاختلاف اسبابها والقضاء بالمجهول متعذر فان مات الشاهدان اوغابا قبل ان يسألهما لا يقضی بشيء كذا في فتاوی قاضيخان
فتاوی عالمگيرية* فی الجلد الثالث صفحه ٤٧٩

١٩٤ شهدا انه ابن الميت ولم يشهدا انالا نعلم له وارثا غيره تلوم القاضي في ذاک وتأنی قد ربما لو كان له وارث يظهر ثم يدفع اليه الميراث* فتاوی سراجية صفحه ٤٧٩

١٩٥ اذا شهد الشهود بوراثة رجل وبينوا سببه ولم يزيدوا عليه فالشهادة مقبولة الا ان القاضي لا يدفع المال الی المشهود له للحال بل يتلوم زمانا لجواز ان يظهر وارث آخر للميت مزاحم للمشهود له او مقدم عليه هكذا فی الذخيرة*
فتاوی عالمگيرية فی الجلد الثالث صفحه ٤٧٩

---

١٩٦ واذا قسم الميراث بين الغرماء فانه لا يؤخذ منهم كفيل ولا من وارث وهذا شيء احتاط به بعض القضاة وهو ظلم وهذا

عند ابي حنيفة رح وقالا يأخذ الكفيل والمسئلة فيما اذا
ثبت الدين والارث بالشهادة ولم يقل الشهود لا نعلم له
وارثا غيره * الهدايـــــــــــة صفحه ٤٨٠

١٩٧ فان كان الوارث ممن يحجب لغيره كالجد والاخ
والعم لا يدفع اليه المال فان كان زوجا او زوجة عند
محمد رح يدفع اليه اوفي النصيبين وهو النصف للزوج
والربع للمرأة وقال ابو يوسف رح اقل النصيبين *
فتاوى سراجيـــــــــــة صفحه ٤٨٠

١٩٨ ثم مما يلي الباب اقسام اربعة احدها ان يكون في المسئلة
جنس واحد ممن يرد عليه عند عدم من لا يرد عليه فاجعل
المسئلة من رؤس سهم كما اذا ترك بنتين او اختين او جدتين
فاجعل المسئلة من اثنين فاعط كل واحدة منهما نصف التركة
لتساويهما في الاستحقاق ورجوع جميع المال اليهما على
السوية فتكون القسمة على عدد الرؤس * سراجية
وشريفيـــــــــــة صفحه ١٠٧ و ١٠٨

١٩٩ والثاني اذا اجتمع في المسئلة جنسان او ثلثة اجناس
ممن يرد عليه عند عدم من لا يرد عليه فاجعل المسئلة من
سهامهم اعني من اثنين اذا كان في المسئلة سدسان

اومن ثلثة اذا كان فيها ثلث وسدس اومن اربعة اذا كان
فيها نصف وسدس اومن خمسة اذا كان فيها ثلثان
وسدس او نصف وسدسان او نصف وثلث *
سراجيـــــــــــــــــة صفحه ١٠٨ و ١٠٩

٢٠٠ كجدة واخت لام لان المسئلة حينئذ من ستة لهما منها
اثنان بالفرضية فاجعل الاثنين اصل المسئلة واقسم
التركة عليهما نصفين فلكل واحدة منهما نصف المال *
شريفيـــــــــــــــــة صفحه ١٠٨

٢٠١ كولدى الام مع الام اذ المسئلة على هذا التقدير ايضا
من ستة ومجموع السهام الماخوذة للورثة المذكورة ثلثة
فاجعلها اصل المسئلة واقسم التركة اثلاثا بقدر تلك السهام
فلولدى الام ثلثان من المال وللام ثلث * شريفية صفحه ١٠٨

٢٠٢ كبنت وبنت ابن اوبنت وام لان المسئلة ايضا من ستة
ومجموع السهام الماخوذة منها اربعة ثلثة للبنت وواحد
لبنت الابن اوللام فاجعل المسئلة من اربعة واقسم
التركة ارباعا ثلثة ارباعها للبنت وربع منها للام اوبنت
الابن * شريفيـــــــــــــــــة صفحه ١٠٩

٢٠٣ كبنت وبنت ابن وام وفى الصورة الثانية قد اجتمعت

جا س ثلثه وسهامهم الماخوذة من الستة خمسة ايضا ثلثة
منها للبنت و واحد لبنت الابن و واحد للام فتقسم التركة
عليهن اخماسا بقدر سهامهن فللبنت ثلثة اخماسها ولبنت
الابن خمس وللام خمس آخر * شريفية صفحه ١٠٩

٢٠٤ والثالث ان يكون مع الاول من لا يرد عليه فاعط فرض
من لا يرد عليه من اقل مخارجه فان استقام الباقي على عدد
رؤس من يرد عليه فيها كزوج وثلث بنات اقل مخارج
فرض من لا يرد عليه اربعة فاذا اعطيت الزوج واحدا منها
بقيت ثلثة وهي مستقيمة على عدد رؤس البنات وهو نظير
مامر في باب التصحيح من انه ان كانت سهام كل فريق
منقسمة عليهم بلا كسر فلا حاجة الى ضرب *
سراجية وشريفية صفحه ١١٠

٢٠٥ وان لم يستقم فاضرب وفق رؤسهن في مخرج فرض من لا يرد
عليه ان وافق رؤس سهم الباقي كزوج وست بنات فان اقل
مخرج فرض من لا يرد عليه اربعة فاذا اعطيت الزوج
واحدا منها بقيت ثلثة فلا تستقيم على عدد رؤس البنات
الست لكن بينهما موافقة بالثلث اذ لا عبرة للمداخلة
كما عرفت فاضرب وفق عدد رؤسهن وهو اثنان

فى الاربعة يبلغ ثمانية فللزوج منها اثنان وللبنات ستة *
سراجية وشريفية ــــــــــــــــــــــــ صفحه ١١١

٢٠٦ والا فاضرب كل عدد رؤسهن في مخرج فرض من لا يرد
عليه فالمبلغ تصحيح المسئلة كزوج و خمس بنات هذه الصورة
كالصورتين السابقتين اصلها من اثنى عشر لاجتماع
الربع والثلثين لكنها يرد مثلهما الى الاربعة التي هي
اقل مخارج فرض من لا يرد عليه فاذا اعطينا الزوج ههنا
واحدا منها بقيت ثلثة فلا تستقيم على البنات الخمس
بل بينها وبين عدد الرؤس مباينة فضربنا كل عدد رؤسهن
في مخرج فرض من لا يرد عليه اى الاربعة فحصلت
عشرون ومنها تصح المسئلة كان للزوج واحد ضربناه
فى المضروب الذي هو خمسة فكان خمسة فاعطيناه اياها
وكانت للبنات ثلثة ضربناها فى الخمسة حصلة خمسة عشر
فلكل واحدة منهن ثلثة * سراجية وشريفية صفحه ١١١

٢٠٧ والرابع ان يكون مع الثاني من لا يرد عليه فاقسم
مابقي من مخرج فرض من لا يرد عليه على مسئلة من
يرد عليه فان استقام فبهــا وهذا في صورة واحدة وهي
ان يكون للزوجات الربع والباقي بين اهل الرد

اثلاثا كزوجة واربع جدات وست اخوات لام *

سراجيـــــــــــــــــــة صفحه ١١٢ و١١٣

٢٠٨ فان اقل مخرج فرض من لايرد عليه اربعة فاذا اخذت امرأة واحدا منها بقيت ثلثة وهي ههنا مستقيمة على مسئلة من يرد عليه لانها ايضا ثلثة لان حق الاخوات لام الثلث وحق الجدات السدس فللاخوات سهمان وللجدات سهم واحد ففي هذه الصورة استقام الباقي على مسئلة من يرد عليه * شريفيـــــــــــــــــة صفحه ١١٣

٢٠٩ وان لم يستقم فاضرب جميع مسئلة من يرد عليه في مخرج فرض من لايرد عليه فالمبلغ مخرج فروض الفريقين *

سراجيـــــــــــــــــــة صفحه ١١٤

---

٢١٠ كاربع زوجات وتسع بنات وست جدات اصل هذه المسئلة على ما سبق من اربعة وعشرين لاختلاط الثمن بالثلثين والسدس لكنها ردية فرددناها الى اقل مخارج فرض لايرد عليه وهو الثمانية فاذا دفعنا ثمنها الى الزوجات بقيت سبعة فلا تستقيم على الخمسة التي هي مسئلة من يرد عليه ههنا لان الفرضين ثلثان وسدس بل بينهما مباينة فيضرب جميع مسئلة من يرد عليه اعني الخمسة في مخرج

فرض من لا يرد عليه وهو الثمانية فبلغ اربعين فهذا المبلغ
مخرج فروض الفريقين واذا اردت ان تعرف حصة
كل فريق منهما من هذا المبلغ الذي هو مخرج فروضهما
فطريقه ما اشار اليه بقوله ثم اضرب سهام من لا يرد عليه من اقل
مخارج فرضه في مسئلة من يرد عليه فيكون الحاصل
نصيب من لا يرد عليه من المبلغ المذكور وذلك لانا
ضربنا مسئلة من يرد عليه في اقل مخارج فرض من لا يرد
عليه فيكون الحاصل من ضرب سهامه من هذا الاقل
في المضروب الذي هو تلك المسئلة حصة من المبلغ الذي
حصل من ضرب هذا المضروب في المخرج الاقل على
قياس ما تحققته فيما مر واضرب ايضا سهام كل فريق ممن
يرد عليه من مسئلتهم فيما بقي من مخرج فرض من لا يرد عليه
فيكون الحاصل نصيب ذلك الفريق ممن يرد عليه وذلك
لان حق كل فريق ممن يرد عليه انما هو في الباقي من
مخرج فرض من لا يرد عليه بقدر سهامهم ففي المسئلة
المذكورة للزوجات من ذلك المخرج واحد فاذا ضربناه
في الخمسة التي هي مسئلة من يرد عليه كان الحاصل خمسة
فهي حق الزوجات من الاربعين وللبنات من مسئلة

من يرد عليه اربعة فاذا ضربناها فيما بقي من مخرج فرض من لا يرد عليه وهو سبعة بلغ ثمانية وعشرين فهي لهن من الاربعين وللجدات من مسئلة من يرد عليه واحد فاذا ضربناه في السبعة كان سبعة فهي للجدات فقد استقام بهذا العمل فرض من لا يرد عليه وفرض كل فريق ممن يرد عليه وان لم يستقم على احاد كل فريق فلذلك قال فان انكسرت السهام الماخوذة من مخرج فروض الفريقين على البعض او الجميع صححت المسئلة بالاصول السبعة المذكورة في باب التصحيح ففي الصورة التي نحن فيها كان من الاربعين نصيب الزوجات الاربع خمسة فبين رؤسهن وسهامهن مباينة فاخذنا مجموع عدد رؤسهن وكانت سهام البنات التسع منها ثمانية وعشرين فبين الرؤس والسهام مباينة فتركنا عدد الرؤس بحاله وكانت سهام الجدات الست منها سبعة وبينهما ايضا مباينة فاخذنا عدد رؤسهن باسره ثم طلبنا بين اعداد الرؤس والرؤس الموافقة فوجدنا ان رؤس الجدات ورؤس الزوجات متوافقة بالنصف فضربنا نصف الاربعة في الستة فبلغ اثنى عشر هي موافقة لرؤس البنات التسع بالثلث

فضربنا ثلث التسعة في اثنى عشر فحصلت ستة وثلثون فضربنا هذا الحاصل فى الاربعين فبلغ الفا واربعماية واربعين فمنها تصح المسئلة على احاد الفرق كان نصيب الزوجات من الاربعين خمسة وقد ضربناها فى المضروب الذي هو ستة وثلثون فبلغ ماية وثمانين فلكل واحدة من الزوجات خمسة واربعون وكان نصيب البنات منها ثمانية وعشرين وقد ضربناها في ذلك المضروب فصار الفا وثمانية فلكل واحدة منهن ماية واثنا عشر وكان نصيب الجدات منها سبعة وقد ضربناها فى المضروب المذكور فصار مايتين واثنين وخمسين فلكل واحدة من الجدات اثنان واربعين * سراجية وشريفية صفحه ١١٤

الباب العاشر فى المناسخة

٢١١ ولو صار بعض الانصباء ميراثا قبل القسمة كزوج وبنت وام فمات الزوج قبل القسمة عن امرأة وابوين ثم ماتت البنت عن ابنين وبنت وجدة ثم ماتت الجدة عن زوج واخوين الاصل فيه ان تصحح مسئلة الميت الاول وتعطى سهام كل وارث من التصحيح ثم تصحح مسئلة الميت الثاني وتنظر بين ما في يده

من التصحيح الاول وبين التصحيح الثاني ثلثة احوال فان استقام

مافي يده من التصحيح الاول علي التصحيح الثاني فلاحاجة الى الضرب

علي قياس مامرفي باب التصحيح من ان سهام كل فريق ان كانت مستقيمة عليهم بلا كسرفلاحاجة الي ضرب فان التصحيح الاول ههنا بمنزلة اصل المسئلة هناك والتصحيح الثاني ههنا بمنزلة رؤس المقسوم عليهم ثمه ومافي يد الميت الثاني بمنزلة سهامهم من اصل المسئلة ففي صورة الاستقامة تصح المسئلتان من التصحيح الاول كما اذا مات الزوج في المثال المذكورعن امراة وابوين علي ماذكرفي الكتاب وذالك لان المسئلة الاولى ردية لان اصلها اثني عشرلا جتماع الربع والنصف والسدس فاذا اخذ الزوج منها ثلثة والبنت ستة والام اثنين بقي منها واحد يجب رده على البنت والام بقدر سهامهما فاذا رددنا المسئلة الي اقل مخارج من لايرد عليه صارت اربعة فاذا اخذ الزوج منها واحدا بقيت ثلثة فلا تستقيم على الاربعة التي هي سهام البنت والام بل بينهما مباينة فتضرب هذه السهام التي هي بمنزلة الرؤس في ذالك الاقل فتحصل ستة عشرفللزوج منها اربعة وللبنت

تسعة والام ثلثة ثم تلك الاربعة التي للزوج منقسمة على ورثته المذكورين فلزوجته واحد منها ولامه ثلث مابقي وهوايضا واحد ولابيه اثنان فاستقام ما كان في يد الزوج من التصحيح الاول على التصحيح الثانی وصحت المسئلتان من التصحيح الاول * سراجية وشريفية صفحه ١٣٠ و ١٣١ و ١٣٢

٢١٢ وان لم يستقم فانظران كانت بينهما موافقة فاضرب وفق التصحيح الثانی في جميع التصحيح الاول * سراجية صفحه ١٣٠

٢١٣ كما اذا ماتت البنت ايضا في ذالك المثال وخلفت كماذكرا بنين وبنتا وجدة فان مافي يدها من التصحيح الاول تسعة وتصحيح مسئلتها ستة وبينهما موافقة بالثلث فيضرب ثلث ستة وهواثنان في ستة عشر فالمبلغ وهواثنان وثلثون مخرج المسئلتين فمن كانت سهامه من ستة عشر اعني ورثة الميت الاول تضرب سهامه تلك في وفق مسئلة البنت وهو اثنان فيكون ماحصل نصيب ومن كانت سهامه من ستة اعني ورثة الميت الثاني تضرب سهامه في وفق ما كان في يد البنت وهوثلثة فماحصل كان

نصيبه وقدكانت لام الميت الاول ثلثة من ستة عشر نضربها في اثنين يبلغ ستة فهي لها وكانت للزوج منها اربعة نضربها في اثنين تحصل ثمانية فهي له ومستقيمة على ورثته فلزوجته منها سهمان ولابيه اربعة ولامه سهمان هما ثلث ما بقي ايضا وان ضربت نصيب كل واحد من ورثته من ستة عشر في ذلك الوفق ثم تختلف الحال وكان لكل واحد من ابنى البنت سهمان من مسئلتها وهي ستة فاذا ضربناهما فى الثلثة صارت ستة فهي له وكان لبنتها من مسئلتها سهم واحد فاذا ضربناه فى الثلثة كان ثلثة فهي لها وكان لجدتها من مسئلتها ايضا واحد نضرب في ثلثة فهي لها وقد كانت لها باعتبار كونها اما لمن مات اولا ستة من اثنين وثلثين ففي يد الجدة حينئذ تسعة *

شريفيـــــــــــــــــــــــــــــــــــة صفحه ١٣٢

٢١٤ وان كانت بينهما مباينة فاضرب كل التصحيح الثاني في كل التصحيح الاول * سراجيـــــــــة صفحه ١٣٣

٢١٥ كما اذا ماتت في ذلك المثال الجدة التي هي ام المرأة المتوفاة اولا وخلفت: وجا واخوين فان ما في يدها تسعة كما عرفت آنفا وتصحيح مسئلتها اربعة وبين التسعة

والاربعة مباينة فاضرب احينئذ الاربعة فى التصحيح السابق اعنى الاثنين والثلثين يبلغ مائة وثمانية وعشرين فهي مخرج المسئلتين فمن كان له نصيب من الاثنين والثلثين يضرب نصيبه فى الاربعة التي هي مسئلة الجدة ومن كان له نصيب من الاربعة يضرب نصيبه منها في جميع ما كان في يد الجدة وهي تسعة فنقول قد كان لامرأة من مات ثانيا وهو زوج الميت الاول سهمان من الاثنين والثلثين فاذا ضربتهما فى الاربعة بلغ ثمانية فهي لها وكانت لابيه منها اربعة تضربها فى الاربعة يبلغ ستة عشر فهي له وكان لامه سهمان فاذا ضربتهما فى الاربعة صار ثمانية فهي لها وكانت لكل واحد من ابني من مات ثالثا وهي بنت الميت الاول ستة من العدد المذكور نضربها فى الاربعة يبلغ اربعة وعشرين فهي لكل واحد منهما وكانت لابنتها ثلثة من ذلك العدد فاذا ضربتها فى الاربعة يبلغ اثنى عشر فهي لها وكان لزوج من مات رابعا وهى الجدة المذكورة من الاربعة التي هي مسئلتها سهمان فاذا ضربتهما فى التسعة التي كانت في يدها تصير ثمانية عشر فهي له وكان لكل واحد من اخوتها من مسئلتها سهم واحد نضربه

فى التسعة فيكون تسعة فهي لكل واحد منهمـا *

شريفيــــــــــــــــــــــــة صفحه ١٣٣

الباب الحادي عشر في ذوي الارحام

٢١٦ وذو الرحم هو كل قريب ليس بذي سهم ولا عصبة كانت عامة الصحابة يرون توريث ذوى الارحام وبه قال اصحابنا وقال زيد ابن ثابت رض لا ميراث لذوى الارحام ويوضع المال في بيت المال وبه قال مالك والشافعي رح *

سراجيــــــــــــــــــــــة صفحه ١٣٧ و ١٣٨

٢١٧ وذو والارحام اصناف اربعة الصنف الاول ينتمي اي ينتسب الى الميت وهم اولاد البنات وان سفلوا ذكورا كانوا او اناثا واولاد بنات الابن كذلك والصنف الثانى ينتمى اليهم الميت وهم الاجداد الساقطون اي الفاسدون وان علوا كاب ام الميت واب اب امه والجدات الساقطات اى الفاسدات وان علون كام اب ام الميت وام ام اب امه والصنف الثالث ينتمي الى ابوى الميت وهم اولاد الاخوات وان سفلوا سواء كانت تلك الاولاد ذكورا او اناثا وسواء كانت الاخوات لاب وام اولاب اولام وبنات الاخوة وان سفلن سواء كانت

الاخوة من الابوين اومن احدهما وبنو الاخوة لام وان سفلوا * سراجية وشريفية صفحه ١٣٩

٢١٨ والصنف الرابع ينتمى الى جدى الميت وهما ب الاب واب الام اوجدتيه وهماام الاب وام الام وهم العمات على الاطلاق فانهن اخوات لاب الميت فان كن اخوات له من الابوين اومن الاب فهن منتمية الى جد الميت من قبل ابيه ان كن اخوات له من امه فهن منتمية الى جدته من قبل ابيه والاعمام لام فانهم اخوة لابيه من امه فهم ايضامنتمون الى جدة الميت من قبل ابيه واعتبر فى الاعمام كونهم لام لان العم من الابوين اومن الاب عصبة والاخوال والخالات فانهم اخوة واخوات لام الميت فان كانوامن ابيها وامها اومن ابيها فهم منتمون الى جد الميت من قبل امه وان كانوا من امها كانوا منتمين الى جدته من قبل امه * سراجية وشريفية صفحه ١٤٠

٢١٩ روى ابوسليمان عن محمد بن الحسن عن ابي حنيفة رحمهما الله ان اقرب الاصناف هوالصنف الثاني وان علوا ثم الاول وان سفلوا ثم الثالث وان نزلوا ثم الرابع وان بعدوا وروى ابويوسف والحسن بن زياد عن ابي حنيفة رح

وابن سماعة عن محمد بن الحسن عن ابي حنيفة رح ان اقرب الاصناف الصنف الاول ثم الثاني ثم الثالث ثم الرابع كترتيب العصبات وهو المأخوذ للفتوى *

سراجية صفحه ١٤١

فصل في الصنف الاول

٢٢٠ اولٰيهم بالميراث اقربهم الى الميت كبنت البنت فانها اولى من بنت بنت الابن * سراجية صفحه ١٤٣

٢٢١ وان استووا في الدرجة فولد الوارث اولى من ولد ذوي الارحام كبنت بنت الابن اولى من ابن بنت البنت * سراجية صفحه ١٤٥

٢٢٢ وان استوت درجاتهم ولم يكن فيهم ولد الوارث اوكان كلهم يدلون بوارث فعند ابي يوسف رح والحسن ابن زياد يعتبرابدان الفروع ويقسم المال عليهم سواء اتفقت صفة الاصول في الذكورة والانوثة او اختلفت ومحمد رح يعتبرابدان الفروع ان اتفقت صفة الاصول موافقا لهما ويعتبر الاصول ان اختلفت صفاتهم ويعطى الفروع ميراث الاصول مخالفا لهما *

سراجية صفحه ١٤٥

٢٢٣ كما اذا ترك الميت ابن بنت وبنت بنت عندهما اي عند
ابي يوسف رح والحسن يكون المال بينهما للذكر مثل
حظ الانثيين باعتبار الابدان اي ابدان الفروع وصفاتهم
فثلثا المال لابن البنت وثلثه لبنت البنت وعند محمد رح
يكون المال بينهما كذلك لان صفة الاصول متفقة في الانوثة
فتعتبر عنده ايضا ابدان الفروع ولو ترك بنت ابن بنت
وابن بنت بنت عندهما يقسم المال بين الفروع اثلاثا باعتبار
الابدان ثلثاه للذكر وثلثه للانثى كما في الصورة السابقة
وعند محمد رح يكون المال بين الاصول اعني في البطن الثاني
الذي هو اول ما وقع فيه الاختلاف بالذكورة والانوثة
وهو بنت البنت وابن البنت اثلاثا وحينئذ يكون ثلثاه لبنت
ابن البنت لان ذلك نصيب ابيها قد انتقل اليها وثلثه لابن
بنت البنت فانه نصيب امه * سراجيـــــة
وشريفيـــــة صفحه ١٤٦

٢٢٤ وهو القول الاول لابي يوسف رح واشهر الروايتين عن
ابي حنيفة رح والظاهر من مذهبه * شريفية صفحه ١٤٦

٢٢٥ واستدل محمد رح باتفاق الصحابة رض على ان
للعمة الثلثين وللخالة الثلث ولو كان الاعتبار بابدان

الفروع لكان المال بينهما نصفين فظهران المعتبر فى القسمة
هو المدلى به فانه الاب فى العمة والام فى الخالة وايضا قد
اتفقنا على انه اذا كان احدهما ولد وارث كان اولى من
الآخر فقد ترجح باعتبار معنى فى المدلى به *
شريفيـــــــــــــــــــــــــــة صفحه ١٤٦

٢٢٦ وكذلك عند محمد رح اذا كانت في اولاد البنات
بطون مختلفة يقسم المال على اول بطن اختلف فى الاصول
ثم يجعل الذكور طايفة والاناث طايفة اخرى بعد القسمة
فما اصاب الذكور يجمع ويقسم على اعلى الخلاف الذي
وقع في اولادهم وكذلك ما اصاب الاناث وهكذا يعمل
الى ان ينتهي * سراجيـــــــــــة صفحه ١٤٧ و ١٤٨

٢٢٧ هذه المسئلة مشتملة على اثنى عشر شخصا من ذوى
الارحام تسعة منها اناث وثلثة منها ذكور وكلهم في درجة
واحدة هي البطن السادس وليس فيهم ولد الوارث فهي
عند ابي يوسف رح ومن وافقه تصح من خمسة عشر لان
كل ابن بمنزلة بنتين فيصير المجموع كخمس عشر بنتا
فعدد رؤسهن تصحيح المسئلة على رائه فلكل واحدة من
البنات التسع سهم واحد ولكل من البنين الثلثة سهمان

واما عند محمد رح فانما تصح هذه المسئلة من ستين وذلک لانا اذا قسمنا المال علی البطن الاول المشتمل علی تسع بنات وثلثة بنين علی قياس ماذكرناه فی الفروع علی مذهب ابي يوسف رح اصابت البنين ستة اسهم والبنات تسعة فاذا جعلنا الذكور الثلثة طائفة وجمعنا مااصابهم اعنی الستة ونظرنا الی ماهواسفل من البطن الاول لم نجد فی البطن الثاني اختلافا بل وجدنا فی البطن الثالث بازاء البنين الثلثة ابناوبنتين فقسمنا الستة عليهم للذكر مثل حظ الانثيين فاصابت للابن ثلثة وللبنتين ثلثة ثم دفعنا نصيب الابن الی آخرفروعه لان البطون المتوسطة بينهما متفقة فی الانوثة وجعلنا البنتين طائفة علی حدة ونظرنا الی ماهواسفل من البطن الثالث فلم نجد فی البطن الرابع اختلافا بل وجدنا فی الخامس بازائهما ابناوبنتافقسمنا الثلثة عليهما للذكر مثل حظ الانثيين فاصاب الابن اثنان والبنت واحدثم دفعنا نصيب كل منهما الی فروعه فی البطن السادس وكذلک اذا جعلنا البنات التسع طائفة وجمعنا ما اصابهن وهوتسعة ونظرنا الی ماهواسفل من البطن الاول لم نجد اختلافا فی البطن الثاني بل فی البطن

الثالث حيث وجد نافيه بازائهن ست بنات وثلثة بنين فاذا
انزلنا كل ابن بمنزلة بنتين كان المجموع كاثنى عشر بنتا
فلا تستقيم عليهن التسعة التي كانت نصيب البنات لكن
بين التسعة وبين عدد رؤسهن اعني اثنى عشر موافقة بالثلث
فضربنا وفق عدد رؤسهن وهو اربعة في اصل المسئلة وهو
خسمة عشر فصار ستين ومنها تصح المسئلة اذ كانت لطائفة
البنتين فى البطن الاول ستة من اصل المسئلة فضربناها
فى المضروب الذي هو اربعة يبلغ اربعة وعشرين ونقسمها
على ما فى البطن الثالث من فروع البنين الثلثة فيعطي
الابن اثنى عشر والبنتين ايضا اثنى عشر ثم ندفع نصيب
الابن الى آخر فروعه من البطن السادس لعدم الاختلاف
ونقسم نصيب البنتين على الابن والبنت الذين بازائهما
فى البطن الخامس للذكر مثل حظ الانثيين فاصابت
الابن ثمانية والبنت اربعة فيدفع نصيب كل منهما الى
فرعه فى السادس وكانت لطائفة البنات فى البطن الاول
تسعة من المسئلة فنضربها في ذلك المضروب اعنى الاربعة
فتحصل ستة وثلثون فاذا نظرنا الى ماهو اسفل من البطن
الاول وجدنا اختلافا فى البطن الثالث اذ كان فيه بازاء

البنات التسع ست بنات وثلثة بنين فقسمنا نصيبهن اعنى
الستة و ثلثين للذكر مثل حظ الانثيين فاصابت البنتين
ثمانية عشر والبنات ثمانية عشر ثم جعلنا الذكور طائفة
والاناث طائفة ولما نظرنا الى ما هو اسفل من الثالث
وجدنا فى الرابع بازاء طائفة البنين ابنا وبنتين فقسمنا
عليهم ما اصاب البنين الثلثة للذكر مثل حظ الانثيين
فاصابت الابن تسعة والبنتين تسعة ثم دفعنا نصيب الابن
الى آخر فروعه لعدم الاختلاف ولم نجد بازاء البنتين
فى الخامس اختلافا بل فى السادس اذ كان فيه بازائهما
ابن وبنت فقسمنا عليهما نصيب البنتين اعنى التسعة
للذكر مثل حظ الانثيين فاصابت الابن ستة والبنت ثلثة
وكذلك وجدنا فى الرابع بازاء طائفة البنات الست
ثلث بنات وثلثة بنين فقسمنا عليهم ثمانية عشر للذكر مثل
حظ الانثيين فاعطينا البنين منها اثنى عشر والبنات ستة
ثم جعلناهما طائفتين ولما نظرنا الى ما هو اسفل من الرابع
وجدنا فى البطن الخامس بازاء البنين الثلثة ابنا وبنتين
فقسمنا نصيبهم الذي هو اثنى عشر للذكر مثل حظ الانثيين
فاصابت الابن ستة والبنتين ستة فدفعنا نصيب الابن الى

فرعه فى السادس وقد وقع فيه بازاء البنتين ابن وبنت فقسمنا نصيبهما عليهما فاصابت الابن اربعة والبنت اثنان ووجدنا فى الخامس ايضا بازاء البنات الثلث اللاتي فى البطن الرابع ابنا وبنتين فقسمنا نصيبهن اعنى الستة عليهم فاصابت الابن ثلثة والبنتين ثلثة فدفعنا نصيب الابن الى فرعه فى السادس ووجدنا فيه بازاء البنتين ابنا وبنتا فقسمنا الثلثة بينهما فاصاب الابن اثنان والبنت واحدا ذا جمعنا هذه الانصباء كلها كانت ستين كما رقمت بازاء الفروع فى البطن السادس * شريفيـــــة صفحه ١٤٨ و١٤٩ و١٥٠ و١٥١

٢٢٨ كذلك محمد رح يأخذ الصفة اى الذكورة والانوثة من الاصل حال القسمة عليه ويأخذ العدد من الفروع يعني انه اذا قسم المال على الاصل يعتبر فيه صفة الذكورة والانوثة التي فيه ويعتبر ايضا فيه عدد الفروع كما اذا ترك الميت ابني بنت بنت وبنت ابن بنت بنت وبنتي بنت ابن بنت بهذه الصـــــــورة

ميـــ

ابني بنت بنت بنت * بنت ابن بنت بنت * بنتي بنت ابن بنت *

عند ابي يوسف رح يقسم المال بين الفروع اسباعا باعتبار ابدانهم لان الابنين كاربع بنات ومعهما ثلث بنات اخرى فالمجموع كسبع بنات فلكل من البنات الثلث سهم واحد ولكل من الابنين سهمان وعند محمد رح يقسم المال على اعلى الخلاف اعني في البطن الثاني اسباعا باعتبار عدد الفروع في الاصول يعني انه يقسم المال على البطن الثاني وفيه ابن وبنتان لكنه يعتبر عدد فروع الابن وهو اثنان في الابن فيجعله كابنين ويعتبر عدد فروع البنت التي في فروعها تعدد فيها فيجعل هذه البنت كبنتين وعلى هذا يكون عدد المجموع في البطن الثاني سبعة لان الابن القائم مقام الابنين كاربع بنات وهناك بنت كبنتين وبنت اخرى هي واحدة فالجميع كسبع بنات فتكون للابن في هذا البطن اربعة اسباع المال وللبنت التي في فروعها تعدد سبعان منها وللبنت الاخرى سبع واحد ثم انه يجعل الذكور طائفة والاناث طائفة اخرى فعنده اربعة اسباعه اي اسباع المال لبنتي بنت ابن البنت اذ هي نصيب جدهما

وهوذلك الابن الذي نزل فى البطن الثاني منزلة ابنين
وعنده ايضا ثلثة اسباعه وهو نصيب البنتين اللتين نزلت
احدىهما منزلة بنتين في ذلك البطن يقسم على ولديهما اعني
فى البطن الثالث انصافا وذلك لان البنت التي فى الثالث
اذا اعتبر فيها عدد فرعها صارت كبنتين فتساوى الابن
الذي فى الثالث فيعطي كل واحد منهما نصف ثلثة الاسباع
وهوسبع ونصف سبع وحينئذ يكون نصفه اي نصف المقسوم
الذي هو ثلثة الاسباع لبنت ابن بنت البنت نصيب ابيها
وهو الابن الذي كان فى البطن الثالث والنصف الآخر
لابني بنت بنت البنت نصيب امهما وهو البنت التي
ساوت الابن فى البطن الثالث وتصح هذه المسئلة من
ثمانية وعشرين * سراجية وشريفية صفحه ١٤١ و١٤٢ و١٤٣

٢٢٩ علماء نارح يعتبرون الجهات فى التوريث غيران
ابا يوسف رح يعتبر الجهات في ابدان الفروع ومحمد رح
يعتبر الجهات فى الاصول كما اذا ترك بنتي بنت
بنت وهما ايضا بنتا ابن بنت وابن بنت بنت *
سراجية صفحه ١٥٤ و١٥٥

٢٣٠ عند ابي يوسف رح يكون المال بينهم اي بين الابن والبنتين

اثلاثا لان البنتين ذواتا جهتين فكانهما بنتان من جهة الام وبنتان اخريان من جهة الاب و حينئذ صار الميت كانه ترک اربع بنات وابنا واحدا فيكون ثلثاه اي ثلثا المال للبنتين ذواتي الجهتين وثلثه للابن ذي الجهة الواحدة *
سراجية وشريفيــــــــــــــة صفحه ١٥٥ و ١٥٦

٢٣١ وعند محمد رح يقسم المال بينهم على ثمانية وعشرين سهما للبنتين اثنان وعشرون سهما ستة عشر سهما من قبل ابيهما وستة اسهم من قبل امهما وللابن ستة اسهم من قبل امه

بيان ذلک انه يقسم عنده المال على البطن الثاني وفيه ابن مثل ابنين وبنتان احدهما كبنتين فصار المجموع كسبع بنات فالمسئلة من عدد رؤسهن فللابن اربعة اسهم وللبنت التي في فرعها تعدد سهمان وللاخرى سهم واحد فاذا جعلنا الذكور طائفة في هذا البطن والاناث طائفة ودفعنا نصيب الابن الى البنتين اللتين فى البطن الثالث اصاب كل واحدة منهما سهمان واذا دفعنا نصيب طائفة الاناث الى من بازائهن فى البطن الثالث لم يستقم عليهم ولان نصيبهن ثلثة اسباع ومن بازائهن ابن وبنتان فالمجموع كاربع بنات وبين الثلثة والاربعة مباينة فضربنا الاربعة التي

هي عدد الرؤس في اصل المسئلة وهوسبعة صار ثمانية
وعشرين منها تصح المسئلة اذا كانت لابن البنت
فى البطن الثاني اربعة فاذا ضربناها فى المضروب الذي
هو اربعة ايضا بلغ ستة عشر فاعطينا كل واحدة من بنتيه
ثمانية وكانت للبنتين فى البطن الثاني ثلثة فاذا ضربناها
في ذلك المضروب حصل اثنى عشر فدفعنا الى ابن بنت
البنت ستة والى بنتي بنت البنت ستة فلكل واحدة
منهما ثلثة فصار نصيب كل بنت فى البطن الاخير احد
عشر ثمانية من جهة ابيها وثلثة من جهة امها * سراجية
وشريفية ——————— صفحه ١٥٦

فصل فى الصنف الثاني

٢٣٢ اولٰهم بالميراث اقربهم الى الميت من اي جهة
كان * سراجية ——————— صفحه ١٥٧

٢٣٣ فاب الام اولى من اب ام الام وكذا اب ام الاب
اولى من اب ام ام الاب واب الام اولى من اب ام
الاب وقس على ذلك حال الجدات * شريفية صفحه ١٥٧

٢٣٤ وعند الاستواء فمن كان يدلي بوارث فهو اولى عند

ابى سهيل الفرائضي وابي فضل الخفاف وعلى ابن عيسى البصري * سراجية صفحه ١٤٧

٢٣٥ فعندهم يكون اب ام الام اولى من اب اب الام لانهما تساويا فى الدرجة لكن الاول يدلى بوارث هو الجدة الصحيحة اعني ام الام والثاني يدلى بغير وارث هو جد فاسدا عني اب الام الذي لايرث مع ام الام فكانت ام الام اقوى فابوها اولى * شريفية صفحه ١٤٧

---

٢٣٦ ولا تفضيل له عند ابي سليمان الجرجاني وابي على البستي ففى الصورة المذكورة يقسم المال عندهما اثلاثا ثلثاه لاب الام وثلثه لاب ام الام * سراجية وشريفية صفحه ١٤٧

٢٣٧ وان استوت منازلهم وليس فيهم من يدلى بوارث اوكان كلهم يدلون بوارث واتفقت صفة من يدلون بهم واتحدت قرابتهم فالقسمة حينئذ على ابدانهم وان اختلفت صفة من يدلون بهم يقسم المال على اول بطن اختلف كما فى الصنف الاول وان اختلفت قرابتهم فالثلثان لقرابة الاب وهو نصيب الاب والثلث لقرابة الام وهو نصيب الام ثم ما اصاب لكل فريق يقسم بينهم كما لو اتحدت قرابتهم * سراجية صفحه ١٤٨ و ١٤٩

فصل فى الصنف الثالث

٢٣٨ الحكم فيهم كالحكم فى الصنف الاول اعني اولٰهم بالميراث اقربهم الى الميت وان استووا فى القرب فولد العصبة اولى من ولد ذوى الارحام كبنت ابن الاخ وابن بنت الاخت كلاهما لاب وام اولاب اواحد هما لاب وام والآخر لاب المال كله لبنت ابن الاخ لانها ولد العصبة * سراجيـــــــــــة صفحه ١٥٩

٢٣٩ ولو كانا اي بنت ابن الاخ وابن بنت الاخت لام كان

المال بينهما للذكر مثل حظ الانثيين عند ابي يوسف رح باعتبار الابدان فان الاصل فى المواريث تفضيل الذكر على الانثى وانما ترك هذا الاصل فى الاخوة والاخوات لام بالنص على خلاف القياس اعني قوله تعالى فهم شركاء فى الثلث وما كان مخصوصا من القياس لا يلحق به ماليس في معناه من جميع الوجوه وليس اولاد هؤلاء في معناهم من كل وجه اذلا يرثون بالفرضية شيئا فيجري فيهم ذلك الاصل وايضا توريث ذوى الارحام بمعنى العصوبة فيفضل فيه الذكر على الانثى كما في حقيقة العصوبة

وعند محمد رح المال بينهما انصافا باعتبار الاصول وهو ظاهر الرواية والوجه فيه ان استحقاقهما للميراث بقرابة الام وباعتبار هذه القرابة لا تفضيل للذكر على الانثى اصلا بل ربما تفضل الانثى عليه الا ترى ان ام الام صاحبة فرض بخلاف اب الام فان لم تفضل الانثى ههنا فلا اقل من التساوي اعتبارا بالمدلي به * سراجيـــــــــة وشريفيـــــــــــــــــــة صفحه ۱٦۰

۲۴۰ وان استووا في القرب وليس فيهم ولد عصبة او كان كلهم اولاد العصبات او كان بعضهم اولاد العصبات وبعضهم اولاد اصحاب الفرائض فابو يوسف رح يعتبر الاقوى في القرابة فعنده من كان اصله اخا لاب وام اولى ممن كان اصله اخا لاب فقط اولام فقط * سراجية وشريفية صفحه ۱٦۱

۲۴۱ ومحمد رح يقسم المال على الاخوة والاخوات مع اعتبار عدد الفروع والجهات في الاصول فما اصاب كل فريق يقسم بين فروعهم كما في الصنف الاول كما اذا ترك ثلثة بنات اخوة متفرقين وثلثة بنين وثلث بنات اخوات متفرقات بهذه الصـــــــــورة

مي

بنت الاخ لاب وام　　بنت الاخ لاب　　بنت الاخ لام
ابن الاخت　　ابن الاخت　　ابن الاخت
بنت　　بنت　　بنت

عند ابي يوسف رح يقسم كل المال بين فروع بني الاعيان ثم بين فروع بني العلات ثم بين فروع بني الاخياف للذكر مثل حظ الانثيين ارباعا باعتبار الابدان * سراجية صفحه ١٦١ و ١٦٢

٢٤٢ عند محمد رح يقسم ثلث المال بين فروع بني الاخياف على السوية اثلاثا لاستواء اصولهم في القسمة فاذا اعتبر عدد الفروع في الاخت لام صارت كانها اختان لام فتأخذ هي ثلثي ثلث المال ويأخذ الاخ لام ثلثه ثم ينتقل نصيبهما الى فروعهما والباقي وهو ثلث المال بين فروع بني الاعيان انصافا لاعتبار عدد الفروع في الاصول فتصير بهذا الاعتبار الاخت لاب وام كاختين من الابوين فتساوي اخاها في النصيب وحينئذ يكون نصفه اي نصف الباقي وهو الثلث لبنت الاخ نصيب ابيها والنصف الآخر من ذلك الباقي بين ولدي الاخت لاب وام للذكر مثل حظ الانثيين

باعتبار الابدان اي ابدان الفروع لعدم الاختلاف في اصول هذين الفرعين ولا شيء لفروع بني العلات لانهم محجوبون ببني الاعيان كما سبق وتصح هذه المسئلة عند محمد رح من تسعة لان اصل المسئلة من ثلثة واحد منها لبني الاخياف الثلثة ولا يستقيم عليهم واثنان لبني الاعيان واحد منهما لبنت الاخ لاب وام وواحد لابن الاخت منهما مع بنت الاخت منهما وهما كثلث بنات لان الابن كبنتين ولا يستقيم الواحد علي الثلث لكن بين رؤس بني الاخياف ورؤس بني الاعيان مماثلة فضربنا احد الثلثين في اصل المسئلة وهو ثلثة ايضا فصارت تسعة فتصح منها المسئلة كان لبني الاخياف من اصل المسئلة واحد ضربناه في الثلثة فكان ثلثة فلكل واحد منهم واحد وكان لبني الاعيان من اصلها اثنان ضربناهما في الثلثة فحصلت ستة دفعنا منها ثلثة الى بنت الاخ واثنين الى ابن الاخت وواحدا الى بنت الاخت * سراجية وشريفيـــــــــــــــــة صفحه ١٦٢ و ١٦٣

٢٤٣ ولو ترك ثلث بنات بني اخوة متفرقين بهذه الصورة

بنت ابن الاخ لاب وام	بنت ابن الاخ لاب	بنت ابن الاخ لام

المال كله لبنت ابن الاخ لاب وام بالاتفاق لانها ولد العصبة ولها ايضا قوة القرابة * سراجيــــــة صفحه ۱۶۳ و ۱۶۴

۲۴۴ وقد زاد بعض الشارحين ههنا مسئلة لاعتبار الجهات وعدد الفروع في الاصول فقال ولوترک ابن بنت اخ لاب وبنتي ابن اخت لاب وهما ايضا بنتا بنت اخت لاب وام وترک ايضا بنت ابن اخت لام بهذه الصورة

اخ لاب	اخت لاب	اخت لاب وام	اخت لام
بنت	ابن	بنت	ابن
ابن		بنتي	بنت

عند ابي يوسف رح المال كله لبنتي بنت الاخت لاب وام لقوة القرابة وعند محمد رح يقسم المال على الاصول التي هي الاخوة والاخوات وتعتبر فيهم الجهات وعدد الفروع فما اصاب كل فريق منهم يقسم على فروعهم فاصل المسئلة عنده من ستة لوجود السدس فيها واحدمنها وهوسدسها للاخت لام واربعة وهي ثلثاها للاخت لاب وام لانا نعتبر فيها

عدد بنتي بنتها فهي كاختين لاب وام فلها الثلثان والباقي منها وهو واحد للاخ والاخت لاب للذكر مثل حظ الانثيين بطريق العصوبة واذا اعتبرنا عدد بنتي ابن الاخت لاب فيها كانت كاختين لاب فالواحد الباقي يكون بينهما وبين الاخ لاب نصفين فاذا ضربنا مخرج النصف وهو الاثنان في اصل المسئلة وهو ستة صار الحاصل اثني عشر كانت للاخت لاب وام من اصل المسئلة اربعة وقد ضربناها في المضروب اعني اثنين بلغ ثمانية اعطيناها بنتي بنتها وكان للاخت لام من اصل المسئلة واحدة ضربناه في ذلك المضروب فكان اثنين فاعطيناهما بنت ابنها وكان للاخ والاخت لاب من اصلها واحد ايضا فضربناه في ذلك المضروب فصار اثنين فقسمناهما بين الاخ والاخت لاب انصافا كما عرفته فلكل واحد منهما واحد فدفعنا نصيب الاخ لاب وهو واحد الى ابن بنته ودفعنا نصيب الاخت لاب وهو واحد ايضا الى بنتي ابنها فلا يستقيم عليهما فاذا ضربنا عددهما في اصل المسئلة وهو اثني عشر صار اربعة وعشرين فمنها تصح المسئلة اذ كانت لبنتي بنت الاخت من الابوين ثمانية من اثني عشر فضربناها في المضروب الذي هو اثنان

فصار ستة عشر فهي لهما وكان لبنت ابن الاخت لام اثنان منها ضربناهما في ذلک المضروب صار اربعة فدفعناها اليها وكان لابن بنت الاخ لاب واحد منها فضربناه في ذلک المضروب فصار اثنين فهماله وكان لبنتي ابن الاخت لاب واحد منها ضربناه في الاثنين فلم يتغير فدفعنا هما اليهما فصار نصيب البنتين من جهتين ثمانية عشر فلكل واحد منهما تسعة *

شريفيـــــــــــــــــــــة صفحه ١٦٤ و ١٦٥

فصل فى الصنف الرابع

٢٣٥ الذي ينتمي الى جدى الميت اوجدتيه وهم العمات على الاطلاق والاعمام لام والاخوال والخالات مطلقا *

شريفيـــــــــــــــــــــة صفحه ١٦٥

٢٣٦ واذا اجتمعوا وكان حيز قرابتهم متحدا كالعمات والاعمام لام اوالاخوال والخالات فالاقوى منهم اولى بالاجماع اعني من كان لاب وام اولى ممن كان لاب ومن كان لاب اولى ممن كان لام ذكورا كانوا او اناثا وان كانوا ذكورا او اناثا واستوت قرابتهم فللذكر مثل حظ الانثيين كعم وعمة كلاهما لام اوخال وخالة كلاهما لاب وام اولاب اولام وان كان

حيز قرابتهم مختلفا فلا اعتبار لقوة القرابة كعمة لاب وام وخالة لام او خالة لاب وام وعمة لام فالثلثان لقرابة الاب وهو نصيب الاب والثلث لقرابة الام وهو نصيب الام ثم ما اصاب كل فريق يقسم بينهم كما لو اتحد حيز قرابتهم* سراجيــــــــــــة صفحه ١٦٦ و ١٦٧

فصل في اولادهم

الحكم فيهم كالحكم فى الصنف الاول اعنى اولٰيهم بالميراث اقربهم الى الميت من اي جهة كان وان استووا فى القرب وكان حيز قرابتهم متحدا فمن كانت له قوة القرابة فهو اولى بالاجماع وان استووا فى القرب والقرابة فولد العصبة اولى كبنت العم وابن العمة كلاهما لاب وام اولاب المال كله لبنت العم لانها ولد العصبة وان كان احدهما لاب وام والآخر لاب المال كله لمن كانت له قوة القرابة في ظاهر الرواية قياسا على خالة لاب مع كونها ولد ذى الرحم وهي اولى لقوة القرابة من الخالة لام مع كونها ولد الوارث لان الترجيح بمعني فيه وهو قوة القرابة اولى من الترجيح بمعني في غيره وهو الادلاء بالوارث وقال بعضهم رح

المال كله لبنت العم لاب لانها ولد العصبة *
سراجيــــــــــــة صفحه ١٦٨ و ١٦٩ و ١٧٠ و ١٧١

٢٤٨ وان استووا في القرب ولكن اختلف حيز قرابتهم
لا اعتبار لقوة القرابة ولا لولد العصبة في ظاهر الرواية قياسا
على عمة لاب وام مع كونها ذات القرابتين وولد
الوارث من الجهتين ليست هي باولى من الخالة لاب
لكن الثلثين لمن يدلي بقرابة الاب فتعتبر فيهم قوة القرابة
ثم ولد العصبة والثلث لمن يدلي بقرابة الام وتعتبر فيهم
قوة القرابة ثم عند ابي يوسف رح ما اصاب لكل
فريق يقسم على ابدان فروعهم مع اعتبار عدد الجهات
في الفروع وعند محمد رح يقسم المال على اول بطن
اختلف مع اعتبار عدد الفروع والجهات في الاصول
كما في الصنف الاول * سراجية صفحه ١٧٢ و ١٧٣ و ١٧٤

٢٤٩ فاذا فرضنا انه ترك ابني بنت عمة لاب وبنتي ابن
عمة لاب هما ايضا بنتا بنت عم لاب وترك مع ذلك
بنتي بنت خالة لاب وابني ابن خالة لاب هما ايضا ابنا
بنت خال لاب بهذه الصـــــــــــــــورة

مي

عمة لاب	عمة لاب	عم لاب	خالة لاب	خالة لاب	خال لاب
بنت	ابن	بنت	بنت	ابن	بنت
ابني		بنتي		بنتي	ابني

فاصل المسئلة ههنا من ثلثة ثلثاها وهما اثنان منها لقرابة الاب وثلثها وهو واحد لقرابة الام لكن عند ابي يوسف رح تصح هذه المسئلة من ثلثين وذلک لان ما اصاب فريق الاب وهو اثنان واعدادهم اذا اعتبر عدد الجهات في الفروع اربعة لان البنتين في هذا الفريق كاربع بنات بنتان من جهة ابن العمة لاب وبنتان من جهة بنت العم لاب لكنا نختصر عدد الرؤس فنجعل هذه البنات الاربع كابنين فهذا الفريق اربعة ابناء ولا استقامة لما اصابهم اعني لاثنين على الاربعة بل هما متوافقان بالنصف فيرد عدد الرؤس الى نصفه وهو اثنان وما اصاب فريق الام واحد واعدادهم اذا اعتبر عدد الجهات في الفروع خمسة لانا نحسب الابنين في هذا الفريق اربعة ابناء ابنان من قبل ابن الخالة لاب وابنان من قبل بنت الخال لاب ونحسب للاختصار البنتين فيهم ابنا واحدا فهذا الفريق خمسة

ابناء ولا استقامة للواحد على الخمسة بل بينهما مباينة
فتركنا الخمسة بحالها ثم نظرنا الى الاثنين الذين هو وفق
رؤس فريق الاب والى هذه الخمسة فوجدناهما متباينين
فضربنا احدهما فى الآخر فصار عشرة فضربناها في اصل
المسئلة الذي هو ثلثة صارت ثلثين ومنها تصح المسئلة
ثلثاها اعني عشرين لفريق الاب عشرة منها لابني بنت
العمة لاب وعشرة للبنتين وثلثها اعني عشرة لفريق الام
ثمانية منها للابنين واثنان للبنتين * شريفية صفحه ١٧٤
٢٤٥ وعند محمد رحمه الله تعالى تصح هذه المسئلة من ستة
وثلثين ...... ومنها تصح المسئلة كانت لفريق الاب اربعة
من اصل المسئلة وقد ضربت في المضروب الذي هو ستة
فصارت اربعة وعشرين فهي نصيب هذا الفريق من الستة
والثلثين واما نصيب احادهم منها فنقول قد ضرب نصيب
بنتي بنت العم لاب من جهة العم وهو اثنان في ذلك
المضروب صار اثنى عشر فلكل واحد منهما ستة وضرب
ايضا نصيبهما من العمة وهو الواحد فى المضروب المذكور
فكان ستة فلكل واحد منهما ثلثة فقد حصلت لكل واحد
منهما تسعة اسهم ستة من جهة العم وثلثة من جهة العمة

وضرب ايضا نصيب ابني بنت العمة وهو واحد في ذٰلك المضروب فكان ستة فلكل واحد منهما ثلٰثة ومجموع هٰذه الانصباء اربعة وعشرون وكان لفريق الام من اصل المسئلة اثنان فاذا ضربناهما في المضروب الذي هو الستة بلغ اثنى عشر فهي نصيب هٰذا الفريق من الستة وثلٰثين واما نصيب احادهم فنقول اذا ضرب نصيب ابني بنت الخال وهو واحد في المضروب اعنى الستة كان ستة فلكل واحد منهما ثلٰثة واذا ضرب نصيب فروع الخالتين وهو واحد ايضا في ذٰلك المضروب كان ستة فلابني ابن الخالة اربعة من تلك الستة فلكل واحد منهما اثنان فقد حصلت لكل من الابنين خمسة ثلٰثة من جهة الخال واثنان من جهة الخالة ولبنتي بنت الخالة اثنان منها لكل واحدة منهما واحد وللابنين عشرة وللبنتين اثنان وجميع هذه الانصباء اثنى عشر فاذا انضمت الى الاربعة والعشرين كان المجموع ستة وثلٰثين * شريفية صفحه ١٧٥

الباب الثاني عشر في الحمل والمفقود والاسير والغرقي والحرقي والهدمي

٢٤١ اكثر مدة الحمل سنتان عند ابي حنيفة رح واصحابه رح وعند ليث بن سعد الفهمي ثلثة سنين وعند الشافعي رح اربع سنين وعند الزهري رح سبع سنين .... واقلها ستة اشهر بالاتفاق * سراجية وشريفية صفحه ١٨٦ و ١٨٧

٢٤٢ وللشافعي رح ما روي ان الضحاک ولد لاربع سنين وقد نبت ثناياه وهو يضحک فيسمى ضحاكا وان عبد العزيز الماجشوني ايضا ولد لاربع سنين وقد اشتهر في نساء ماجشون انهن يلدن كذلک وروي ان رجلا غاب عن امرأته سنتين ثم قدم وهي حامل فهم عمر رض ان يرجمها فقال له معاذ وان كان لک سبيل عليها فلا سبيل لک على ما في بطنها فتركها حتى ولدت ولدا وقد نبت ثناياه وشبه اباه فقال الرجل هذا ابني ورب الكعبة فاثبت عمر رض نسبه منه مع انه ولد لاكثر من سنتين وقال لولا معاذ لهلک عمر والجواب عن الاول ان الضحاک وعبد العزيز ما كانا يعرفان ذلک من انفسهما ولا عرفه غيرهما اذ لا اطلاع

لاحد علی ما فی الرحم سوی الله سبحانه تعالیٰ و یجوز
ان یکون ذٰلک لانسداد فم الرحم لمرض علی سبیل
الندرة فلا اعتداد به و من الثاني ان المراد غیبته عنها
قریبا من سنتین و اثبات النسب کان باقرار الزوج *
شریفیــــــــــة صفحه ۱۸۷

۲۵۳ لنا حدیث عایشة رض فانها قالت لایبقی الولد في رحم
امه اکثر من سنتین ولو بفلکة مغزل و مثل هذا لایعرف
قیاسا بل سماعا من رسول الله صلعم * شریفیة صفحه ۱۸۷

۲۵۴ فان کان الحمل من المیت وجاءت بالولد لتمام اکثر مدة
الحمل او اقل منها ولم تکن اقرت بانقضاء العدة یرث
ویورث عنه وان جاءت بالولد لاکثر من اکثر مدة الحمل
لا یرث ولا یورث عنه وان کان الحمل من غیره وجاءت
بالولد لستة اشهر او اقل یرث وان جاءت بالولد لاکثر من
اقل مدة الحمل لا یرث * سراجیـــــة صفحه ۱۹۰

۲۵۵ اذا لم یتیقن علوقه حینئذ ولا ضرورة ههنا الی تقدیر
وجوده في زمان الموت بخلاف ما اذا کان الحمل منه فان
العلوق هناک یستند الی اکثر اوقات الحمل لضرورة
اثبات نسبه من المیت بعد ارتفاع النکاح بالموت اما اذا کان

الحمل من غيره فنسبه ثابت من ذلك الغير فلا ضرورة
ههنا الى اعتبار اكثر الاوقات بل يجب الاقتصار على
ما هو اقل مدة الحمل وما دونه حتى يتيقن بوجوده
حال الموت * شريفية صفحه ١٩١

٢٥٦ وطريق معرفة حيوة الحمل وقت الولادة ان يوجد منه
ما يعلم به الحيوة كصوت او عطاس او بكاء او ضحك
او تحريك عضو * شريفية صفحه ١٩١

٢٥٧ فان خرج اقل الولد ثم مات لا يرث وان خرج اكثره
ثم مات يرث فان خرج الولد مستقيما فالمعتبر صدره وان
خرج منكوسا فالمعتبر سرته * سراجية صفحه ١٩١

٢٥٨ ويوقف للحمل عند ابي حنيفة رح نصيب اربعة بنين
او اربع بنات ايهما اكثر وتعطي لبقية الورثة اقل الانصباء
وعند محمد رح يوقف نصيب ثلثة بنين او ثلثة بنات ايهما
اكثر رواه عنه ليث بن سعد رح وفي رواية اخرى
نصيب ابنين وهو قول الحسن رح واحدى الروايتين
عن ابي يوسف رح رواه عنه هشام رح وروى الخصاف رح
عن ابي يوسف رح انه يوقف نصيب ابن واحد وبنت
واحدة وعليه الفتوى ويوخذ الكفيل على قوله *

سراجيــــــــــــــة صفحه ١٨٨ و ١٨٩

٢٥٩ الاصل في تصحيح مسائل الحمل ان تصحح المسئلة على تقديرين اعني على تقديران الحمل ذكر و على تقدير انه انثى ثم تنظر بين تصحيح المسئلتين فان توافقا بجزء فاضرب وفق احدهما في جميع الآخر وان تباينتا فاضرب كل احدهما في جميع الآخر فالحاصل تصحيح المسئلة *

سراجية وشريفيــــــــــــة صفحه ١٩١

٢٦٠ ثم اضرب نصيب من كان له شيء من مسئلة ذكورته في مسئلة انوثته على تقدير التباين او في وفقها على تقدير التوافق و اضرب ايضا نصيب من كان له شيء من مسئلة انوثته في مسئلة ذكورته او في وفقها على ذينك التقديرين *

سراجية وشريفيــــــــــــة صفحه ١٩٢

٢٦١ ثم انظر في الحاصلين من الضرب ايهما اقل يعطى لذلك الوارث والفضل الذي بينهما موقوف من نصيب ذلك الوارث * سراجيــــــــــة صفحه ١٩٢

٢٦٢ كما اذا ترك بنتا وابوين و امراة حاملا فالمسئلة من اربعة وعشرين على تقديران الحمل ذكر لانه اجتمع فيها حينئذ ثمن وسدسان ومابقي فللزوجة ثمنها وهو ثلثة ولكل واحد من الابوين

السدس وهو اربعة وللبنت مع الحمل الذكر الباقي وهو
ثلثة عشر والمسئلة من سبعة وعشرين على تقديرانه انثى لانه
اجتمع فيها على هذا التقدير ثمن وسدسان وثلثان فهي
منبرية وتعول من اربعة وعشرين الى سبعة وعشرين
فللابوين ثمانية وللمرأة ثلثة وللبنت مع الحمل الانثى
ستة عشر وبين عددي تصحيح المسئلتين اعني اربعة
وعشرين وسبعة وعشرين توافق بالثلث لان مخرجه
وهو ثلثة يعدهما معا فاذا ضرب وفق احدهما اي ثلثة وهو
ثمانية من الاول وتسعة من الثاني في جميع الآخر صار
الحاصل مايتين وستة عشر سهما ومنها تصح المسئلة اذ على
تقدير ذكورته للمرأة سبعة وعشرون ولكل واحد من الابوين ستة
وثلثون وذلك لان سهام المرأة من مسئلة الذكورة
اعني اربعة وعشرين ثلثة كما عرفت فاذا ضربت في وفق
مسئلة الانوثة وهي تسعة بلغ سبعة وعشرين وسهام كل
من الابوين من مسئلة الذكورة اربعة فاذا ضربناها
في ذلك الوفق بلغ ستة وثلثين وعلى تقدير انوثته للمرأة
اربعة وعشرون لان سهامها من مسئلة الانوثة اعني سبعة
وعشرين ثلثة ايضا فاذا ضربت في وفق مسئلة الذكورة

وهوثمانية صار اربعة وعشرين ولكل واحد من الابوين اثنان
وثلثون لان سهام كل منهما من مسئلة الانوثة اربعة ايضا
فاذا ضربناها في وفق مسئلة الذكورة وهوثمانية صار اثنين
وثلثين فتعطي للمراة من مايتين وستة عشر اربعة وعشرون
لانها اقل نصيبها على تقديري ذكورة الحمل وانوثته
وتوقف من نصيبها ثلثة اسهم وهي الفضل بين النصيبين الى
ان تنكشف حال الحمل وتوقف من نصيب كل واحد من
الابوين اربعة اسهم اي يعطي من المبلغ المذكور كل منهما
اقل النصيبين وهواثنان وثلثون ويوقف الفضل الذي
بينهما فقد جعل الحمل في حق الزوجة والابوين انثى *
سراجية وشريفية صفحه ١٩٣

٢٦٣ وتعطي للبنت ثلثة عشر سهما لان الموقوف في حقها
نصيب اربعة بنين عند ابي حنيفة رح واذا كان البنون
اربعة فنصيبها سهم واربعة اتساع سهم من اربعة وعشرين
مضروب في تسعة فصار ثلثة عشر سهما فهي انها *
سراجية صفحه ١٩٤

٢٦٤ فان ولدت بنتا واحدة او اكثر فجميع الموقوف للبنات
وان ولدت ابنا واحدا او اكثر فيعطي للمرأة وللابوين

ما كان موقوفا من نصيبهم فما بقي يقسم بين الاولاد
وان ولدت ميتا فيعطي للمرأة والابوين ما كان موقوفا
من نصيبهم وللبنت الى تمام النصف وهو خمسة وتسعون
سهما والباقي للاب وهو تسعة اسهم لانه عصبة *
سراجيـــــــــــــة صفحه ١٩٤

٢٦٥ واعلم ان الميت اذا ترك من لا يتغير فرضه بالحمل
فانه يعطي فرضه كما اذا ترك جدة وامرأة حاملا فانه
يعطي الجدة السدس وكذا اذا ترك امرأة حاملا وابنا
فللمرأة الثمن * شريفيـــــــــــة صفحه ١٩٦

٢٦٦ وان الوارث اذا كان ممن يسقط في احدى حالتى
الحمل فانه لا يعطي شيئا لان اصل استحقاقه مشكوك ولا
توريث مع الشك كما اذا ترك امرأة حاملا واخا وعما
فلاشيء للاخ او العم لجواز ان يكون الحمل ابنا فما قررناه سابقا
انما هو فيمن يتغير فرضه من الورثة * شريفية صفحه ١٩٦

فصل فى المفقود

٢٦٧ وهو الغائب الذي انقطع خبره ولا تدرى حيوته
ولا موته * شريفيـــــــــــة صفحه ١٩٦

٢٦٨ ويوقف ماله حتى تصح موته او تمضي عليه مدة واختلفت الروايات في تلك المدة ففي ظاهر الرواية انه اذالم يبق احد من اقرانه حكم بموته * سراجية صفحه ١٩٧

٢٦٩ وروى الحسن ابن زياد عن ابي حنيفة رح ان تلك المدة مائة وعشرون سنة من يوم ولد فيه وقال محمد رح مائة وعشر سنين وقال ابويوسف رح مائة وخمس سنين * سراجية صفحه ١٩٧

٢٧٠ وهاتان الروايتان لم توجدا في الكتب المعتبرة * شريفية صفحه ١٩٧

٢٧١ وقال بعضهم تسعون سنة لان الزيادة عليها في زماننا غاية الندرة فلا تناط بها الاحكام الشرعية التي مدارها على الاغلب قال الامام التمرتاشي رح وعليه الفتوى * سراجية وشريفية صفحه ١٩٧

٢٧٢ واذاتم له مائة وعشرون سنة من يوم ولد حكمنا بموته قال علي رض وهذه رواية الحسن عن ابي حنيفة رح وفي ظاهر المذهب يقدر بموت الاقران وفي المروي عن ابي يوسف رح بمائة سنة وقدره بعضهم بتسعين والاقيس ان لايقدر بشيء والارفق ان يقدر بتسعين واذا حكم

بموته اعتدت امرأته عدة الوفاة من ذلك الوقت *
الهـــــــــــــــداية صفحه ٣٦١

٢٧٣ لا يفرق بينه وبين امرأته وحكم بموته بمضي تسعين
سنة وعليه الفتوى وفي ظاهر الرواية يقدر بموت اقرانه
فاذا لم يبق احد من اقرانه حيا حكم بموته ويعتبر موت
اقرانه في اهل بلده كذا في الكافي والمختار انه يفوض الى
رأى الامام كذا في التبيين * فتاوى عالمگبريـــة
في المجلـــــــــــد الثاني و صفحه ٤٠٥

٢٧٤ فقيل المعتبر اقرانه في بلده وقيل جميع البلدان والاولى
الاصح كما ذكر في فرائض الامام التمرتاشي رح ان يعتبر
اقرانه في بلده لان الاعمار مما تتفاوت باختلاف الاقاليم
والبلدان وايضا اعتبار جميع الاقران فيه حرج عظيم *
شريفيـــــــــــــــــة صفحه ١٩٧

---

٢٧٥ وقال بعضهم مال المفقود موقوف الى اجتهاد الامام
في موته وهو مذهب الشافعي رح فانه قال اذا مضت
مدة يقضي القاضي بان مثله لا يعيش اكثر من هذه المدة
حكم بموته ويقسم ماله على ورثته الموجودين حال
الحكم به * سراجية وشريفيـــــــة صفحه ١٩٧

٢٧٦ المفقود حي في ماله حتى لا يرث منه احد وميت في مال غيره حتى لا يرث من احد لثبوت حيوته باستصحاب الحال وهو معتبر في ابقاء ما كان على ما كان دون اثبات مالم يكن ولهذا لا يثبت استحقاق ورثته لماله * سراجية وشريفيـــــــــة صفحه ١٩٦

٢٧٧ وموقوف الحكم في حق غيره حتى يوقف نصيبه من مال مورثه كما في الحمل * سراجية صفحه ١٩٨

٢٧٨ فاذا مضت المدة فماله لورثته الموجودين عند الحكم بموته وما كان موقوفا لاجله يرد الى وارث مورثه الذي وقف من ماله * سراجيـــــــــة صفحه ١٩٨

٢٧٩ الاصل في تصحيح مسائل المفقود ان تصحح المسئلة على تقدير حيوته ثم تصحح على تقدير وفاته وباقي العمل ماذكرنا في الحمل * سراجيـــــــــة صفحه ١٩٨

٢٨٠ فاذا تركت مثلا زوجا حاضرا واختين لاب وام حاضرتين واخا لاب وام مفقودا فعلى تقدير كون المفقود ميتا يكون للزوج النصف وللاختين الثلثان فالمسئلة من ستة لكنها تعول الى سبعة وعلى تقدير كونه حيا للزوج النصف غير عائل وللاختين الربع لان اصل المسئلة

على هذا التقدير اثنان واحد للزوج وواحد للاخ مع الاختين فلا يستقيم عليهم وهم كاربع اخوات فتضرب الاربعة في اصل المسئلة فبلغ ثمانية اربعة منها للزوج واثنان للاخ واثنان آخران للاختين لكل واحدة واحد فموت المفقود خير للاختين من حيوته وهو ظاهر وحيوته خير للزوج اذ له حينئذ نصف من المال بلا عول فتعتبر حيوة المفقود في حق الاختين فلا يصرف اليهما الا ربع المال ويعتبر موته في حق الزوج فلا يعطي الا ثلثة اسباع المال ويوقف الباقي وهذه المسئلة تصح من ستة وخمسين لان مسئلة الحيوة من ثمانية ومسئلة الوفات من سبعة وبينهما مباينة فتضرب احدهما في الاخرى فيبلغ ستة وخمسين كان للزوج من مسئلة الحيوة اربعة فاذا ضربت في مسئلة الوفات وهي سبعة حصلت ثمانية وعشرون وكانت له من مسئلة الموت ثلثة فاذا ضربت في مسئلة الحيوة وهي ثمانية بلغت اربعة وعشرين فتعطي للزوج اربعة وعشرون لانها اقل الحاصلين وهو النصف العائل ونوقف من نصيبه اربعة وكان للاختين من مسئلة الحيوة اثنان فاذا ضربنا في السبعة حصلت اربعة عشر

وكانت لهما من مسئلة الوفات اربعة فاذا ضربت
فى الثمانية صار الحاصل اثنين وثلثين فيصرف اليهما
اقل الحاصلين وهواربعة عشر وهوربع الستة والخمسين
فلكل واحدة منهما سبعة وتوقف من نصيبهما ثمانية عشر
فجميع مايصرف الى الزوج والاختين ثمانية وثلثون
والباقي من الستة والخمسين وهو ثمانية عشر موقوف
فان ظهران المفقود حي تدفع الى الزوج الاربعة الموقوفة
ليتم له نصف المال وهو ثمانية وعشرون ويكون الباقي
وهواربعة عشر للاخ حتى يكون النصف الآخر بين الاخ
والاختين للذكر مثل حظ الانثيين وان ظهرله انه ميت
تدفع الى الاختين الثمانية عشر الموقوفة من نصيبهما
حتى تتم لهما اربعة اسباع المال وهي اثنان وثلثون
واما الزوج فقد اخذ نصيبه كملا وهواربعة وعشرون *

شريفيــــــــــــــــة صفحه ۱۹۹

فصل فى الاسير

۲۸۱ حكم الاسير كحكم سائر المسلمين فى الميراث مالم
يفارق دينه فان فارق دينه فحكمه حكم المرتد فان لم تعلم

ردته ولا حيوته ولا موته فحكمه حكم المفقود*
سراجيــــــــــــــة صفحه ۲۰۳

فان ادعي ورثته انه ارتد في دار الحرب لا تقبل في ذلك ۲۸۲
الا شهادة مسلمين عدلين فاذا شهدا حكم القاضي
بوقوع الفرقة بينه وبين امرأته وقسم ماله بين ورثته لانه
ميت حكما عند قضاء القاضي * شريفية صفحه ۲۰۴

فصل في الغرقي والحرقي والهدمي

اذا ماتت جماعة بينهم قرابة ولا يدرى ايهم مات اولا كما ۲۸۳
اذا غرقوا في السفينة معا او وقعوا في النار دفعة او سقط عليهم
جدار او سقف بيت او قتلوا في معركة ولم يعلم التقدم
والتأخر في موتهم جعلوا كانهم ماتوا معا فمال كل واحد منهم
لورثته الاحياء ولا يرث بعض هؤلاء الاموات من بعض هذا
هو المختار * سراجية وشريفيــــــــة صفحه ۲۰۴

وقال علي وابن مسعود رضي الله عنهما في احدى ۲۸۴
الروايتين عنهما يرث بعضهم من بعض الا فيما ورث
كل واحد منهم من صاحبه * سراجية صفحه ۲۰۵

واذا غرق اخوان اكبر واصغر وخلف كل منهما ٢٨٥
اما وبنتا ومولى وترك كل منهما تسعين دينارا فعندنا تقسم تركة كل واحد منهما فيعطي لام كل واحد منهما سدس تركته وهو خمسة عشر وابنت كل منهما النصف وهو خمسة واربعون ولمولاه مابقي وهو ثلثون وعند علي وابن مسعود رضي الله عنهما في احدى الروايتين منهما يحكم بموت الاكبر اولا فتقسم تركته فللام السدس وهو خمسة عشر وللابنة النصف وهو خمسة واربعون وللاصغر ما بقي وهو ثلثون ثم يحكم بموت الاصغر فتقسم تركته كذلك فقد بقي من تركة كل واحد منهما ثلثون وهو ما ورث كل منهما من صاحبه فللام من ذلك الباقي السدس وهو خمسة وللابنة كل منهما نصفه وهو خمسة عشر والباقي للمولى لان كلا منهما لا يرث من صاحبه ما ورث منه فقد اجتمع لام كل منهما عشرون ولبنته ستون ولمولاه عشرة * شـــــريفية صفحه ٢٠٦

٢٨٦ ثم ينتقل هذا الحكم الذي ذكرناه مفصلا في عمومة الميت وخؤلته وفي اولادهم الى جهة عمومة ابويه وخؤلتهما ثم الى اولادهم ثم ينتقل الى جهة عمومة ابوي ابويه وخؤلتهم ثم الى اولادهم كما في العصبات يعني اذا لم توجد عمومة الميت وخؤلته واولادهم انتقل حكمهم المذكور الى عم اب الميت لام وعمته وخاله وخالته والى عم ام الميت وعمتها وخالها وخالتها فان انفرد واحد منهم اخذ المال كله لعدم المزاحم وان اجتمعوا واتحد حيز قرابتهم فالاقوى منهم اولى ذكرا كان الاقوى او انثى وان استوت قرابتهم فللذكر مثل حظ الانثيين وان اختلف حيز قرابتهم فلقرابة الاب الثلثان ولقرابة الام الثلث الى آخر ما مر هناك فان لم يوجد هؤلآء كان حكم اولادهم حكم اولاد الصنف الرابع فان لم توجد اولادهم ايضا انتقل الحكم الى عمومة ابوي الميت وخؤلتهم ثم الى اولادهم وهكذا الى ما لا يتناهى واشار بقوله كما في العصبات الى ان توريث ذوي الارحام باعتبار معنى العصوبة كما سلف فيعتبر بحقيقة العصوبة وما عرف في حقيقة العصوبة الحكم

في اعمام الميت نقل ذلك الحكم الى اعمام ابيه
ثم الى اعمام جده فكذا الحال في معنى العصوبة *
سراجية وشريفيـــــــــــــــــة صفحه ١٧٧

والثالث يلبسه في داره يكفن بالثاني لان الاول أعلى والثالث ادنى فالمتوسط اولى * شريفية صفحه ٣

٣ وانما كان قضاء الدين مؤخرا عن الكفن لانه لباسه بعد وفاته فيعتبر بلباسه في حيوته الا ترى انه يقدم على دينه اذ لا يباع ما على المديون من ثيابه مع قدرتـــــه على الكسب * شريفية صفحه ٤

٤ واعلم ان الابتداء بالكفن ليس مطلقا كما تشعر به عبارة الكتاب بل كل حق للغير تعلق بعين التركة فانه مقدم على تكفينه كالدين المتعلق بالمرهون اذا لم يكن للميت شيء سواه فيقضى منه دينه اولا * شريفية صفحه ٤

٥ واذا اقر الرجل في مرض موته بديون وعليه ديون لزمته في صحته وديون لزمته في مرضه باسباب معلومة فدين الصحة والدين المعروف بالاسباب مقدم لانه لا تهمة في ثبوت المعروف بالاسباب اذا المعاين لا مرد له مثل بدل ما يملكه واستهلكه وعلم وجوبه بغير اقراره اوتزوج امرأة بمهر مثلها وهذا الدين مثل دين الصحة لا يقدم احدهما على الآخر * الجوهرة النيرة في كتاب الاقرار

٦ واما اذا اقر في مرضه بدين علم ثبوته بطريق المعاينة

الفرائض

على

مذهب ابي حنيفة

الباب الاول

فى التركة وما يتعلق به من الحقوق

١ قال علماءنا رحمهم الله تتعلق بتركة الميت حقوق اربعة
مرتبة الاول يبدء بتكفينه وتجهيزه بلا تبذير ولا تقتير ثم تقضى
ديونه من جميع مابقي من ماله ثم تنفذ وصاياه من ثلث مابقي
بعد الدين ثم يقسم الباقي بين ورثته * سراجية صفحه ٣

٢ امّا باعتبار العدد فتكفين الرجل باكثر من ثلثة اثواب
والمرأة باكثر من خمسة تبذير وباقل مما ذكر تقتير
واما باعتبار القيمة فاذا كان يلبس في حيوته ماقيمته عشرة
مثلا فلو كفن بما قيمته اقل او اكثر منها كان تقتيرا او تبذيرا
واذا كان له ثوب يلبسه فى الاعياد والثاني يلبسه بين اقرانه